Nietzsche and the Metaphysics of the Tragic

Also available from Continuum

Nietzsche – Gianni Vattimo and Nicholas Martin
Nietzsche and Philosophy – Gilles Deleuze
Nietzsche and the Vicious Circle – Pierre Klossowski
Nietzsche's Philosophy – Eugene Fink
On Nietzsche – Georges Bataille

Nietzsche and the Metaphysics of the Tragic

Nuno Nabais

Translated by Martin Earl

continuum

Continuum International Publishing Group
The Tower Building   80 Maiden Lane, Suite 704
11 York Road   New York, NY 10038
London
SE1 7NX

© Nuno Nabais 2006

All rights reserved. No part of this publication may be reproduced or transmitted in any form or by any means, electronic or mechanical, including photocopying, recording, or any information storage or retrieval system, without prior permission in writing from the publishers.

Nuno Nabais has asserted his right under the Copyright, Designs and Patents Act, 1988, to be identified as Author of this work

British Library Cataloguing-in-Publication Data
A catalogue record for this book is available from the British Library.

ISBN: 0-8264-6677-X (hardback) 0-8264-6678-8 (paperback)

Library of Congress Cataloguing-in-Publication Data
A catalog record for this book is available from the Library of Congress.

Typeset by YHT Ltd, London
Printed and bound in Great Britain by Biddles Ltd, King's Lynn, Norfolk

Contents

	Translator's Preface	vii
	Introduction	xi
1	Nietzsche's Place in the Aesthetics of Postmodernity	1
2	The Individual and Individuality in Nietzsche	37
3	Necessity and Contingency in Nietzsche's Early Writings	65
4	Nietzsche and Stoicism	85
5	The Role of the Idea of the Eternal Recurrence in the Genesis of the Project for the Revaluation of All Values	99
6	Nihilism According to Nietzsche	133
	Notes	159
	Bibliography	185
	Index	195

To Olga Pombo, who
taught me everything
about Nietzsche …
and then some.

Translator's Preface

When Nuno Nabais's *Metafísica do Trágico* was published in Portugal in 1997 it was the first full-length study of Friedrich Nietzsche to appear in a country which has – when compared with other European countries – no philosophical tradition to speak of. Published by Relógio d'Água, the book won the PEN Club Award in the essay category for that year. Now, with the publication of *Nietzsche and the Metaphysics of the Tragic*, English-speaking readers of Nietzsche will be able to benefit from a study which questions the fundamental canonical interpretations of the evolution of Nietzsche's thought and the subsequent impact of his principal notions on the twentieth-century world.

There is no other nineteenth-century philosopher whose ideas, whose style of writing and, indeed, whose life, have proved so fertile for subsequent generations of not only philosophers, but also poets, novelists, playwrights and the general reading public. Ideas such as the Eternal Recurrence, nihilism and the will to power continue to modulate our sense of who we are.

Of these three notions, the Eternal Recurrence is certainly Nietzsche's most glaring contribution to the cultural vocabulary of the twentieth century. Like Freud's uncovering of the subconscious mind, or Warhol's fifteen minutes of fame, Nietzsche's notion of an unending recycling of the substance of life has become self-proliferating, taking on a life independent of Nietzsche himself. It belongs not only to the history of philosophy, but also to the history of popular culture. Like all such notions, its power lies in its ease of appropriation, its fetching mutability. Like all truly important philosophical ideas, there lies at its centre a certain impenetrability. During his (for us) tragically brief writing life, Nietzsche tended to move rapidly from one major idea to the next, almost as though they were a series of poetic flukes. He dropped them as quickly as he received inspiration for new ones. In fact, one of the initial concerns of *The Metaphysics of the Tragic* is with the vapour trail left in the wake of Nietzsche's first important abandonment, his Wagner-inspired analysis of the silence of the Greek chorus in *The Birth of Tragedy*.

The Eternal Recurrence occupied Nietzsche for approximately five years, providing the central premise for *The Gay Science* and *Thus Spoke*

Zarathustra. But then it disappears as a functional concept nearly as quickly at it had appeared. This must have happened sometime during that resonantly brief hiatus between the publication of *Thus Spoke Zarathustra* and *Beyond Good and Evil,* published a year later. And yet, Nietzschean scholarship, like the popular mind, has tended to elevate the Eternal Recurrence, to see it as the fulcrum of the Nietzschean project. The book in hand takes a starkly different approach and proposes a corrective reading of Nietzsche's late philosophy.

How, one is bound to wonder, could such an original interpretation as readers will find below, come out of Portugal, a country situated on the margins of contemporary intellectual trends? And yet perhaps it is precisely this particular geointellectual positioning which has afforded the difference. Often, the smaller and more debilitated the country, the greater the fascination for the book. This is something I had noticed upon arriving in Portugal in 1986, and which I found once again when I visited the former GDR in 1991. In fact, one of the tangible differences between West and East Berlin that first grabbed my attention was, in contrast to the general flattening of architectural standards, the bookish splendour of my friend's apartments on the city's eastern side. It was explained to me that, for the last half century, there had been nothing else to do. Also, reading was one of the few activities into which the state could not pry. While the West was watching television, the East had spent half a century reading.

Some of this dynamic – a bookish intensity combined with geographical remoteness, or indeed the political remoteness of the state – is fused with the figure of the contemporary philosopher in one of the European Union's least affluent countries. Nabais's predicament is predicated upon, on the one hand, Portugal's historic isolation from Europe, and, on the other, the internal isolation of the intellectual classes from a largely working-class population. University in Portugal is still only reached by around 11 per cent of the population; it is an institution which, though broadly esteemed, has little to do with the lives of most Portuguese. Professors – of whatever – remain a coddled, almost priestly class, their erudition undiluted by the workaday world that surrounds them. This double isolation combines conveniently with yet another factor, the role of Portuguese itself.

While Portuguese is a world language, thanks to the country's fifteenth- and sixteenth-century imperial expansion (it is almost more widely spoken than both French and German combined), its linguistic footprint on the European continent is tiny. Consequently, Portugal's intellectuals, especially its humanists, are almost preternaturally polyglot. Fluency in three languages is commonplace. Their bibliographies reflect broad reading of the European and Anglo-American canon in its original languages. More so than in England – because more isolated – an ability in this country to speak, to read, to write and to translate foreign tongues into Portuguese is part of every intellectual's arsenal. Here, a kind of language refractor is built into the basic condition of being a scholar. This necessarily produces a different reading of primary texts. That difference is part of the story, part of the exception.

It is quite possible that Nietzsche is today more widely read in English than he is in German. As a translator, this fact alone gives me reason to pause. What is the effect of reading Nietzsche in the English prose of, among others, Walter Kaufmann, R. J. Hollingdale, or Duncan Large – all of them translator/scholars who now appear in Nabais's *Metaphysics of the Tragic*? Their versions of Nietzsche were of course not in the original book. There all citations from primary and secondary texts were translated by Nabais himself, from the German, French, Italian and English into Portuguese. That was part of his labor, organic to the scholarship itself. In a world hooked on English, the fact alone of now having to bring numerous philosophers – from Nietzsche to Schopenhauer to Kant to Deleuze, all of them translated by different hands – under one lingual roof in order to provide for a monoglot public, has, paradoxically, introduced a certain babel into the texture of the present book.

Certainly, I am complicit, having signed up for the task of translating and, and in a sense, mediating this volume. George Steiner reminds us in *Errata: An Examined Life* of Spinoza's view on the subject: "On a higher plane, attempts to search out the truth, to formulate it and teach it – the philosophic enterprise – run into the fog of language(s). Spinoza affirms that error, controversy, mutual misinterpretation, arise ineluctably from the incapacity of different languages to grasp, to translate rightly, each other's vocabulary and grammar."[1] This complex of problems becomes particularly acute in Nietzsche's case. As Walter Kaufmann posited in his introduction to the *Basic Writings of Nietzsche*, even if Nietzsche had died at the age of thirty-seven, after the publication of *The Gay Science* and before he "came into his own during the last six years of his creative life," ... "he would be remembered as one of the greatest masters of German prose ... cited as proof that the German language can be used to write lucidly, penetratingly, wittily and beautifully about topics on which German professors, from Kant down to Heidegger, have written without a trace of wit or beauty."[2] To what extent is Nietzsche these days lost in translation, as the saying goes, and how might this loss be recompensed in Nietzsche scholarship, a good proportion of which is now conducted exclusively in English? Has the expansion of Nietzsche beyond his German context in the latter half of the twentieth century led to his being not necessarily misunderstood but, perhaps, opportunistically understood, creating a situation in which, as Peter Gay says, "his ideas have been most things to most men?"[3]

There is no doubt in my mind that in translation Nietzsche's texts create certain problems, not only mechanical but also "philosophical" ones. John Keats, in one of his greatest odes, has the Grecian Urn tell us that "Beauty is truth, truth beauty," which speaks to, among other things, the ancient indivisibility of form from content. In a translated world such separation is inevitable. Beauty is often the first victim, while content suffers the more hidden, "collateral" damage. Certainly one of my concerns here was to find a language to suit the tonal substratum of a book that does not agree with the canonical reading. But, on the other hand, one of my observations about the book as a reader (and translation is the deepest form of reading) was how the author's immersion in Nietzsche's German, as both a scholar and a translator of Nietzsche, might have sponsored that disagreement in the first place, by allowing him to penetrate further that matrix of thought and expression, where ideas are meshed with syntax, verbal texture, and the tropic energy of wit and irony. This world – the inner life of the German language, as expressed by a master – is increasingly unavailable to new generations of Nietzsche scholars and students who cannot read him in the original. In this book, however, they will have the benefit of one who can.

Introduction

Nietzsche completely transformed our experience of the Greek tragedy by drawing our attention to the inherent muteness of its legacy. But his first book, *The Birth of Tragedy*, revealed much more than the disappearance of the word, or the evanescence of the discourse of the hero, tongue-tied before calamity, or the wordless speech of the chorus in the mourning ritual. Behind the silence of the drama there is another yet more unbridgeable one, which Nietzsche was quick to articulate – the abyssal silence of the music. With the total loss of the musical compositions of Aeschylus, Sophocles and Euripides, the whole of tragic theatre has been rendered mute. For all that we do to stage the words of Orestes, Oedipus, Antigone and Ajax, what they give back is simply an immense emptiness. We are left listening to the absence of that deep background of harmonies, rhythms and dissonances onto which all of the voices had originally been melded. And this silence is absolute. It reduces what's left of the tragic poets to ruins.

It was the Attic silence that *The Birth of Tragedy* wanted to make heard. Nietzsche tried to retrace each of the hero's words against the gestures of the chorus, and the gestures of the chorus against the dissonance of the Dionysiac delirium, carrying the Aristotelian thesis, according to which tragedy had originated with the chorus, to its ultimate consequences. It was enough to compare the *Bacchantes* and its maenads to the choruses of Tannhäuser to suddenly make the Greeks' deafening silence obvious.

But in 1872 German classical philology could hardly deal with the trial of their precious object in the court of Wagnerian musical theatre. Nietzsche's elucidation of one silence was met with another: the academic community was rendered mute. Only one young philologist, Wilamowitz-Möllendorff spoke out. In two slight treatises he claimed that Nietzsche had reduced the Greeks to a rehash of Schopenhauerean metaphysics and Wagnerian motifs, to a metaphor for the primordial nothingness of the philosophy of pessimism, or a counterpoint to the orchestral stridencies of Wagner.

Wagner even tried to publicly shield *The Birth of Tragedy*. In an open letter to Nietzsche published in a small newspaper, he definitively shifted the interpretation of Greek tragedy to within the controversy over German opera. The result was disastrous. In the following semester not one student enrolled in Nietzsche's course on Classical Philology at the University of Basel. His book on tragedy and his philological territory expropriated by the scholars and by Wagner, Nietzsche chose exile. In 1879, at the age of thirty-five, he abandons the University to become an itinerant thinker, wandering ceaselessly between Turin, Nice, Venice and the Engandine region of Switzerland. The theme of tragedy disappears completely from his texts, giving way to a new experience of silence, in which all trace of his early work has completely vanished. In the books published between 1878 and 1882 it is as though Nietzsche had never written a single line on Aeschylus and Sophocles.

This silence will only be tenuously interrupted in 1883. This occurs at the end of *The Gay Science*. After the penultimate aphorism had for the first time revealed the idea of the Eternal Recurrence in the form of a terrifying enigma that a devil has suddenly been placed before each of us, obliging us to live each instant as though we wanted to return to relive it an infinite number of times, the last aphorism issues forth with the title "*Incipit tragoedie.*"

What is proclaimed here is the arrival of the figure of Zarathustra, the prophet of the idea of the Eternal Recurrence. Paradoxically, *Thus Spoke Zarathustra*, published during the subsequent two years, once again keeps silent about the subject of tragedy or the tragic. We know how Zarathustra's ascension, apogee and fall are constructed from beginning to end as a repetition of the progress of Oedipus, the decipherer of enigmas and destroyer of all gods. We know as well that his fundamental centre is in the idea of the Eternal Recurrence, and that this idea is presented in the same tragic tones, appealing to an absolute affirmation of each instant of existence, which we found in the descriptions of the Dionysian experience in *The Birth of Tragedy*. Nevertheless, in order to embody the new evangelist in this archaic prophet out of the East, Nietzsche must abandon the Dionysiac/Socratic and the Hellenistic/Christian oppositions that had framed his readings of tragedy. In spite of this, *Thus Spoke Zarathustra* will forever remain Nietzsche's tragic testimony, the libretto for a new kind of tragedy, which lets us hear in each word a new musical essence, that very silence which Richard Strauss, Mahler, Schoenberg and so many others would try to make real.

Thus Spoke Zarathustra reconciled Nietzsche with his reading of the tragedies. In 1886 he agreed to write an *Attempt At Self-Criticism* to be included as a preface to a new edition of *The Birth of Tragedy*. In 1887, in the second essay of *The Genealogy of Morals* he constructed a new phenomenology of tragic guilt and, therefore, a new theory of tragedy as the representation of cruelty between men offered up for the eyes of the gods. And in 1888, in *Ecce Homo* – his nearly posthumous autobiography – he defines himself as the only tragic philosopher and *The Birth of Tragedy* as the first work of the revaluation of all values, the first step beyond nihilism. Some weeks after sending *Ecce Homo* to the editor, Nietzsche sank into delirium, or rather, submitted himself definitively to silence. In the subsequent eleven years, from the vantage of his total muteness, Nietzsche would see his youthful reading of tragedy come to be discovered as the great aesthetic revolution of modernity.

*

If there is a theory of the tragic in Nietzsche it is probably more present in the texts that remain silent on the subject of tragedy than in those in which Sophocles and Euripides are the subjects.

The chapters that follow dwell on that silence. Instead of reading what Nietzsche wrote about the Dionysian, the music of the chorus, the metamorphoses of the hero, they try rather to trace the interior contours of his interpretation of the tragic. The theory of tragedy is viewed in terms of the Romantic tradition (of Kant, Schiller and Schopenhauer). It is also measured against the aesthetic debates of postmodernity that centre on the significance of figures of the sublime and of the unrepresentable. This is where the first chapter of this book, "Nietzsche's Place in the Aesthetics of Postmodernity," situates itself. But it was also necessary to closely follow the sixteen years of Nietzsche's theoretical work so as to root out the lines of fracture and hesitation that would lead to a new understanding of that immense absence of the tragic which follows the publication of *The Birth of Tragedy* in 1872 and is only broken with *Ecce Homo* in 1888. The chapters that traverse the stations of the Nietzschean theory of the tragic concentrate on the following:

- The concepts of the *individual* and *individuality*.
- The different figures of *necessity* and *contingency*.
- The relation between Stoic ethics and the tragic maxim of *Amor fati*.
- The place of the idea of the Eternal Recurrence in the evolution of the Nietzschean oeuvre.

Each of these notions is developed haphazardly so as to better cleave to the internal ruptures of Nietzsche's own thinking. But they take in five moments, which can be schematized in the following fashion: (a) before Schopenhauer; (b) following the reading of *The World as Will and Representation*; (c) the break with Schopenhauer and commitment to the Renaissance programme of natural sciences; (d) works marked by the inspiration of the Eternal Recurrence; and (e) theory of the will to power and the diagnosis of the decadence of European culture and the resulting nihilism.

Gradually, as we trace the wiles of Nietzsche's philosophical journey a thesis will emerge, which will only be fully justified in the final chapter. This has to do with the idea of the Eternal Recurrence. In the final chapter we will look closely at Nietzsche's abandonment, beginning in 1886, of that idea which had been, through his middle period, a controlling philosophical notion. After the publication of *Beyond Good and Evil* it disappears from his works, even as the first sketches of the project for the revaluation of all values and the provisional creation of the metaphysics of the will to power begin to appear in his notebooks. As we will show, by the time he is composing *The Genealogy of Morals*, Nietzsche's attentions have turned away from the Sils-Maria vision. His new understanding of a moral revolt against life, which fills this 1887 work, has superseded the complex theories of the will, of time and of causality which fell under the rubric of the image of an eternal repetition.

This book is thus an attempt to demonstrate that Nietzsche's culminating idea is not the idea of the Eternal Recurrence. All of the major notions in his project for a tragic justification of existence, such as the metaphysical basis of individuation, the aesthetics of the unrepresentable, the psychology of guilt and the poetics of necessity find their most rigorous formulation in the major typology of offended wills and in the story of their self-destructive logic, that is, in the metaphysics of the will to power and the genealogy of nihilism. The Eternal Recurrence is merely a moment in this genealogy – that moment of its self-exhaustion.

The metaphysics of the tragic, which first announces itself even before *The Birth of Tragedy*, is only fulfilled within the ambit of another silence: that which, after 1886, befalls the idea of the Eternal Recurrence. But, in this case, the silence must be respected. For it cast a light over the books written by Nietzsche in the final period before his collapse in Turin.

1

Nietzsche's Place in the Aesthetics of Postmodernity

"Here, when the danger to his will is greatest, *art* approaches as a saving sorceress, expert at healing. She alone knows how to turn these nauseous thoughts about the horror or absurdity of existence into notions with which one can live: these are the *sublime* as the artistic taming of the horrible, and the *comic* as the artistic discharge of the nausea of absurdity."

The Birth of Tragedy[1]

I. The Sublime and Postmodernity

1. Kant between the beautiful and the sublime

Immanuel Kant might have delighted in the fact that his Critiques were destined to become a linchpin in the postmodern debate and that two of the principal exponents of that debate would, in each their own ways – and somewhat at the expense of Friedrich Nietzsche – become neo-Kantians. Jürgen Habermas's "transcendental-pragmatic," with its call for a "*sensus communis*," and Jean-François Lyotard's "negative representation" with its version of a nihilistic sublime, created out of Kant, by way of Nietzsche, a postmodern dissonance. The differences in their respective readings of the *Critique of Judgment* did much to fuel the theoretical divisiveness in political, epistemological and aesthetic thought of last two decades of the twentieth century. This conflict, between, on the one hand, the pragmatics of taste and taste's capacity to engender agreement and, on the other, the eclipsing capacities of the sublime and the failure of consensus in creating a workable telos, are still with us today. It is as though, woven into Kant's aesthetic tapestries, strands of those same categories, which have come to either legitimize or antagonize our own shared experience, anticipate, by two hundred years, current ideas of *truth* and *ethicality*.

It was Habermas who first brought a Kantian tone to the debate over postmodernity. For him, the *Critique of Judgment* had discovered the *a priori* aesthetic of a truly "transcendental-pragmatic." By making explicit those political utopias which are postulated in all judgments of taste, Kant furnished the criteria for a rational admissibility of our models of truth and of justice. By presenting its criteria of appreciation throughout the thesis as universally valid, the judgment of taste reveals the principle for the establishment of a super-sensible community based on communication, free from mediation by laws or by concepts; for Habermas, the *Critique of Judgment* creates the necessary condition for a true Manifesto for aesthetic modernity, and becomes a *regulative utopia* with both a practical and theoretical reach. This idea of an objectivity of aesthetic experience defines the moment in which the Enlightenment truly establishes the programme of modernity.[2] We know how Kant raises the specificity of the judgment of taste to a *fact of reason* – as disinterested satisfaction and as the objectification of a self-affirming subjectivity. For Habermas it is precisely this specificity of the judgment of taste that defines the project – increasingly self-conscious from Baudelaire onwards – for the aesthetic founding of modernity. This would occur principally in the institutionalization of a form of artistic creation that was independent of the market and in the invention of a criticism of art which functioned, not as a praxis of description, but as a process of inscription – into the work itself – of new worlds of signification produced at the moment of public reception.

For Jean-François Lyotard, the Kantian aesthetic also furnishes the categories for the interpretation of contemporary experiments of art, and through them, of science and politics. Yet Lyotard thinks that Habermas's reading of the third *Critique* is insufficient, since it is oriented strictly toward the aesthetic of the beautiful. If it is true that (in our approach to the beautiful) disinterested pleasure in the contemplation of the forms of the object always reveals that aspiration toward the universal sharing of feeling, which is fundamental to the intersubjective community, it would follow that the beautiful does not entirely exhaust the structure of the aesthetic experience.[3] To raise this feeling of the beautiful into a paradigm for aesthetic experience would be to forget that, along with the analysis of the *beautiful*, Kant developed an analysis of the *sublime*, or, in other words, a description of the conditions for the possibility of this other aesthetic experience which he called "negative representation." For Kant, the sublime is the impossibility of the figuration of either a colossal object in space and time, or of the infinity of power as pure idea.[4] According to Lyotard, it is precisely the experience of the sublime that has illustrated the condition of contemporary art for the last century. The Kantian theory of the sublime reveals to what extent contemporary art has long ceased to be oriented by the categories of the beautiful. This is especially true of its more minimalist and abstract variations, as much as in the absolute autonomy of artistic creation and the criticism of art, by which we define the vanguard.[5] Likewise, such an experience of something "that happens" as a work, but which refuses figuration, does not correspond to the idea of a community of judgment, or of a *"sensus communis."*[6] For Lyotard, far from permitting direct communication between subjects of the same judgment of beauty, exercising reflective judgment in the experience of the *sublime* wakes in us the sense of a promised community which is invariably deferred – of a utopia which no longer has a regulating value. Instead of ending up with a philosophy of *"sensus communis"* and of intersubjectivity free of a concept which is presupposed in the theory of the beautiful, the theory of the *sublime* in the *Critique of Judgment* "fractures constituted norms, shatters consensus and reanimates a sense of disagreement."[7]

The emergence of an aesthetic of the *sublime* in Kant, as a theorization of the disaster of the imagination in the experience of the work of art, signals a discovery: the failure of the normative value of the judgment of taste, and the end of its pretensions towards a utopian representation. For Lyotard, Kant's theory of the *sublime* finally reveals the destitution of modernity's theoretical programme and the scuttling of its logic of legitimization, which had been based on the shared forms of existence inherited from the French Revolution. It excludes all interpretation of judgment of taste as the *a priori* of the validating pretensions of theoretic and practical reason. The *sublime* ceases being the place where respect for the unrepresentable moral law was legitimized in the community of the judgment of taste. On the contrary, as Lyotard says: "In this way the sublime is nothing other than the sacrificial announcement of the ethical in the aesthetic field."[8]

2. Aesthetic education and political utopia

This disagreement over the significance of Kantian aesthetics which occupied a large part of the philosophical debate of the eighties – and which I have only attempted to outline here[9] – is not entirely new. The most important aesthetic plot in the debate over postmodernity concerns the significance of the utopian potential found in the experience of the art of each epoch. Yet we should recall that this potential was first pronounced by Schiller in his reading of Kant's aesthetics. In this sense, it can almost be said that the theoretical debates of the eighties, and preeminently in the argument between Habermas and Lyotard, repeated Schiller's reinvention of the *Critique of Judgment* in his *Letters on Aesthetic Education*.

We know that in the *Critique of Judgment* Kant discovered that all judgment of taste and all criticism of art presume that a shared outlook is possible. This point of view is not conceptual, but indeterminate, or rather, it is the connection between a particular feeling and a universal

Idea conducted through reflection with the view of establishing direct communication between individuals, or a "shared feeling" which is not, however, conceptually founded. As Kant said, "That is precisely why someone who judges with taste (provided he is not mistaken in this consciousness and does not mistake the matter for the form, i.e., charm for beauty) is entitled to require the subjective purposiveness, i.e., his liking for the object, from everyone as well, and is entitled to assume that his feeling is universally communicable, and this without any mediation by concepts."[10] In this sense there is, in the judgment of taste, a "universal communicability of the sensation (of liking or disliking) – a universal communicability that is indeed not based on a concept."[11] In the ability to experience a work of art, each individual is involuntarily raised to the condition of membership in a rational community guided by principles of mutual recognition of the criteria of judgment, and is thus carried beyond the limits of subjectivity and its aporias.

But it is Schiller – and not Kant – who, transforms the aesthetic theory elaborated in the *Critique of Judgment*, in order to overcome the limits of modern political reason. In his *Letters on Aesthetic Education* he analyses the schisms that will inaugurate modernity and that critical philosophy had expressed for the first time in a rigorous fashion by distinguishing between the *theoretical, practical* and *aesthetic* ambits of reason. According to Schiller, only the radicalization of the theory of reflexive judgment – which had been presented in the *Critique of Judgment* as the midpoint between the *judgment of taste* and *teleological judgment*, that is, between the explanation of the universal character of a work of art and the explanation of the conditions of representation of organisms as finalized structures – would lead to a surpassing of the antinomies of reason, and, in particular, the antinomies of political reason (general will/individual will, national sovereignty/cosmopolitan state, constitutionality/the right to revolution, etc.). In the theory of reflexive judgment and in the autonomy that Kant attributed to the sphere of aesthetical-teleological reason, Schiller discovers the principles of an aesthetic utopia, which attributes to art the role of the unifying power and constituent of general will. Instead of *religion*, it is now *art* which must institute intersubjective relations, *art* as the *medium* for the education of the human race. Art transforms itself into an experience wherein conflicts are resolved: those which dwell as much in theoretic reason (where the natural constraints of the human condition are revealed) as they do in practical reason (where the link to the sphere of moral obligation is established). As Schiller writes, "In the midst of the fearful kingdom of forces, and in the midst of the sacred kingdom of laws, the aesthetic impulse to form is at work, unnoticed, on the building of a third joyous kingdom of play and of semblance, in which man is relieved of the shackles of circumstance, and released from all that might be called constraint, alike in the physical and in the moral sphere."[12] This "third kingdom" of the human condition, this utopia in which humanity is liberated by art, is constructed through aesthetic education, and via the reconstitution of a *sensus communis*, which, because it is not conceptual, can be neither theoretical nor practical, but is rather realized in the shared character of the judgment of taste as it operates before each work of art.[13] Kant and Schiller had perceived that the normative character of any utopia derives from an aesthetic faculty, and that it was therefore important to cultivate the faculty of taste in each citizen in a programme of scientific and ethical emancipation.

In *The Philosophical Discourse of Modernity*, Habermas showed us to what extent this programme of linking political utopia to aesthetic education, as a project for overcoming the antinomies of modern reason, persisted as a point of orientation throughout the whole of romanticism, continuing to exert influence even over Lukács, Marcuse, and Hannah Arendt. What is more: out of Schiller's *Letters* – which he defines as the "the first programmatic work toward an aesthetic critique of modernity"[14] – Habermas formulates a basis for the recuperation of the promises of rational emancipation inherited from the Enlightenment, those promises that had been stripped of their regulating power by the critique of metaphysical presuppositions (or of metaphysical destiny) of modern rationalism, especially in the work of Nietzsche and Heidegger and, most recently, in those thinkers, such as Adorno, Derrida, Foucault and Lyotard, who recognize themselves in the founding experience of modernity: precisely in this critical corrosion of the metaphysical.

Habermas transforms Kant and Schiller into a bulwark against this aesthetic shattering of the pretensions of the universal validity of value judgments initiated by Nietzsche. The "metaphysics of artists" from *The Birth of Tragedy*, and its recent prolongations in the works of Derrida and Lyotard, signify, for Habermas, nothing less than the return to politically conservative positions. In the famous 1980 lecture "Modernity : an Unfinished Project?" Habermas considers that the spirit of Nietzsche, as it was rediscovered in the 70s, is the inspiration behind political neoconservatism in Europe. As he says:

> The *Young Conservatives* essentially appropriate the fundamental experience of aesthetic modernity, namely the revelation of a decentered subjectivity liberated from all the constraints of cognition and purposive action, from all the imperatives of labor and use value, and with this they break out of the modern world altogether. They establish an implacable opposition to modernism precisely through a modernist attitude. They locate the spontaneous forces of imagination and self-experience, of affective life in general, in what is most distant and

archaic, and in Manichean fashion oppose instrumental reason with a principle accessible solely to evocation, whether this is the will to power or sovereignty, Being itself or the Dionysian power for the poetic.[15]

In Schiller's *Letters on Aesthetic Education* Habermas finds the antidote to the aesthetic dissolution of modernity's political utopia carried out by Nietzsche and by the Nietzscheans of the 70s. To fulfil the promises of emancipation contrived by the unfinished project of modernity, Habermas returns to that moment in which Schiller invents the figure of art as the unifying power of reason; that is where, for the first time, a true communicative reason had been conceived for the aesthetical State of the future, as the resurrection of a common sense destroyed by the illusions of dogmatic reason. It is in the idea of an "aesthetically reconciled society" that the basis for the programme of an ethics of communicative action is to be found. This is where Schiller, in Habermas's version, says "[each person] dwells quietly in his own hut, communing with himself and, as soon as he issues from it, with the whole race."[16]

It is not surprising that the project to rehabilitate modernity – with which Habermas counters the "postmodernists" – has placed the Kantian/Schillerean link between *political utopia* and *aesthetic education* at the center of the philosophical debate of the 1980s.

3. Problems

The goal of this chapter is not to add fuel to the controversy between Lyotard and Habermas over their different readings of the texts of Schiller and Kant, but rather to achieve a more rigorous understanding of the plots by which Kant's aesthetic has come to be a site of explication for contemporary thought.

The first problem which is posed by the return to the *Critique of Judgment*, whether by Habermas or by Lyotard, is Nietzsche's place in that paradigm of return. For Habermas, something in the emancipationist destiny of the Kantian programme went awry; somehow a detour or an interruption occurred in the critical and utopian potential of the non-conceptual, non-legislating universality proclaimed through a theory of art which would validate the judgment of taste. That is why it is urgent to once again piece together what it was that led to our detour from Kant. We know that in his diagnosis of the dissolution of the promises of modernity – whose last two hundred years Habermas has monumentally recreated in *The Philosophical Discourse of Modernity* – Nietzsche occupies the fissile point in our divergence from the Kantian legacy, that moment in which the prospect for a rational legitimization of modernity is abandoned.[17] The chapter dedicated to Nietzsche ("The Entry into Postmodernity:

Nietzsche as a Turning Point") demonstrates how that schism is the result of a political and hermeneutic assault on the tradition of critical philosophy. For Habermas, returning to Kant is a way to outflank Nietzsche and all of the mechanics of mockery he directed against modernity – which he achieves by paying more attention to Nietzsche's philosophical legatees (Heidegger, Bataille, Adorno, Derrida, Deleuze, Foucault and Lyotard) than to Nietzsche himself. It is however significant that when Nietzsche's positions are referred to, it is almost invariably *The Birth of Tragedy* which is adduced. This is understandable. Habermas knows that *The Birth of Tragedy* contains a great many of the premises of postmodern aesthetic theory and that, from the 70s, via so-called "French Nietzscheanism" – which, in addition to Derrida, Deleuze, Foucault and Lyotard, included, among others, Klossowski, Lacoue-Labarthe, Sarah Kofman, Bernard Pautrat, Jean-Michel Rey, and Jean-Luc Nancy – this work became Holy Writ for the movement to aesthetically dismiss the foundational pretensions of the metaphysics of modernity.[18]

However, the opposition which Habermas would like to highlight between Kant and Nietzsche, between the aesthetic programme of the *Critique of Judgment* and that of *The Birth of Tragedy*, seems nothing more than a forced dramatization of the antinomies that inhabit the very experiments themselves of the art of modernity. This opposition utterly loses its pertinence when we try to reckon it with the works of the French Nietzscheans. In fact, why would Lyotard, and with him Lacoue-Labarthe and Nancy, among others, have plunged directly into a commentary on the *Critique of Judgment*, instead of using *The Birth of Tragedy* to reaffirm their positions? Why don't they couple their rediscovery of the plots of the Kantian theory of the sublime with a demonstration that this postmodern "turning point" inaugurated by *The Birth of Tragedy* does not take the form of a "detour," or an "abandonment" of the promises of the Kantian critique of reason, but rather respects the true destiny of art in the West, that is, expresses something of Art's epochal condition? It is after all precisely these same philosophers of the so-called school of "French Nietzscheanism," who had made *The Birth of Tragedy* the fulcrum of the Nietzschean oeuvre, who, in the 80s, would discover the importance of the aesthetic of Kant and, in particular, the Kantian theory of the sublime. We can even say that if today the sublime occupies one of the central positions in the contemporary philosophical debate, and has become a category which contemporary art criticism pretty much takes for granted, this is due in large measure to the renovative readings of the chapter entitled "Analytic of the Sublime" in the *Critique of Judgment* realized precisely by, among others, Lyotard, Lacoue-Labarthe and Nancy.[19] Is there not something indeed absurd in this whole situation? Habermas, in *The Philosophical Discourse of Modernity*, refutes the postmodern aesthetic through a refutation of the "metaphysics of the artist" as it is formulated by Nietzsche. It was by this same mechanism that the Parisian Habermasians (Luc Ferry, Alain Renaut, Vincent Descombes and André Comte-Sponville) were led in 1991 to publish a collective manifesto against the postmodern discourse eloquently entitled *Why We Are Not Nietzscheans*.[20] "Postmodernism" and "Nietzsche" became exchangeable labels for the same concept. Yet, those Nietzscheans/postmodernists that Habermas and the Parisian Habermasians were attempting to confute, had completely abandoned any reference to Nietzsche, and in turn became specialists, amazingly enough, in the theory of the sublime as expressed by Kant and the Romantics. The border between modernity and postmodernity was thus redrawn within Kant's oeuvre itself. Lyotard shows us already fully fledged in Kant's own aesthetic the programme, which will be the one we will discuss in Nietzsche, of transforming aesthetic experiments into sites that mocked modern reason, thus disarming those who make out of Kant's aesthetic a site of resistance to the theoretical models of postmodernity.

This abandonment of *The Birth of Tragedy* as a reference created a real conundrum within the debate over postmodernity. Could Habermas have incorrectly read the corrosive effects of Nietzsche's aesthetic? Might he have exaggerated in claiming that Nietzsche was the "turning point" in modernity? And if such were the case, how do we explain the lack of response on Lyotard's or Nancy's part, within the framework of this same aesthetic in Nietzsche, showing that the Nietzschean aesthetic is not reducible to aporias of the theory of the beautiful as Habermas insists? Or might Habermas's reading be correct? The silence of the postmoderns would then signify that they no longer saw themselves reflected in the work of Nietzsche, recognizing that he still belonged to the philosophical universe of classicism and to the opposition between truth and appearance that Habermas was trying to refute? But, even if this is the case, the equivocation remains. Habermas's thesis, according to which *The Birth of Tragedy* constitutes a fundamental reference in the postmodern discourse, still makes no sense. How can we create a mechanism to critique the philosophical programme of postmodernity out of an analysis of the errors in Nietzsche's aesthetic if the postmodernists themselves no longer recognize themselves in *The Birth of Tragedy*, having traded it for the *Critique of Judgment* as their key text?

It is also bewildering to wonder why these same "Nietzscheans" who today recognize themselves in the Kantian theory of the sublime never attempted to determine what role the aesthetic of the sublime could have played in *The Birth of Tragedy*.[21] Neither Lyotard, nor Lacoue-Labarthe, nor even Nancy, attempted to reconstruct the phases in their own shift in position, nor did they attend to the general transformation of a Dionysian aesthetic of intensities into an aesthetic of an irrepresentable sublime. As such they misrepresent the terms of the controversy over the sublime. Because they read the "Analytic of the Sublime" from a Nietzschean perspective – which is never made explicit – they are able to undermine the Kantian fortress from the inside. Against Habermas, against his appeal for the renovation of the promises of an ideal community of communication inscribed in the Kantian idea of objective aesthetic reason, Lyotard excludes the *Critique of Judgment*, separates it from Habermas's anti-Nietzschean reading. But this reading is, in turn, built upon an unspoken assumption. It is never clarified to what extent this "Nietzschean" reading of the *Critique of Judgment* is nothing more than a returning to Kant of that which for a long time had been attributed to Nietzsche. What is dodged is the very recognition that the Kantian sublime can only be subjected to a postmodern interpretation because the actual postmodern models – with their Nietzschean roots – are nothing more than a peculiar elaboration of the theory of the sublime in the *Critique of Judgment*. It is by ignoring the fact that the figures of the Dionysian are a metamorphosis of the Kantian figures of the sublime that Lyotard can believe that he has discovered in Kant a ratification that anticipates the aesthetic of the unrepresentable that would come to define postmodernity.

An analysis of the category of the sublime in the aesthetic of *The Birth of Tragedy* has never been written.[22] What is more, there has been no attempt to reconstruct the various metamorphoses of the Kantian sublime up to the point of its application by Nietzsche in his interpretation of the Greek tragedy as a musical drama. And this vacuum is more than just another of those inevitable lacunas in philosophical historiography. The absence of a description of the Nietzschean origins of the postmodern reading of the Kantian sublime is so paradoxical that it might even be seen as symptomatic of something else: it shows us to what extent this real permutation of the Nietzscheans into Kantians, or the permutation of the *Dionysian* aesthetic into the sublime, is predicated upon the fact that no one has yet contemplated the tradition of the sublime itself in *The Birth of Tragedy*.[23] In fact, this must be one of the more curious phenomena in the narrative of postmodern discourse. It is as though a repressed Kantianism has returned to disrupt the arrogance of the Nietzschean aesthetic – for too long secure in its usurpation of the whole tradition of the philosophy of art inaugurated by Kant and prolonged by Romanticism.

This leads us to another paradox. If it is the Nietzscheans who discovered the site of explication for a postmodern aesthetic in the Kantian theory of the sublime, how should we treat the fact that this same theory of the sublime is not used to read the programme of aesthetic dismissal of the modern figures of rationality which orient the work of Nietzsche and in this way clarify to what extent aesthetic Nietzscheanism is nothing more than a detour or an escape hatch from the programme proposed by the

Critique of Judgment? Might we not find, in the postmodernist's very silence on the subject of their own evolution, a way to understand the aesthetic implications of the debate over postmodernity?

4. Hypotheses

Thanks, at least in part, to *The Birth of Tragedy* – a text which moves well beyond the consequences of the Schillerean reading of the *Critique of Judgment* – our understanding of the condition of art and criticism in contemporary culture still leans greatly on the Kantian distinction between an *aesthetic of the beautiful* and an *aesthetic of the sublime*.

The aesthetic theory of *The Birth of Tragedy* is nearly incomprehensible when separated from the tradition of the sublime. This is because the true model for the fundamental *Dionysian/Apollonian* polarity is the difference between the *sublime* and the *beautiful* as it was formulated by Kant, later developed by Schiller and, above all, transformed by Schopenhauer into the paradigmatic experience leading to the pessimist vision of existence. However, this latter-day reinstatement of the concepts of the *sublime* and the *beautiful* in the guise of the *Dionysian* and *Apollonian*, while it shifts the attempt, inaugurated by Kant and Schiller, to justify modernity in aesthetic terms from the plane of practical to aesthetic reason, still contains nearly all of the premises of the postmodern discourse: (a) because the *Dionysian/Apollonian* pairing reproduces the Kantian *thing-in-itself/phenomenon* distinction, the equivalence between the *Dionysian* and the *sublime* – which only seems valuable as a theory of art – leads to the identification between the *sublime* and *truth*, in that way transforming truth itself, not into the basis – apophantic or regulating – for aesthetic appearance, but into the negative site of the reality of a work of art. Dionysian art, the ecstatic experience of contemplating the horror of existence that annuls the aspiration to beauty and the illusion of the aesthetic subject, reveals its own poietic reality in this impossibility for figuration, in this case its condition of baseless appearance – its truth is contained in its non-representationality; (b) at the same time, with the concept of the Dionysian work of art, Nietzsche transforms the truth itself, this appearing of the irrepresentable, into an object of aesthetic experience, as the experience of the absolute absence of representation; (c) in this way the sublime loses its moral destiny. It is transformed into a fact of knowledge, but a knowledge which knows nothing else but the disappearance of its object into its unfigurability; (d) in the thesis which makes the world into an artistic phenomenon, if Nietzsche is once again inspired by Schillerean romanticism, this inspiration manifests itself above all in the autonomization of the sublime as the intensive inverse of reason, as that which is revealed in the ecstatic, in the dissolution of individual subjectivity before the grandiosity of nature. Knowledge objectified, in yielding to nature, would not be banished to the margins of the aesthetic. On the contrary, it returns to inscribe itself in the very center of the artist's metaphysic – by virtue of the way in which it transforms itself into an experience of the sublime.

*

This summary of how the reinstatement of the *Apollonian/Dionysian* pairing over that of the *beautiful/sublime* anticipates some of the premises of the postmodern theory of the *sublime* serves, among other things, to underline just how strange the indifference is which recent readings of Nietzsche show for the subject of the sublime. How can we explain that the place of the sublime in *The Birth of Tragedy* has been neglected in postmodern discourse, this same discourse which locates its two inaugural moments in Kant's theory of the sublime and in Nietzschean metaphors of the Dionysian? Only an analysis of the small differences in the interpretation of Kant by the modernists and the postmodernists and of their modes of using Nietzsche will be able to clarify this question.

It is crucial to reconstruct some of the arguments which come into play in the debate over postmodernity in order to bring to light the role which *The Birth of Tragedy* plays in forging two separate interpretations of Kant's aesthetic. Yet, because Nietzsche's use of Kantian categories of the sublime is quite rare, almost secretive, elucidating the Nietzschean theory of the sublime calls for an elliptical reading. In other words, we will first need to present the theory of the sublime in Schopenhauer, for that is where we find the true catalyst for the postmodern inscription of Nietzsche's theory of the Dionysian in the aesthetic of Kant. As such, Schopenhauer must inevitably be seen as the linchpin in any description of the sublime in Nietzsche and of the permutation of the Dionysian aesthetic into the sublime. As we have tried to show here, in the metaphysical interpretation of the sublime, in its elevation to the paradigmatic experience of the ethic of pessimism, in the hesitations surrounding its own condition of truth and, certainly, in the radical dislocation that Schopenhauer produces in the Kantian and Romantic tradition of the sublime, each one of Nietzsche's principal metaphysical theses of the aesthetic of the tragic, which he will employ to write *The Birth of Tragedy*, are already at work. For this reason, to understand Nietzsche, or better, to understand how his aesthetic of the tragic has its roots in the Kantian theory of the sublime, is to understand the theory of the sublime in Schopenhauer. But that's not all. It is also necessary to understand Wagner's use of the Schopenhauerean theory of the sublime, as an ontology for the unrepresentable in music, since the *The Birth of Tragedy* actually originated in Nietzsche's thesis on the sublime condition of music. This notion was established in metaphysical and aesthetic axioms for the first time in Wagner's 1870 text, *Beethoven*. This description of the sublime in the Nietzschean metaphysic of the tragic will have to venture in that direction as well.

To understand some of the aesthetic plots in the debate between Habermas and Lyotard we must return to that moment of transition between Kant and Nietzsche, or better, to the transformation of the aesthetic theory of the *Critique of Judgment* into the metaphysical premises of *The Birth of Tragedy*. Which is to say, we have to return to Schopenhauer, to examine exactly how his aesthetic of pessimism developed out of his metaphysical interpretation of the Kantian sublime. Unfortunately, there is still much work to be done in this area. Because the Schopenhauerean interpretation of the sublime, in spite of being central to his philosophy, maintains a nearly secret status within the group of his works that treat the aesthetic, it has been invariably forgotten. That is why we must take a closer look at Schopenhauer.

II. Ontology of the Sublime in Schopenhauer

1. From the beautiful to the sublime

Paragraph 39 of *The World as Will and Representation* is entirely dedicated to the difference between the beautiful and the sublime. It is worth citing at length from Schopenhauer's text. It contains, with nearly ingenuous transparency, all that joins him to the Kantian Tradition and, at the same time, it contains each of the lines of inspiration that lead to the aesthetic of *The Birth of Tragedy*.

> Now so long as it is the accommodation of nature, the significance and distinctness of its forms, from which the Ideas individualized in them readily of mere relations serving the will into aesthetic contemplation, and thus raises us to the will-free subject of knowing, so long is it merely the *beautiful* that affects us, and the feeling of beauty that is excited. But these very objects, whose significant forms invite us to a pure contemplation of them, may have a hostile relation to the human will in general, as manifested in its objectivity, the human body. They may be opposed to it; they may threaten it by their might that eliminates all resistance, or their immeasurable greatness may reduce it to nought. Nevertheless, the beholder may not direct his attention to this relation to his will which is so pressing and hostile, but, although he perceives and acknowledges it, he may consciously turn away from it, forcibly tear himself from his will and its relations, and, giving himself up entirely to knowledge, may quietly contemplate, as pure, will-less subject of

knowing, those very objects so terrible to the will. He may comprehend only their Idea that is foreign to all relation, gladly linger over its contemplation, and consequently be elevated precisely in this way above himself, his person, his willing, and all willing. In that case, he is then filled with the feeling of the *sublime* [*Erhaben*]; he is in the state of exaltation [*Erhebung*], and therefore the object that causes such a state is called *sublime*.[24]

At first sight it seems that Schopenhauer is simply repeating Kant's position. We know how in the *Critique of Judgment* the beautiful and the sublime are often depicted as symmetrical. For Kant, what they have in common is the fact that they please on their own, being both independent of determinant judgments (judgments of knowledge or moral judgments); they imply a necessary pleasure; they both lay claim to being universal and, finally, they are present in the eyes of a subject with no mediation via the concepts of understanding.[25] But there are, at the same time, decisive differences. The beautiful refers to the form of an object, while the sublime is found in the formless object – that is, in an object that is not delimited.[26] This is why the sublime is essentially maladapted to the imagination: the sublime wreaks violence upon the imagination. For this reason, pleasure in the sublime is negative, or better, passive. The sublime forces us to admire it and to respect it. While the beautiful gives birth directly within us to a feeling of the intensification of life, the sublime never appears as an attraction or a seduction. Faced with the sublime, the spirit experiences a moment of inhibition and a moment of expansion.[27]

Schopenhauer returns to this Kantian formulation in which the *beautiful* and the *sublime* mirror each other. There is, however, an essential difference. Schopenhauer breaks with the transcendental terrain of the *Critique of Judgment*, that is, with Kant's refusal to base the aesthetic on the supposedly non-subjective characteristics of the object, characteristics such as harmony in the experience of the beautiful, and grandiosity or monstrosity in the experience of the sublime. For Kant, an ontological doctrine of the *beautiful*, or one of the *sublime*, was out of the question: neither the *beautiful* nor the *sublime* are real determinations of the object. They are ideal properties of aesthetic judgment. As reflexive judgments, the beautiful and the sublime "simply lay claim to the feeling of pleasure, and not any cognition of the object."[28] On the contrary, Schopenhauer proposes constructing a positive doctrine of the objects of aesthetic experience, reestablishing a metaphysics of art through an analysis of the objective characteristics of artistic forms (or formlessness) that are either beautiful or sublime.

2. The sublime between the ontology and the aesthetic

In this reification of the beautiful and the sublime, Schopenhauer thinks that he is not being led back to a pre-critical position, or to a metaphysical realism similar to what we find in Baumgarten's *Aesthetics*. It is exactly the transcendental overcoming of such a realism that is considered by Schopenhauer as the great merit of Kant's aesthetic. We can find this apology of Kant's transcendental approach in Schopenhauer's "Critique of Kantian Philosophy" (published as an appendix to the first edition of *The World as Will and Representation*).[29]

But this recognition fades completely in the context of an objection that, at first sight, seems to contradict earlier theses formulated by Schopenhauer.

> He [Kant] suggested the method for this investigation, paved the way, but otherwise missed the mark. . . . in this *Critique of Aesthetic Judgement* he does not start from the beautiful itself, from the direct, beautiful object of perception, but from the *judgement* concerning the beautiful, the so-called, and very badly so-called, judgement of taste. This is the problem for him. His attention is specially aroused by the circumstance that such a judgement is obviously the expression of something occurring in the subject, but is nevertheless as universally valid as if it concerned a quality of the object. It is this that struck him, not the beautiful itself. He always starts only from the statement of others, from the judgement concerning the beautiful, not from the beautiful itself.[30]

Here Schopenhauer completely falsifies Kant's theory of reflexive judgment. In Kant's discovery of a vocation for the universal validity of the judgment of taste, Schopenhauer sees aesthetic appreciation as heteronymous. The universality of the aesthetic would in that case have a conventional foundation; it would mean having to accept the validity of a judgment made by a subject that is not me.

Schopenhauer's refutation of the caricature, which he himself made, of Kant's aesthetic, is too facile. He proposes a realist subjectivism instead of one that would sacrifice, by convention, the immanent determinations of the object to transcendental intersubjectivity. If the beautiful is not a property of the object or a property of the intuition – as Baumgarten would have it – then it is also not a property of judgment – given that judgment always expresses the Other's point of view as arbitrary. The beautiful, for Schopenhauer, is the way in which certain – beautiful – properties of the object affect my mood (*Gemüt*), the way they affect my faculty for aesthetic emotion in all its uniqueness. In Schopenhauer the mark of the universal disappears into each aesthetic feeling, while the aesthetic itself recoils within feeling.

Schopenhauer's aesthetic is an ontology of the work of art and an anthropology of feeling. Because of this, the determination of the *sublime* and the *beautiful* addresses in the first instance the structure of the respective objects and only later the forms of affection. It is certain, for example in the sublime, that the feeling of transport is only produced when the individual is raised to the condition of pure subject which is able to abstract itself from the hostility directed at his own body by the object. Yet the condition for the possibility of feeling this emotion occurs in the object. There are immanent aesthetic characteristics in the *sublime* object; it is these that demand a change in the observer: that is, he must abstract himself from precisely this empirical relationship to hostility. Yet, even this abstraction, which leads to the annulment of one's will, bursts forth from the object. Its terrifying character annuls individual will, which in turn transports the viewer, transforming him into one who contemplates nature, serenely yet ecstatically.

This reification of the aesthetic is riddled with paradoxes. The first one has to do with the ontological condition of the aesthetic determinations of objects. Because Schopenhauer retains the distinction between *phenomenon* and *thing-in-itself*, the effects themselves of the object upon the subject of representation must be thought of as mere appearances, without any footing whatsoever in the truth of the world. The harmonious or terrifying aspects which forms display to the eye of the observer exist only in his own angst; they are simply a means for affecting himself as condition of the possibility for representation. In the contemplation of a storm or of some terrifying situation of chaos, when I am crushed beneath that overwhelming sense of my form's corporal fragility, I am at once raised to a level from whence the discovery of the illusion of this experience becomes possible: the threatening object is nothing more than mere fiction constructed out of the pure forms of sensibility, and I am revealed to myself in my condition of illusion, as a phenomenon of will, an ephemeral and occasional manifestation of a will that exists beyond space and time and that, for some unfathomable metaphysical reason expresses itself by shattering itself within individuals in space and time, that is, in individuals endowed with a body and a discrete will that manages to exist by maintaining this illusion of being real, of being a thing-in-itself.

For Schopenhauer, the characteristic ambivalence of the feeling of the sublime – at once *terrifying and transporting* – results precisely in this paradox of a representation that, the more real it appears, the more strongly it reveals its condition as a mere appearance. It is precisely at that very moment in which I feel crushed by the grandeur of that which I contemplate, in the moment that I find myself reduced to a state of absolute fragility and insignificance, that the only meaning I can give to this annulment of self is that of a mere illusion. If I am nothing, then everything I produce in my activity of representing is also nothing, and that very same object that reveals to me my condition of being *nothing* can also not be otherwise than *nothing*, just the dream of the dreamer, but of a dreamer who, nevertheless, only exists in a dream. It is the peak of this experience of fragility that the sense of expansion, or that relief of one who has woken from an anguishing dream, is produced. "The feeling of the sublime arises here through our being aware of the vanishing nothingness of our own body in the presence of a greatness which itself, on the other hand, resides only in our representation, and of which we, as knowing subject, are the supporter. Therefore, here as everywhere, it arises through the contrast between the insignificance and dependence of ourselves as individuals, as phenomena of will, and the consciousness of ourselves as pure subject of knowing."[31]

3. The aesthetic and theory of knowledge

We must always bear in mind that the subjectivist realism of Schopenhauer's aesthetic – which will be decisive in *The Birth of Tragedy* – is the result of a double transformation of critical philosophy. The first has to do with the theory of knowledge, the second with the theory of will. We know Kant plays a paradigmatic role in the Schopenhauerean exposition of the nature of knowledge. The concepts of "representation" and of "will" (the world's two modes of existence) are an exact tracing of the distinction between "phenomenon" and "thing-in-itself". Throughout the four books of *The World as Will and Representation*, Schopenhauer's various theses are built upon the foundation of this duality, whether they are about the nature of sensibility, the structure of the color spectrum, the reality or visual qualities of the objects of experience, or about the types of figurative art, or even about the possible basis of a non-imperative morality. It is primarily this duality ("representation"/"will") that leads Schopenhauer to his most important break with Kant: the rejection of the Kantian triad of the faculties. Instead of the distinction between *intuition/ understanding* and *reason*, Schopenhauer propounds the *intuition/ understanding* duality. Intuition is always intellectual, that is, it is always an expression of understanding. To know is to apprehend matter beyond the forms of space and time. Matter, while perennial activity and nothing more than activity, manifests itself as causality whose subjective correlative is the principle of sufficient reason, which is only apprehensible via understanding. All intuition thus presupposes the participation of sensibility and understanding. Thus all intuition is intellectual intuition.[32]

This intellectuality of the intuition will lead Schopenhauer to transform the metaphysics of art into a propaedeutic to knowledge. The principle of sufficient reason manifests itself in the subject of knowledge in twofold fashion: as *principle of causality* in the understanding as faculty of knowledge, and as *motivation* in the will of the practical subject. However, the principle of causality is metaphysically dependent on the structure of motivation. Individual will affirms itself in each moment by constructing intuitive representations out of the objects that surround it. Intuitive knowledge expresses a will; it is the materialization of an interest, of the will's survival strategy in the confrontation with other wills which it likewise constitutes as objects in its representation. These objects are not anything more than the will's mode of appearing to other wills, nothing more than objectifications of will as representation.[33] But, in and of itself, as *thing-in-itself*, or rather, metaphysically, the will is unique. The plurality of given objects presented in representation have the value of phenomena, of apparitions of this will. However, this will, which is, in essence, unrepresentable, allows for degrees of objecthood (*Objektitaet*). The less immediate is defined in Kantian terms: it corresponds to individual given objects in representation, when subordinated to the forms of time, space and causality. Schopenhauer derives his notion of immediate objecthood expressly from the Platonic metaphysic: it is an "idea" (*Idee*). This is why he can say: "Now if for us the will is the *thing-in-itself*, and the *Idea* is the immediate objectivity of that will at a definite grade, then we find Kant's thing-in-itself and Plato's Idea ... to be, not exactly identical, but yet very closely related, and distinguished by only a single modification."[34] Ideas are the forms and the original and immutable properties of all natural bodies constituted in representation. They manifest themselves in a plurality of individuals in space, time and causality, but they are atemporal, non-spatial, causal and undetermined.

How can we gain access to the sphere of Ideas, if they do not let themselves become objectified in the intuition? Schopenhauer's response will directly link his metaphysics of the will to the anthropology of motivation in the *Critique of Judgment*. Since representation exists uniquely for a subject conditioned by his individual will, that is, by the motivation for knowledge, then placing himself beyond representation and apprehending Ideas implies an annulment of the condition of the subjective possibility of representation, it implies an annulment of the individual will, an annulment of individuality.[35] The form of this suppression of individuality too freely repeats the theory of "interest" (*Interesse*) in the *Critique of Judgment*. Kant, in §§ 41 and 42, had emphasized a modification in his vision of motivation in the judgment of taste. If the judgment of taste expresses an interest, it is an immediate interest for the simple existence of the object of judgment, as though this object were an end unto itself. In this total absorption of interest in the contemplated object, Schopenhauer sees the mechanism itself for the annulment of individual will. When faced with a beautiful form, I suspend my relation, based in motivation, to the world of representation, suspending my will and elevating myself to the condition of pure and disinterested subject. That which I contemplate is no longer the unique and beautiful object, but the idea, of which the object is the phenomenon.[36] The experience of beauty is a cognitive experience, not of the empirical object that offers itself to me in its harmonious forms, but of the Idea that this object exemplifies.

There are therefore two modes of fusion between the knowledge and the experience of beauty. Beauty is a determination of the empirical object; it is a property of its forms as they offer themselves up in time, space, and causality. In the experience of the beautiful I know something of the object, I know its beauty. It is that beauty which, a moment later, will liberate me from my individuated will, that will annul the interested condition of my knowledge and elevate me to the condition of pure subject, subject of the disinterested contemplation of beautiful forms. What is then revealed is no longer the beautiful empirical object, but the intelligible idea that it expresses. In both experiences art is the real point of entry into the sphere of knowledge: knowledge of empirical beauty, knowledge of the Idea through empirical beauty.

This process is repeated in the experience of the sublime. In the sublime I am also elevated to the intuitive contemplation of Ideas, freed from my relation to and motivation vis-à-vis the objects of representation. The difference between the beautiful and the sublime resides in the process of transition between the sphere of representation to that of Ideas. As Schopenhauer wrote:

> Thus what distinguishes the feeling of the sublime from that of the beautiful is that, with the beautiful, pure knowledge has gained the upper hand without a struggle, since the beauty of the object, in other words that quality of it which facilitates knowledge of its Idea, has removed from consciousness, without resistance and hence imperceptibly, the will and knowledge or relations that slavishly serve the will. What is then left is pure subject of knowing, and not even a recollection of the will remains. On the other hand, with the sublime, that state of pure knowing is obtained first of all by a conscious and violent tearing away from the relations of the same object to the will which are recognized as unfavourable, by a free exaltation, accompanied by consciousness, beyond the will and the knowledge related to it.[37]

4. The sublime as an ethical experience

As it was for Kant, the ambivalence of the feeling of the *sublime* is the site *par excellence* for showing the human condition in its finitude. Firstly, finitude of sensibility. Herein resides one of the most inspiring motifs of Schopenhauer's aesthetic: there is nothing except representation, that is, artistic construction by a subject who only exists to the extent that he permanently creates representations. But here finitude is not the reverse of the infinitude of the Ideas of reason. It exists with respect to, not the limits of the imagination in its own impossibility of representing the totality of the Idea which would correspond to the grandiosity of the object, but to the limits of the will of the individual who contemplates. Because the aesthetic subject is essentially will and the aspiration to continue to exist in permanent struggle against other wills, the discovery of its limits, before coinciding with the recognition of its condition as intuitive subject and thus a prisoner of the forms of space and time, is the discovery of the fragility of its existence which is exposed at every moment to the dangers of other forces. The sublime reveals this fragility in its extreme, in its absolute form, and so dissolves it, as a sentiment of nullity before the colossal force of nature, or before works of crushing grandiosity – just as it also dissolves the individuality of the spectator, transforming it into pure consciousness, into an eternal and incorporeal subject of pure knowledge.

The consciousness of finitude produced in the experience of the sublime does not, however, lead in Schopenhauer to the immediate subordination of the ethical by the aesthetic, as inclusion of the imagination's limits in the infinitude of a supra-sensible faculty which can be conjectured in the moral Idea. This difference is found precisely in the analysis of the concept of the "mathematical sublime." There we can see an essential inadequacy between the purely quantitative infinitude of space and time as *a priori* forms of the sensibility and the infinitude of the Idea, which is not revealed in the intuition. They are two infinitudes which lead in parallel fashion to the experience of the sublime.

In this same paragraph, after referring to Kant and to the distinction Kant makes between the "dynamic sublime" and the "mathematic sublime," a distinction Schopenhauer considers to be correct, he goes on to say that "... although we differ from him entirely in the explanation of the inner nature of that impression, and can concede no share in this ... to moral reflections."[38] What separates Schopenhauer from Kant is the way the experience of the sublime closes in upon itself. The mathematical sublime, which corresponds to the grandiosity of space and time in its condition as non-objective determinations of experience and, as such, its immeasurability, has an annihilating effect on the subject of aesthetic contemplation, without directing his spirit toward the moral sphere. It certainly produces a change in the point of view, but only within the sphere of knowledge:

> If we lose ourselves in contemplation of the infinite greatness of the universe in space and time, meditate on the past millennia and on those to come; or if the heavens at night actually bring innumerable worlds before our eyes, and so impress on our consciousness the immensity of the universe, we feel ourselves reduced to nothing; we feel ourselves as individuals, as living bodies, as transient phenomena of will, like drops in the ocean, dwindling and dissolving into nothing. But against such a ghost of our own nothingness, against such a lying impossibility, there arises the immediate consciousness that all these worlds exist only in our representation, only as modifications of the eternal subject of pure knowing. This we find ourselves to be, as soon as we forget individuality; it is the necessary, conditional supporter of all worlds and of all periods of time.[39]

Schopenhauer repeats Kant's description of a tension brought on by a greatness which, seeming to fill us entirely, attracts us and, at the same time, because it is formally endless, unsuited and inappropriate to our own faculty of representation, ends up by repelling us. But in Kant, the immeasurability of the sublime calls for a certain measure to be taken, an experience of respect for the immeasurable, that immeasurable which is none other than the Idea of practical reason. Because of this, Kant sometimes transforms the sentiment of the sublime into an exclusively moral experience.[40] In Schopenhauer the sublime does not heighten, it only annuls – it annihilates aesthetic consciousness. The thesis that all forms in space and time are illusory inevitably leads to the discovery of the unreality of the colossal as well, namely that the sublime object itself is an illusion. Kant's notion that the senses are of no importance in the experience of the sublime (which he sees as a negative pleasure that suspends the game of the imagination and imposes the seriousness attributed to moral law, thereby confirming the essential relationship between morality and the violence done to the senses) is precisely that which in *The World as Will and Representation* leads from knowledge of the sphere of representation to knowledge of the sphere of the *Idea*. Nevertheless, the abyss of representation, the scuttling of the forms of the sensibility, does not lead to the sphere of the supra-sensible. The sublime leads to insensibility before the colossal, before the infinitely large and terrifying. For Schopenhauer the sublime is more than an opposition to the senses: it is the only experience that totally frees the subject from the prison of sensibility. The experience of the aesthetic, as a process, is thus an *anaesthetic* experience, it uses the senses against the senses and in this way opens the consciousness to a metaphysical experience.

5. The truth of the sublime

Although Schopenhauer declares that the *beautiful* and the *sublime* are both ways to reach the sphere of Ideas – in the beautiful via the intensification and later suspension of pleasure in the object, in the sublime via the immediate suspension of interest before the hostility of the object – examples of the experience of the sublime reveal a fundamental difference. The sentiment of the beautiful never exceeds the sphere of Ideas. It raises itself out of individual beautiful forms to a form of intelligible beauty of which they are the manifestation in space and time. In the sentiment of the sublime, which, by definition, "is an exaltation beyond our own individuality [*Erhebung über das eigene Individuum*], a feeling of the sublime"[41] the violent annulment of my individuality is also an annulment of my finitude and, therefore, the metaphysical conversion of my gaze. I find myself essentially merged with the world. In the sublime I attain the knowledge of the Vedas, the feeling that "we are one with the world, and therefore not oppressed but exalted by its intensity."[42] In other words, in the sublime what is given are not Ideas – objectifications of the will – but the will itself, one and eternal. In the contemplation of a colossal object I am plucked from the empirical world in order to attain the world as *thing-in-itself*. Yet, what kind of knowledge could correspond to an experience which does not belong to the world of representation, does not take as its goal the intelligible world of Ideas?

In chapter 39 of the 1819 edition – dedicated completely to the idea of the sublime – Schopenhauer does not respond to this question. Here the sublime seems only to have an effect through privation, that is, it simply excludes the reality of something that occurs through representation. This is the value that is emphasized precisely at that moment in which Schopenhauer expels mere pleasure for the form of an empirical object from the aesthetic field. When he wants to distinguish the pure aesthetic experience (which frees the subject of his motivational relations with the world of representation) from the trivial aesthetic experience, or rather, that experience of immediate pleasure that, on the contrary, binds the subject of experience more intensely to empirical stimuli and so makes his illusory condition even worse, Schopenhauer does not use the beautiful as an example, but rather the sentiment of the sublime. It is the sublime that becomes the counterpoint to the "pretty" (*das Reizende*). "The feeling of the sublime arose from the fact that something positively unfavourable to the will becomes object of pure contemplation. This contemplation is then maintained only by a constant turning away from the will and exaltation [*Erhebung*] above its interests. ... On the other hand, the charming or attractive draws the beholder down from pure contemplation, demanded by every apprehension of the pretty, since it necessarily stirs his will by objects that directly appeal to it."[43] In the experience of the infinitely great or threatening the aesthetic pleasure is pure, entirely disinterested, because in this experience the object is "unrealized," as it were, as its representation is reduced to illusions. If the beautiful frees me as well from representation because it absorbs my vision in Ideas, these still maintain the marks of the empirical forms for which they are the Platonic model. There is both a metaphysical and an aesthesic continuity between the unique beautiful object and the universality of the Idea that it, the object, expresses as its phenomenon in space and time. Because the beauty of the object touches me, in my vision of it I separate it from its function, that which in it might satisfy some project of my will, in order to preserve it alone in its metaphysical condition of an appearance, the apparition of something else, the manifestation of an Idea. In the sublime this transition has no continuity. There is an abrupt severing in the sphere of representation (I move from the representable to that which refuses figuration) and a complete inversion in the motivational sphere (what is terrifying, hostile, repugnant, transforms itself into a sentiment of pleasure as a species of abstracted contemplation of an illusion that seems to exist for my own eyes alone). Unrepresentable and attractive, but without being an attraction by the unrepresentable – that is the mystery of the sublime within Schopenhauer's system of pessimism. And this is what distances it from the Kantian theory of the sublime. Because it is atheological and because it refuses the imperative model of morality, the sublime in Schopenhauer leads only to an experience of undefined unrepresentability, since it neither refers to the invisibility of a god, nor does it want for foundational experiences of respect for invisibility, or for the unrepresentability of the law. Pessimism lacks a metaphysic of the sublime, parallel to the metaphysic of beauty; it lacks a doctrine that establishes the nature of the objects which correspond to the experience of pure contemplation, i.e. which are revealed through the collapse of the individual will, that which is produced from the annihilation of the reality of the grandiose, or colossal reality, given in representation.

In the 1819 edition the silence about the metaphysical correlative of the sentiment of the sublime left open the way for two theses central to Schopenhauer's aesthetics. They would only come to be articulated in the 1844 edition and would play a decisive role in the metaphysics of the tragic in *The Birth of Tragedy*. They are: (a) the privileged place of tragedy in the hierarchy of those works of art which occur in the sphere of representation; and (b) the value of the truth of music.

6. Tragedy, symbol of the sublime

In chapters 43 to 51 of the 1819 edition, Schopenhauer elaborated a general cartography of the forms of art, from architecture and the art of garden design to literature, poetry and the drama and including, among other things, painting, sculpture, and the goldsmith's art. This poietic plurality is organized along the lines of a musical scale or like a chemical table that starts from the densest chemicals until it reaches the most ethereal. Architecture and its organization of large masses of stone represents the baseline, the first degree. On the other extreme we have poetry, a true architecture of significations. Within poetry Schopenhauer distinguishes *subjective* poetry from the *objective*, and in this he includes the novel, epic poetry, and the drama. And, going back to canonical classifications, he allows for two fundamental kinds of drama – comedy and tragedy. Here, according to Schopenhauer, we reach the extreme point in the hierarchy of the arts: "Tragedy is to be regarded, and is recognized, as the summit of poetic art, both as regards the greatness of the effect and the difficulty of the achievement."[44] This superiority has yet another justification, this time non-canonical: it is also a metaphor par excellence of the world, the visible figuration of its unjust essence and of injustice as its essence. The "purpose of this highest poetical achievement is the description of the terrible side of life. The unspeakable pain, the wretchedness and misery of mankind, the triumph of wickedness, the scornful mastery of chance, and the irretrievable fall of the just and the innocent are all here presented to us; and here is to be found a significant hint as to the nature of the world and existence."[45] If all forms of art are manifestations of an Idea, only tragedy expresses the world itself, only tragedy is "a significant hint as to the nature of the world and existence" (*ein bedeutsamer Wink über die Beschafenheit der Welt und des Daseins*).

In the 1819 edition the relation between the tragic experience and the category of the sublime is never established. In the examples of objects of the sublime presented in chapter 39 in the 1819 edition Schopenhauer does not include the tragedy. It is significant that, in addition to natural phenomena and colossal examples of architecture like the pyramids or Saint Peter's Basilica in Rome, he used a metaphor of tragic theatre when he refers to that which he calls "sublime character" (*erhabene Charakter*). As an example of a tragic character, he recalls the figure of Horatio as he is described by Hamlet in Shakespeare's play: "As one, in suffering all, that suffers nothing;/A man, that fortune's buffets and rewards/Hast ta'en with equal thanks" (Act III, Sc.2.).[46] And in chapter 51, dedicated to tragedy, even though it doesn't establish a specific link between the form of tragedy and the aesthetic of horror, the description that he gives of the effects the work of art has on the spectator is an exact repetition of the definition of the experience of the sublime:

> Here and there it reaches thoughtfulness and is softened more or less by the light of knowledge, until at last in the individual case this knowledge is purified and enhanced by suffering itself. It then reaches the point where the phenomenon, the veil of Maya, no longer deceives it. It sees through the form of the phenomenon, the *principium individuationis;* the egoism resting on this expires with it. The *motives* that were previously so powerful now lose their force, and instead of them, the complete knowledge or the real nature of the world, acting as a *quieter* of the will, produces resignation, the giving up not merely of life, but of the whole will-to-live itself.[47]

Everything seems to lead Schopenhauer to the thesis of the tragic condition of the sublime or of the sublime condition of the emotion which is produced in the contemplation of the tragedy. But this thesis will only come to be formulated in 1844 when Schopenhauer adds a new volume of supplements to *The World as Will and Representation*. In chapter 37 of these Supplements, which is entitled "Aesthetics of Poetry," the tragic drama is recognized as expressly belonging to, not the aesthetic of the beautiful, but to the sublime.

> Our pleasure in the *tragedy* belongs not to the feeling of the beautiful, but to that of the sublime; it is, in fact, the highest degree of this feeling. For, just as at the sight of the sublime in nature we turn away from the interest of the will, in order to behave in a purely perceptive way, so in the tragic catastrophe we turn away from the will-to-live itself. Thus in the tragedy the terrible side of life is presented to us, the wailing and lamentation of mankind, the dominion of chance and terror, the fall of the righteous, the triumph of the wicked; and so that aspect of the world is brought before our eyes which directly opposes our will. At this sight we feel ourselves urged to turn our will away from life, to give up willing and loving life.[48]

In the 1819 edition, the only examples of the sublime are natural phenomena of frightening grandiosity and violence, colossal examples of architecture and the ethical sublime of character (which is illustrated by the tragic personage). By this time the whole of tragedy as work of art has been given a privileged status in the aesthetic of the sublime. Artistic representation of the essence itself of the world, of the unjust condition of existence conditioned, as it is, by the will to live, tragedy is the materialization itself of the infinite power of its unrepresentability.[49] This tie between tragedy and the experience of the sublime will lead Schopenhauer to make a positive determination of the validity of the truth of this experience. In fact, returning to the doctrine in the *Critique of Judgment*, he will see the sublime as based on the idea of *negative representation*.

Tragedy sets two experiences of the sublime in motion. The first is when the spectator, at the pinnacle of that terror which crushes him in his identification with the misfortune of the tragic hero, discovers that everything is nothing more than a representation, that is, dramatic illusion, and because of this he suspends his interest in the destiny of the characters, raising himself to the serenity of a pure contemplative subject of the work of art. "At the moment of the tragic catastrophe, we become convinced more clearly than ever that life is a bad dream from which we have to awake. To this extent, the effect of the tragedy is analogous to that of the dynamically sublime, since, like this, it raises us above the will and its interest, and puts us in such a mood that we find pleasure in the sight of what directly opposes the will."[50] The second experience of the sublime is like a transference of the first experience from the sphere of the stage to existence in its entirety. The spectator suddenly sees himself as though he were a mere figure in a tragic play, since tragedy is nothing more than the figuration on stage of the cruel and illusory essence of existence.[51] The metaphor of theatre, which oriented Schopenhauer's work right from the beginning with its duality between the world as will and the world as representation, finds its most perfect expression in tragedy.[52]

7. The sublime and the unrepresentable

Tragedy as an art form arouses in the spectator a terror vis-à-vis existence itself; the spectator is transported directly into the realm of the sublime where the unrepresentable experience of the world is conveyed through the tragic representation, or through the tragedy of the unrepresentability of the world. Through this experience, the sentiment of another existence beyond the representable makes itself felt. This negation of life is actually an affirmation and a demand for a different form of existence, one which occurs intuitively and only allows itself to be represented as a *negative representation*. "We become aware that there is still left in us something different that we cannot possibly know positively, but only negatively, as that which does *not* will life. Just as the chord of the seventh demands the fundamental chord; just as a red colour demands green, and even produces it in the eye; so every tragedy demands an existence of an entirely different kind, a different world, the knowledge of which can always be given to us only indirectly, as here by such demand."[53] Schopenhauer has previously never come so close to the Kantian definition of the sublime: a representation of the unrepresentable. In the 1819 edition the sublime is simply a conversion of our vision of the terrifying or colossal phenomena, a conversion that transforms representation into representation of the second degree, into the representation of a representation, therefore into a *re-presentation* of sublime objects in their condition as mere *representations*. There is a neutralization of the object, but it remains in the intuition as represented. In this chapter, in the 1844 edition, Schopenhauer wants to explore the reverse side of the unrepresentability of the representation of the object as it corresponds to the sentiment of the sublime in the precise moment that it reveals itself as sublime. In the two examples presented here, the Other of representation is considered in its condition as non-representable, non-figurable, though in spite of everything, presentable in its non-representability. So, just as it is the positive representation of the dominant seventh chord that lets us negatively apprehend the fundamental chord, as the solution, the redemption of the disharmony of an interval of sound, so in the positive representation of the disharmony of existence, of the perpetual struggle between individual wills, the indirect knowledge of that which is demanded by this existence is present – in its inverse – that is, its harmony, the dissolution of the *principium individuationis* at the heart of the unified and eternal will.

In the experience of the beautiful I am led to the positive intuition of the Idea that the beautiful form (natural or artistic) is the phenomenon; in the sublime I arrive at a negative intuition of the actual thing-in-itself, the knowledge of the will of the world itself in its unrepresentability. The beautiful belongs to the dominion of representation. There is in it a metamorphosis of the empirical representation of unique objects subjected to the forms of space, time, and causality in the purely intellectual representation of universal, eternal, and unconditional Ideas. On the contrary, in the sublime, we are rooted in a world of empirical representation in order to demand a world that is completely Other which we know simply as a correlative of this demand, as the Other of representation, therefore as that which is in its essence unrepresentable.

If Schopenhauer repeats Kant in the concept of *negative representation*, there is nevertheless a double subversion of the Kantian theory of the sublime. The sublime is always the experience of the unrepresentable as a correlative of the feeling of demanding something else beyond the representable – but this unrepresentable is not an Idea. Ideas do not need the sublime in order to appear, since they are the object of intelligible intuition. For Schopenhauer what occurs in the sublime is the actual world of the in-itself, that which is beyond all representation: the unified will, that same will that each individual discovers all at once in himself as spontaneity, as vital impulse which manifests itself in motives for acting, but which therein reveals itself to be deformed by its individual condition.

And the world of the in-itself occurs as non-gift, as a negative gift, as a gift of that which cannot possibly be given, therefore as the gift of a non-gift.[54]

8. Music

What is important now is to ask a retrospective question about the metaphysics of the sublime that organized the 1819 edition. As we have indicated, (a) there is a lack therein of an actual characterization of the metaphysical condition of the sublime – frequently muddled together with the experience of the beautiful by being seen as also having the world of Ideas as its object – and (b) tragedy is never expressly incorporated within the aesthetic of the sublime. Between these two phenomena there is a rigorous parallel. The aesthetic of the sublime already points toward the unrepresentable, without this unrepresentable ever having been determined: likewise, tragedy is placed at the highest end of the hierarchy of the arts of figuration (those arts that produce or induce spatio-temporal images), which already signals a transition to a world beyond sensibility. These two points of suspension (the fact that the sublime presupposes the unrepresentable and the fact that tragedy is held in suspension between the figurative arts and the non-figurative) are present in chapter 51 of the 1819 edition. They encompass the figurative goal of art and its vocation for the intuition of Ideas via material forms. Chapter 52 completely shifts this particular analysis of art. It begins with the almost solemn declaration:

> We have now considered all of the fine arts in the general way suitable to our point of view. We began with architecture, whose aim as such is to elucidate the objectification of the will at the lowest grade of its visibility, where it shows itself as the dumb striving of the mass, devoid of knowledge and conforming to law; yet it already reveals discord with itself and conflict, namely that between gravity and rigidity. Our observations ended with tragedy, which presents to us in terrible magnitude and distinctness at the highest grade of the will's objectification that very conflict of the will with itself. After this, we find that there is yet another fine art that remains excluded, and was bound to be excluded, from our consideration, for in the systematic connexion of our discussion there was no fitting place for it; this art is *music*. It stands quite apart from all the others. In it we do not recognize the copy, the repetition, of any Idea of the inner nature of the world. Yet it is such a great and exceedingly fine art, its effect on man's innermost nature is so powerful, and it is so completely and profoundly understood by him in his innermost being as an entirely universal language, whose distinctness surpasses even that of the world of perception itself...[55]

The passage from chapter 51 to 52, or rather that which remains in suspension in the earlier and which in the latter is brought to completion, reveals a central ambiguity in the Schopenhauerean theory of art. In chapter 51 the analysis of the sublime speaks of the representation, not of ideas, but of something else from the dominion of the non-representable, that non-representable which is evoked various times as the world itself, beyond both the empirical and intelligible objectifications of it. In chapter 52 this non-representable is paradoxically seen as representable: and music is that representation. What's more: Schopenhauer knows that by modulating his notions in such a way he is formulating a thesis that he cannot justify. "I recognize, however, that it is essentially impossible to demonstrate this explanation, for it assumes and establishes a relation of music as a representation to that which of its essence can never be a representation, and claims to regard music as the copy of an original that can itself never be directly represented."[56] Music then, as a copy of an inexistence, furnishes a solution for the mystery of the sublime. What is essentially of the order of the unrepresentable becomes representation. But what could represent a representation of that which can never be the object of a representation? Will it still be representation? Might not Schopenhauer, in order to avoid the paradox of a copy without a model, have removed music from the condition of mimesis to which he attributes all forms of art? It is the double orientation – metaphysical and anthropological – of Schopenhauer's theory of art which makes it impossible to think of music as the pure presentation of itself alone, absorbing into its manifestation that model which it lacks. But, at the same time, it is exactly this orientation which makes of music the material correlative of the experience of the unrepresentable which occurs in the sublime. The sublime is that which opens sentiment to something beyond representation, and beyond Ideas, that is, to the abyss of the world's will as thing-in-itself. Negative representation, representation of that which in representation is denied – our gaze swallowed by the abyss that annuls the whole of the visible and toward which negative representation caused it to turn. The world is, in essence, the unrepresentable. But this overwhelming of the visible produces in turn a metaphysical revelation, a conversion of knowledge into pure contemplation, a conversion of vision into listening, in a word, the conversion of *negative representation* that defines the experience of the sublime into *representation without an object* which defines the work of musical art.[57]

Neither in the edition of 1819, nor in that of 1844, do we find any link between the metaphysic of music and the aesthetic of the sublime. Music is never expressly presented in its condition as perceivable resonance of the unrepresentability established by the negative representation of the sublime experience. However, it is this music/sublime dyad which lies concealed, as it were, at the centre of *The World as Will and Representation* – and it is in the form of the *music/tragedy/sublime* triad that this work will be transformed by Nietzsche into the programme for a renaissance of the tragedy through the opera of Wagner. And it will be Nietzsche who will attempt to create a unified vision of these three faces of the aesthetic of pessimism, to test the invisibility of *music* through a unified theory of artistic creation, the terrifying grandiosity of *tragedy* and the transfiguration of the subject of contemplation which is exclusive to the *sublime*. But this unity which Nietzsche will call the "dionysian experience" depended directly on Wagner. It was Wagner who gave substance to the thesis that the metaphysical uniqueness of music, that which distinguishes it from all of the other forms of art, was the result of its own aesthetic regime, or rather, the fact that it alone belongs to the sphere of the *sublime*, while all other arts should be understood through the category of the *beautiful.*

9. Music and the sublime in Wagner

We know that Wagner offers the best path towards reconstructing precisely how Nietzsche's aesthetic theory is derived from Schopenhauer's metaphysics. However, this path is far from being transparent. On the one hand, we do not know to what extent the aesthetic of pessimism really influenced Wagner's production.[58] On the other, it is also difficult to determine from which moment Nietzsche himself began to furnish Wagner with certain of his own theoretical intuitions, intuitions which were later incorporated into *The Birth of Tragedy*, as though they had been inspired by the experience of Wagnerian opera.[59]

It is in the context of this indetermination that we must read the only text in which Wagner formulated the thesis which contained in latent form the whole of Schopenhauer's aesthetic – that is, the thesis of the sublime character of music. We refer to his essay *Beethoven*, written in 1870 to commemorate the centenary of the birth of the composer. This is the only place in all of Wagner's writings where we find an elaboration of a doctrine of the sublime, formulated here in the attempt to discover the essence of Beethoven's instrumental music and through it the essence of all music. After *Beethoven*, Wagner would never again defend the correlation between music and the sublime. And, what is more significant, the doctrine of the sublime is not only constructed according to Schopenhauer's principles, but it also anticipates the articulation between tragedy (as musical drama) and the Dionysian aesthetic (as an aesthetic of rhythmic and melodic dissonance) which Nietzsche would elaborate a year later. Wagner's *Beethoven* functions as a true bridge between Schopenhauer and Nietzsche. At the same time, it is surprising that in *The Birth of Tragedy* this doctrine on the sublime condition of music, even though it serves to organize the whole reading of the Dionysian/Apollonian opposition, only appears obliquely. It is as though Wagner, having appropriated the interpretation of the theory of the sublime, which structured the Nietzschean reading of the universe of classical tragedy, had forced Nietzsche into silence about his own intuitions. In fact, we can imagine that, recognizing Wagner's expropriation in *Beethoven* of his theses on the link between music and the sublime, Nietzsche did not take them up again explicitly in order to avoid raising the question of precedence. This would explain why the central theses of *The Birth of Tragedy* on Greek culture did not appear to repeat Wagner's aesthetic positions; Nietzsche may have preferred to exclude the explicit formulation of his theory of the sublime and, as such, condemned his reading of classic tragedy to theoretical stillbirth. What is more, no other text by Wagner after *Beethoven* repeats the thesis on the sublime in music. One might be led to speculate that Wagner, conscious of his appropriation of the positions of this young professor of classical philology from Basel, was anxious to erase forever the marks of his "crime." Of course, these questions outstrip the bounds of the present work. Nevertheless, they do tend to hover around any parallel reading of *Beethoven* and *The Birth of Tragedy*.

In *Beethoven* the thesis on the sublime condition of music responds to a very particular aesthetic problem: the determination of the metaphysical nature of the "musical drama." Wagner wants to establish an objective basis for joining music with other art forms (poetry, set design, the dance, and the art of acting) in a single and "total" work of art. The plurality of materials and languages which converge in the realization of each opera cannot be the result simply of mechanisms of juxtaposition. They must occur as a real organic unity, one which is indissoluble. Only in this way can they provoke a single affect in the spectator. Wagner found his solution in Schopenhauer's interpretation of Kant's establishment of the difference between the *beautiful* and the *sublime* in the *Critique of Judgment*:

> Music ... can be judged, as far as it is properly concerned, only after the category of the *Sublime*, for, as soon as it touches us, we are filled with the highest ecstasy of the consciousness of illimitability. That which *results* from our being absorbed by the perception of a work of plastic art, i.e., the effect of *Beauty*, produced by the temporary emancipation of the intellect from the service of the individual will (which takes place whilst the connection of the will with the object perceived is severed), *that* effect music produces *at once*; for, as soon as it strikes the ear, it draws the intellect away from any apprehension of the relations of external things, it shuts us off, as it were, from the outer world, and causes us to look inwards, as into the essential nature of all things.[60]

The canonical characteristics of the sublime spelled out by Schopenhauer are here attributed to the musical experience: (a) the consciousness of a gift of something formless, limitless, in a word, the absence of the figuration of experience; (b) freeing the intellect from its link with the individual will; (c) contrary to the beautiful, the sublime produces its effect on one's spirit instantaneously, brusquely plucking the intellect from the dominion of thingness (perceivable or ideal); (d) penetration of the world as thing-in-itself, access to the intimate and essential dimension of all things. As a structuring thesis, this reflects the need to distinguish between the *sublime* and the *beautiful*.

Wagner's appropriation of the sublime should also be read as a transposition of the opposition between the sublime and the beautiful, which the Schopenhaurean metaphysics of music prepared for but never performed. By establishing this connection between music and the sublime, Wagner wants to ignite a radical break between modes of aesthetic experience, he wants to eliminate the controversy with Hanslick over the ontological and aesthetic condition of the musical object, a distinction which is much more than simply a speculative construction. By including the musical experience in the sphere of the sublime, Wagner frees himself with a single blow from all of Hanslick's objections to his expressionist definition of music.

It should be recalled that Eduard Hanslick, the music critic who most vehemently resisted Wagnerianism, was also the founder of the formalist aesthetic.[61] In 1854 he had declared, in his *Von Musikalisch-Schönen*, that what defines music as an object of art are not the feelings that it expresses, the more or less violent experiences of ecstasy or the elevation of the spirit, but the determinations of its form, that is, its beauty as an inherent property of the architecture of sounds.[62] Grounding his arguments in the classical identification between beauty and form, Hanslick concludes that musical beauty can be nothing more than the way in which the form of sounds exist, even if this form seems imperceptible, something that is beyond the sentiments that it awakens.[63]

Hanslick does not reject the existence of sentiments associated with music. However, he considers that they are not inherent to audible matter. For this reason, as he writes, "the faculty that apprehends the beautiful is not the emotions, but the imagination, as an act of pure intuition."[64] It is obvious that Wagner's compositions and, above all, the way in which he legitimated his investment in the sphere of pure expression of the feelings, was the principal target of *Von Musikalisch-Schönen*.[65]

The distinction between the *beautiful* and the *sublime* provided Wagner with an apparently simple refutation of this formalism. The subjection to forms and to their rules, in the way that Hanslick intends, according to Wagner, is a crude transposition of the aesthetic of the plastic arts – and therefore of the beautiful – to musical art. Wagner rescues the autonomy of sentiment at the same time that he locates it in the essence of musical creation as a subjective correlative to the *sublime*. Hanslick's whole theory as it is proposed in *Von Musikalisch-Schönen* is bluntly reduced to a limited point of view of music, as Wagner shows that he has only captured its condition as a work of *belle art*. The aesthetic of the sublime which Wagner employed allowed him to make ecstasy, the sudden transport from the sphere of representation to the heights of the unrepresentable, the transport which goes further than all of the forms, the centre of the musical object. "If we survey the progress which music has made under Beethoven from an historical point of view, we may briefly describe it as the attainment of a faculty which had previously been denied to it: by virtue of this faculty music, from the confines of aesthetical beauty, strides into the sphere of the Sublime; and in this sphere it has been released from all constraint of traditional or conventional forms, and it completely penetrates and animates these forms with its proper spirit."[66] With Beethoven, or rather, with purely instrumental music and with the "symphonic poem," the faculty of the sublime was conquered. Instead of Hanslick's architecture of sounds, we have the animating of musical forms by something which is far beyond them. And this beyondness represents a "spirit," the "spirit of music" (*Geist der Musik*).

Wagner did not limit himself to using the concept of the sublime exactly as he found it in Schopenhauer. He surpasses the Schopenhauerean metaphysics of music insomuch as he finds a way to include within it the polarity between the sublime and the beautiful. Although he defines the metaphysical condition of music exactly according to the canons of *The World as Will and Representation* – a representation of the essence of the world as irrepresentable – he never questions the fact that Schopenhauer did not establish at any point a correspondence between *music* and the *sublime*. It is clear that Schopenhauer was unable to achieve such a thing; for him the concept of the sublime still belonged to the dominion of the arts, to the dominion of representation which produced an aesthetic effect by starting with the forms of space and time. This effect would then lead to the contemplation of Ideas or to simple resignation. That did not impede Wagner from using the vocabulary of pessimism – its ethical tone and its appeal for resignation – to describe the experience of music as *sublime*. As to the symphonies of Beethoven, especially those composed in the later period when he was completely deaf, Wagner has the following to say: their effect upon the hearer is that of setting him free from the sense of guilt, just as their after-effect is a feeling of "paradise lost," with which one again turns toward the world of phenomena. Thus these wonderful works preach repentance and atonement in the deepest sense of a divine revelation. The aesthetic idea of the *Sublime* is alone applicable here: for the effect of serenity passes at once far beyond any satisfaction to be derived from mere beauty.[67] Wagner gets to the fundamental heart of the aesthetic of the *sublime* and to that which truly comprises its tradition, from Longinus to Kant, from Schiller to Schopenhauer: its theophanic condition. Art moves us only to the extent that it is experienced as the unrepresentable presence of the absolute, of the divine. As Kant insisted, the oldest organizing law of artistic creation is the Mosaic law on the interdiction of all images of God. About the sublime, the Mosaic law speaks the truth. It says that there can be no possible representation of the metaphysic or of the absolute. That which is invisible in the work of art is its divine character; it is that which touches us as divine revelation. *Beethoven* marks another turning point in Wagner's work – a change toward the mystical, which, more than anything else, Nietzsche will denounce at the moment of their rupture. In Wagner's concept of the sublime as divine, he abandons the romantic project to transform the forms of art into a new religion. Instead, it is suddenly religion that is proffered as art's escape valve.[68]

There is yet another goal behind Wagner's characterization of music according to the category of the sublime. Conceived of as the representation of the unrepresentable in representation, the sublime provides the key rationale for the total work of art, that is, the unification of music with drama. In the "musical drama" sound and image come together, or even better, fuse into a new aesthetic and metaphysical existence, leaving the perceivable universe of both – the condition of their materiality – unaffected. Music is at once the truth and the non-presence of the drama. It is music that makes the drama into a representation, not of human actions, but of something absolute, in itself utterly unrepresentable. In this way Wagner explicitly fuses the romantic tradition of tragedy and the Schopenhauerean metaphysics of music – "Music which does not represent the ideas contained in the phenomena of the world, but is itself an Idea, indeed, a comprehensive Idea of the world, embraces the drama as a matter of course, since that the drama, again, represents the only Idea of the world adequate to music. The drama reaches beyond the confines of poetic art, as music reaches beyond those of other arts, the plastic arts especially, since its effects lie solely in the region of the Sublime."[69] Music is itself the essence of the world, that is, its Idea. But because it is unrepresentable in itself, the Idea can only be really seen in the drama as its expression, which becomes its palpable expression. The drama goes beyond poetry by inscribing it in the visible space of the actor's body and on the stage itself. Music, in turn, inscribes the drama in the underlying invisibility of the world's essence. It is because tragic drama belongs to the sublime, as Schiller and, after him, Schopenhauer had revealed, and because music, as Wagner contended (carrying the aesthetic of pessimism to its limit), is itself a form of the art of the formless, of the non-visible, the unrepresentable, that the total work of art, the musical drama, is metaphysically possible. Music and drama pour forth out of this common abyssal depth that is the intimate essence of things, the actual *thing-in-itself*, from this underlying formless world, which sustains the surface of appearance, the dramatic appearance of the characters, the audible appearance of melody, of harmony and rhythm.[70] Here is the perfect resonance of Schopenhauerean polarities within a single work of art, the "musical drama" – from the thing-in-itself to the phenomenon, from music to the drama, the formless to form, Wagner brings all of the spheres of art together, aligning them along that fundamental fault-line that distinguishes between the sublime and the beautiful.

10. Nietzsche

All the facts are in the open. It remains for Nietzsche to unite them in a single vision of the Greek Tragedy as musical drama. Apollo, the divinity of the forms of appearance, Dionysus, who spreads the vision of the formless, of chaos, the true vision of the essence of this cruel world – they will be the symbols of this long metamorphosis of the difference between the beautiful and the sublime. After Kant, Schiller, Schopenhauer, and Wagner, the Nietzschean moment in the history of the sublime is nearly insignificant. He will have to take this small step in the elaboration of this ambivalent experience of pain that leads to a more elevated pleasure. Yet this step marks the separation of two traditions. In *The Birth of Tragedy* the sublime speaks the language of Schopenhauer and of Wagner, though its consequences differ. The terror which the disciple of Dionysus feels in that moment in which, led by music and dance, he immerses his vision in the world's essence, fails to drive him to resignation, to the negation of will. Crushed beneath the cruelty of existence, which is revealed in the experience of the sublime, he does not aspire to another existence, he doesn't attempt to raise himself to a negative representation of that which lies beyond all representation, beyond the realm of forms, beyond life. According to Nietzsche, the Greeks had discovered that at the pinnacle of the sublime it is possible to aspire to the beautiful, to appearance, to the return to the serenity of forms. And this would have been the discovery that engendered tragedy. Apollo as the vestibule to Dionysus, the dream that prepares for the revelation of the intimate essence of things. And a revelation that, because it is intolerable, demands once again the pleasure of appearance.

The beautiful that redeems the sublime is Nietzsche's invention. In a Dionysus which aspires to the state of Apollo, there lies the ecstatic experience which aspires to be itself, which is justified by itself alone. The end of the sublime as an ethical experience, the beginning of the aesthetic as an experience of the sublime. This will be a small step in the history of the sublime. But it will be enough to remove the aesthetic, from its condition as the path to the ethical, in the way that Kant, Schiller, Schopenhauer, and Wagner had imagined.

It is now possible in this lengthy story to write the chapter on Nietzsche.

2

The Individual and Individuality in Nietzsche

> The pessimistic condemnation of life by Schopenhauer is a moral one. Transference of herd standards into the realm of metaphysics.
>
> The "individuum" meaningless. ... We are paying for the fact that science has not understood the individuum.
>
> Friedrich Nietzsche,
Posthumous Fragments; The Will to Power[1]

For Nietzsche nihilism is the extreme consequence of that ineffable condition of the singular that defines philosophy beginning with Plato. Whether as the One (as in the figures of the Platonic *Idea*, as Spinoza's *Divine Substance*, as Hegel's *Spirit*, or Schopenhauer's *One Will*, within which the singular is delimited as a copy, a mode, a moment or a phenomenon), or as Law, which confers truth and intelligibility upon singular phenomena, or, lastly, as the Good or the Common Interest, which determines the value of individual actions, the West has always reduced the singular to the condition of a simple Archimedean point of one reality, of one truth and of one morality. Nihilism, that indisposition of European conscience at loggerheads with the fictional character of all knowledge, was the result of the emergence of the scandal of singularity and the discovery of the "all-too-human" nature underlying all of the figures of the universal. Yet, at the same moment in which the individual frees himself from the reality of the universal, he deprives himself of his own truth. The collapse of the One, the Truth and the Good – which Nietzsche condensed into the idea of the "death of God" – and around which human essence, knowledge, and will had gravitated, threatens each individual's self-confidence. From that point on, all individuality seemed groundless, all phenomena chaotic, and all actions vain.

For Nietzsche, the inversion of values is an affirmation of the radically individual character of each being and a denial of the thesis of a Universal which exists in and of itself; it is the denial of a Being apart. But it is as well the immanent quest in each individual being for his own individuality, for some inner law that connects him to his predicates, states, and modifications. It is this law that constitutes the foundation of his biography and his own internal principle of differentiation as he faces other individuals. In spite of the fact that Nietzsche considered himself – in his struggle to intensify singularity – as totally outside the history of philosophy, in essence he is returning to a certain metaphysical tradition, one which, as in Aristotle and Leibniz, attributed absolute ontological primacy to the individual. "There are only individuals,"[2] Nietzsche never tired of affirming; only the individual being is a real being, or, as Leibniz had said, "ce qui n'est pas véritablement *un* estre, n'est pas non plus véritablement un *estre*."[3]

However, what we call Nietzsche's "ontology" lacks – like all the rest of his fundamental concepts – an explicit explanation of the idea of the individual.[4] This fact is due most importantly to the deliberately non-systematic character of his texts. While dozens of aphorisms take on the theme of singularity, they always do so laterally, sporadically, and in a nearly concealed fashion. But there are two more decisive reasons for the obscurity of Nietzsche's explanation of the individual. One is the fact that he took as his starting point those paradoxes of individuation which run through the metaphysics of Schopenhauer; the second lies in the fact that Nietzsche would attempt to dissimilate this inheritance and escape it through a process of permanent internal reformulation of his own anti-Schopenhauerean positions.

To understand Nietzsche we must pursue the consequences of this link to Schopenhauer, whether it is in those texts written between 1872 and 1885, marked, as they are, by the paradigms of pessimism, or in those which, after 1885, decisively break with these paradigms and are contemporaneous with Nietzsche's formulation of the theory of nihilism and the will to power.

While we should underscore the superiority of the images of individuation proposed by the theory of the will to power, the theory itself falls short of the solution to the problem that Nietzsche was trying to address. It did allow him to overcome the paradoxes that he had inherited from Schopenhauerean metaphysics and to create a basis for his project of the inversion of all values, that is, the ethical and ontological justification for individual existence. But he was never able to produce a determination of the individual that would be simultaneously intrinsic and exhaustive. But neither, for that matter, has anyone else.

I. Meditation on the Individual in the Period Preceding the Theory of the Will to Power

1. The paradox of individuality in Schopenhauer

The essential incommunicability between *individuality* (*Individualität*) and *individuation* (*Individuation*) remains one of the central paradoxes of Schopenhauerean metaphysics; and it is the one which most hindered the autonomous development of the Nietzschean theory of the individual.

Schopenhauer defines the principle of individuation in exclusively spatial and temporal terms: a single individual cannot begin to exist twice in time, just as two individuals cannot occupy the same space simultaneously. He goes so far as to call space and time "*principium individuationis*" because, as he says, "it is only by means of time and space that something which is one and the same according to nature and its concept appears as different, as a plurality of co-existent and successive things."[5] Since Schopenhauer, following Kant, refuses to give space and time the character of real determinants of the objects of experience, there can be no objective principle in the differentiation between two individuals, or between two moments of the same individual. Thus each individual's individuation is reduced to mere appearance.

Nevertheless, along with phenomenal individuation, Schopenhauer affirms that for each individual there is a real essence, the sign of his uniqueness and the foundation of the identity of his existence in time and space beyond the diversity of forms. In natural beings this essence is generic, the expression of an Idea. If on a level of existence in space and time two animals of the same species can only be differentiated through appearance, on the level of essence they are totally indistinguishable. This is not, however, the case with two individuals endowed with consciousness. Their essence is individual. Each person, while just an illusory individuation in existence, is a real individuality in essence. Schopenhauer's conception of this individuality is based explicitly on the Kantian concept of "intelligible character," as he employs it in the solution of the third antinomy of the *Critique of Pure Reason* in order to reconcile mathematical regularity of phenomena on the temporal plane with human freedom.[6] Schopenhauer adopts the Kantian solution, even considering it as the point at which critical philosophy serves as an introduction to his metaphysic of the will.[7] Yet what in Kant was merely *law* is interpreted in Schopenhauer as *thing*. Indeed, Schopenhauer actually reifies "intelligible character," identifying it as the will as it is manifested in each individual. In this way, more than being a problematic concept, or an ideal correlate of the unity of apperception, or a casual and intelligible rule for acting, the *thing-in-itself*, according to Schopenhauer, is actually, in an immediate and intuitive way, the will of each individual. But the paradox lies therein. This reification of the *thing-in-itself* implies that while embodied in a multiplicity of particular wills, it is still subject to space and time – forms which are the exclusive property of phenomena. Overcoming this contradiction is left up to the thesis of the unity of will, as *thing-in-itself*, beyond the multiplicity of its spatio-temporal embodiments (the central thesis of Schopenhauerean metaphysics). Not only does a real distinction between numerically distinct individuals not exist, from an empirical point of view, but the existence of such a multiple is considered to be phenomenal and, as such, unreal. The result of all this is that Schopenhauer generally comes to see the individual as, on the one hand, the double incarnation of the *thing-in-itself* – as much "intelligible character" as will – and on the other, pure phenomenon. From the empirical point of view, therefore, the individual is not only not a real particular, he is not endowed with individuality.

What then is the real basis of each human being's individuality for Schopenhauer? For, as Kant did before him, he considers individuality to be the condition that makes any judgment of imputability possible and, as such, that which clears the way for a personal ethics. This question is not answered in his metaphysics. Schopenhauer is aware of this when he writes in one of his final works: "*Individuality* does not rest on the *principio individuationis* alone and therefore is not through and through mere *appearance*. Rather, it is rooted in the thing in itself, in the will of the individual: for its character is itself the individual. How deep its roots go here, however, belongs to the question which I do not attempt to answer."[8]

An absolute criterion for individual differentiation exists only from the standpoint of intelligibility. On the simple plane of representation, there is no distinction save the numerical.

This paradox of individuation is freighted with ethical consequences. Since for Schopenhauer no real difference exists from the point of view of the multiplicity of individual wills, the unremitting struggle for survival between them is considered essentially groundless.

From the perspective of the *thing-in-itself*, it is the same will, one and indivisible, "which digs its own teeth into itself."[9] Therefore, surmounting injustice and sundering appearances can only be achieved, according to Schopenhauer, through the nullification, by each individual, of his own individuality and of his own individual will, raising it to the generic status of pure subject of knowledge.

2. Individuation between the aesthetic and the ethical

The works of Nietzsche's first period (1872–8) are profoundly marked by this paradox which lies at the root of individuality in Schopenhauer's metaphysics. They adopt the fundamental distinction between the *thing-in-itself* and phenomenon, just as Schopenhauer in his fashion (using it as the paradigm for a series of oppositions such as one/multiple, essence/existence, reality/appearance) adopted it from Kant. Already in the first chapter of *The Birth of Tragedy*, published in 1872, Nietzsche makes no bones about specifying the metaphysical principles from which he is about to launch himself. "Philosophical natures even have a presentiment that hidden beneath the reality in which we live and have our being there also lies a second, quite different reality; in other words, this reality too is a semblance."[10] In another passage he goes so far as to characterize this appearance as "absolute inexistence."[11] Yet, admitting to the unreal nature of the forms of space and time, wherein the existence of each individual being unfolds, will be equally consequential for Nietzsche's meditation on the individual and his individuality. In Nietzsche's eyes the empirical individual will always be doubly groundless, whether he is particular, before the One of universal will of which he is only an ephemeral manifestation, or singular, before his own individuality, which renders his empirical action a simple, imperfect and chaotic copy of the intelligible law it embodies.

The Birth of Tragedy builds itself precisely upon the figures of Dionysus and Apollo, around the opposition between the One and the Multiple, while the *Untimely Meditations*, especially the third one, entitled "Schopenhauer as Educator", published in 1874, try to overcome the radical incommunicability between individuality and empirical individuation.

However, like all great disciples, Nietzsche is no mere parrot of his master. Already in these works the fault-lines that signal a rupture with Schopenhauer's thinking have begun to appear precisely in Nietzsche's search for a justification of individual empirical existence. Nietzsche breaks not only with Schopenhauer's definition of the principle of individuation, but also with the ethical consequences of the absence of any real empirical correlative for individuality. In this way, even though he acknowledges that individual existence is an injustice against the One, Nietzsche tries to justify the plane of appearance and, with it, the empirical existence of each individual, instead of proposing, like Schopenhauer, a process of ascetic negation of the individual will. How does he do this? He establishes a dialectic tension between Truth and Appearance, a vision of the One and an affirmation of the Multiple, a knowledge of the Intelligible and an apology for the Empirical. In *The Birth of Tragedy*, for example, if Dionysian ecstasy represents the state of aesthetic fusion with the "Primal One" (*das Ur-Ein*) which, as Schopenhauer had affirmed, is reached in the disinterested contemplation of the Whole beyond all personal motivations,[12] that ecstasy is nevertheless offset by the figure of Apollo, "the magnificent divine image [*Götterbild*] of the *principium individuationis,*" as Nietzsche precisely calls him,[13] who seeks through the apology for the forms of appearance and dreams to justify the individualized character of human existence.[14] For Nietzsche, the mystery of Greek tragedy consisted precisely in the fact that at the heart of the drama there was this tension, between the One of mystical fusion with the universe in Dionysian delirium and the Multiple of the characters of Apollonian drama as they struggled to affirm the hero's individuality.

Similarly, in the third of his *Untimely Meditations,* Nietzsche seeks to justify the empirical existence of each individual. He adopts an interior point of view, conceiving the individual not only as one, but as unique according to his individuality. Early on in this work, he defines each individual as a "unique miracle" (*ein einmaliges Wunder*), endowed with an absolute "uniqueness" (*Einzigkeit*). This uniqueness, regarded as being truly the "quick of his being" (*der Kern seines Wesen*), is conceived, as well, according to the model of "intelligible character." It is the "fundamental law" (*Grundgesetz*) that comprises the principle of his individuality and confers unity upon the biography of each individual because it regulates the condition of its manifestation.[15] Even though he admits, as Schopenhauer does, to the fickle and spurious nature of the empirical existence of each individual, Nietzsche does not deny this existence, but seeks to endow it with dignity and imbue it with intelligibility by purifying it of its empirical determinations in such a way that it becomes an exact mirror of the individuality which it embodies "Be yourself! The totality of what you are is not what you do, think, desire."[16]

In both *The Birth of Tragedy* and the third of the *Untimely Meditations,* whether from the standpoint of individuation, or of individuality, Nietzsche seeks to overcome Schopenhauer's condemnation of individual existence. Nonetheless, he still, at this stage, remains the victim of his "educator's" metaphysical paradigms. In fact, even though Nietzsche grounds the figure of Apollo in the multiple, thereby rescuing it from the vertigo of the One,[17] this is not because of a different conception of individuation, but simply to invoke life's need for appearance.[18] Since he continues to consider that space and time originate in the subject of representation, Nietzsche's solution ends up being reduced to a simple value judgment: he simply inverts the Truth–Appearance hierarchy and leaves the formative principle of their differentiation unquestioned. He rescues the individual from the abyss of truth but only by maintaining the sphere of illusion as the place of aesthetic justification of existence.

Also in the third of his *Untimely Meditations,* individuality – because he still conceives of it from within the framework of Schopenhauerean metaphysics – becomes irreconcilable with empirical existence which Nietzsche set out to justify through it. Contrary to what would take place after 1885 with the theory of the will to power, the "fundamental law," which defines the individuality of each person and which grounds his identity in time, is still not thought of as a serial law containing all of the states of the individual's biography and for which temporality would, therefore, be immanent. As Schopenhauer did, the 1874 text conceives of individuality as the atemporal rule that manifests itself as a reiterated point within the series of events that constitutes the existence of each individual; because individuality, in its immutability, is unconditioned, it remains essentially distinct from this same existence. The evolution and the mutability of each biography are not contained within the law, but are merely the aftermath of the diversity of external conditions which make up the empirical framework of its manifestation. As such, the only way that an individual can recover his true individuality is by abstracting his existence from empirical determinations, transforming each moment of his biography into the exact expression of his meta-empirical individuality. "That heroism of truth" – writes Nietzsche – "consists in its one day ceasing to be its plaything. In the process of becoming all is hollow, deceitful, vain, worthy of our contempt; the puzzle which man ought to solve, he can only release from being, in being such and not other, in the everlasting. Now he begins to check how deeply he is united with becoming, how deeply he is united with being – an enormous task wells up before his soul; to destroy all being, to illuminate all falsity in things."[19] By identifying with this everlasting individuality which constitutes the pith of all that he is, and which secures his identity in its becoming, that is, his status as a *being*, the individual is reduced to a pure and petrified essence, to a disembodied spirit, while at the same time the spatio-temporal plane against which his biography unfolds, condemned as it is to being "vain and deceitful," still lacks inherent consistency, no longer, as it were, before the One, but before the individual and atemporal law of which it is considered a mere sensory manifestation.

In the works of this first period Nietzsche is never quite able to work out a positive concept for either the individual or individuality. The most he can do is to invert the ethical consequences of Schopenhauer's paradox of intelligible individuality to which no empirical individuation corresponds, without questioning the metaphysical postulates which establish it. The individual that Nietzsche would justify remains divided between an extrinsic definition (as a particular in the heart of the spatio-temporal Multiple, where all differentiation as such is considered unreal) and an intrinsic definition, an atemporal individuality which reduces the individual to an abstract entity, in other words, between a merely numerical differentiation and one which is real yet abstract.

3. The individual without qualities

With the publication of *Human, All Too Human* in 1878, an open break with Schophenhauer's metaphysics took place, which, according to what Nietzsche believed, implied a break with metaphysics in general. The principal target of this break would be precisely the distinction between a "metaphysical world" and a "world of representation." "It is true, there could be a metaphysical world; the absolute possibility of it is hardly to be disputed," Nietzsche wrote at the time, "for one could assert nothing at all of the metaphysical world except that it was a being-other, and inaccessible, incomprehensible being-other; it would be a thing with negative qualities."[20] What we now have before us is not just a simple hierarchy; the world of representation is suddenly seen as autonomous from the world of metaphysics. Nietzsche even declares solemnly: "We are in the realm of representation [*Vorstellung*], no 'intuition' can take us any further."[21]

This autonomy conferred upon the forms of space, time, and causality brings with it the reality of the principle of individuation pitted against the illusion of the undifferentiated One. The spatio-temporal dimension ends up creating an objective principle of individuation. The individual is no longer considered to be a mere phenomenon: "There are only individuals."[22]

In the works of this period – *Mixed Opinions and Maxims, The Wanderer and His Shadow, Daybreak* and *The Gay Science* – the concept of the individual occupies a central position. Nietzsche seeks to determine the historical conditions that permitted the appearance of sovereign individuals, who struggled for their own individuality and whose model he discovers in the Italian Renaissance man.[23] Yet, this autonomy of representation compromises the basis of the individuality of each singular being. In fact, to reject the possibility of an unconditioned world, which comprises the principle of intelligibility of the empirical world, implies stripping individuality of its status as immutable law, removing the basis not only for the identity of each individual in time, but for his internal principle of individual differentiation. On the strict level of representation, the individuality of human action is necessarily diluted by the empirical constraints of his biography. Nietzsche even considers that the biographical sequence of each individual is determined in the long chain of causality in such a way that, as he indicates, "if one were all-knowing, one would be able to calculate every individual action, likewise every advance in knowledge, every error, every piece of wickedness. The actor himself, to be sure, is fixed in the illusion of free will; if for one moment the wheel of the world were to stand still, and there were an all-knowing, calculating intelligence there to make use of this pause, it could narrate the future of every creature to the remotest ages and describe every track along which this wheel has yet to roll."[24]

On the level of representation, all internal laws of action disappear. The individual can no longer live according to his own law, nor can he even be himself. The only law that remains is one which regulates the multiplicity of individual biographies. This is the principle of causality, which mechanically determines all of the events on the "wheel of the world," as a function of its position in the order of simultaneity and of succession.

Individuality is no longer just a matter of introspection. On the strict level of forms of space and of time there are only external relations; in this way, the "interior" of each particular being is nothing more than an extension of these relations and, as Nietzsche says, "We have transferred 'society' into ourselves, diminished it, and withdrawing into oneself is no escape from society; rather it is often a meticulous *clearing up* and *interpretation* of our [inner] processes according to the schema of earlier experiences."[25]

If representation is declared to be the only plane of reality, then numerical difference will come to be considered objective. Individual difference then becomes simply a question of numbers rather than an individual and internal principle of differentiation. The individual is condemned to being nothing more than a generality, a simple internal reproduction of the empirical framework within which his existence unfolds.

What, then, would be the basis of individuality that allows for each particular being to construct himself as a person, as an autarkic individual? Nietzsche's solution will be aporetic: because individuality is not an original given that each individual finds within himself, it must be conceived of as a task to be accomplished. Numerical difference must become real difference through a process by which one renounces one's general features. Accordingly, Nietzsche even declares: "My moral would be ever more to deprive men of their universal character, and to specialize in it, up to a degree incomprehensible for the others to achieve."[26] Individuality now becomes a model to construct and to be realized by each individual: "The point is, however: that *each* designs his own model-image and actualizes it – the individual model."[27] Yet, this conception of the individual is also clearly incompatible with Nietzsche's reduction of the whole structure of reality to the plane of representation and its particular set of laws. The dynamism implicit in each being's movement toward his own model of individuality contradicts the reduction of all causal processes to one single process (that which comes into play in the strictly mechanical concatenation of all events on the "wheel of the world"). That would be to admit that the real cause of human action came from a tendency toward an individual *telos* whose existence is merely fictional. Nietzsche himself realizes that there is a contradiction when he asks: "How does the model relate itself to our evolution? To that which we must necessarily strive for? Is the model at best an anticipation? But why then necessary?"[28]

Nietzsche ends up denying any power of causation to the individual model, in which he had seen an alternative to the "intelligible character" paradigm. This model, as Nietzsche said, was limited to being "*a representation of the ego*" (*Vorstellung vom "Ich"*).[29]

The concept of the construction and realization of an individual model, which will come to substitute the concept of discovering and living by a fundamental law, is, finally, as illusory as its precursor paradigm. If individuality cannot be conceived as the interior of each individual, as the formal cause of his identity in time – since this would presuppose a real conditioning relationship between the intelligible plane of law and the empirical plane of action – then, correspondingly, individuality can also not be conceived as merely external, something to be achieved and which, as a final cause, would guarantee the identity of each individual. The individual model, as a *telos*, transcends the plane of representation as thoroughly as did the a-temporal law conceived as its intelligible formal cause.

Given that Nietzsche wants to remain on the level of representation, refusing to fall back on "metaphysical institution" which, according to him, are characterized precisely by the postulation of ideal entities to explain empirical phenomena (such as laws, forms, finalities), the real basis of individuality is for the moment not pursued at all.

If Schopenhauer had – as a way of saving individuality – condemned the individual to the status of mere appearance by considering individuation to be exclusively founded in the forms of representation, Nietzsche, in his turn, guided by the search for a justification for individuality within empirical individuation, saves the forms of representation by viewing them as the only real plane. Yet, by doing so, individuality is condemned to the status of mere appearance, to being a simple representation which the "ego" creates out of itself, petrified as it is within the causal chain of events in time. Nietzsche remains the victim of Schopenhauer's metaphysics, precisely because of the fashion in which he rejects them.

The first time Nietzsche will undertake to resolve this aporia, between an individuality without individuation and an individuation without individuality, will be with the idea of the Eternal Recurrence.

4. Individuality as identity in repetition: the doctrine of the Eternal Recurrence

The image of a long chain of causation, the "wheel of the world" upon which all events are rigorously connected, steered Nietzsche, in 1881, toward the idea of the Eternal Recurrence. According to him, the entire series of the world's events cannot have had a beginning in time; nor is it acceptable that it could tend toward some final state. Such being the case, this series would have to be eternal in the sense that it would always have existed and would always continue to exist.[30] However, since Nietzsche starts from the principle that the number of possible events within this chain of causation is finite – as the totality of the force of the universe is constant – he concludes that becoming is circular in character. Each episode in the biography of each individual is absolutely equal to an infinite number of other events in these biographies already lived in earlier phases of the great recurrence of all things. "Thus the development of this moment must be a repetition, and also that which generated it, and that which arises from it, as so forward and backward again!"[31]

The idea of an eternal recurrence of all events allows Nietzsche to innovatively reformulate the basis of each individual's individuality, though the result will be terribly paradoxical.

We have seen how, by reducing reality to the plane of representation, Nietzsche does not contest Schopenhauer's principle of individuation; he simply considers it objective, that is, as the real determination of the objects of experience. Yet, we have also seen how this principle limits us to thinking about numerical difference and not real difference. After 1878, the individual is conceived objectively as a particular being, numerically distinct from other beings, though not distinct in terms of individuality. What constitutes the individual, as such, is simply the fact that he cannot have two separate beginnings in time and cannot occupy two different points in space simultaneously. Because an individual continues to be conceived of exclusively as a function of his place in an order of succession and simultaneities, Nietzsche concludes that temporal differences are necessarily translated into individual differences. Just as the same individual cannot be in two places at once, he can likewise not be present in two different moments. From one moment to the next he is other. Thus, "there is no Individual, in the shortest instant it is something other than in the next, and its conditions of existence are those of innumerable individuals."[32] The impact that the idea of Eternal Recurrence will have on the basis of individuality is to confer individuality upon each individual. This happens by simply prolonging *ad infinitum* the spatio-temporal definition of individuation. Because time is considered to be not only real, but infinite, the individual in time is now endowed with new determinations – he will be defined as the infinite repetition of himself.[33] If via this continual succession of instants, the identity of the individual – who is obliged in each new moment to become another – is dissolved in time, it is also through time that this same individual, with the passing of each new instant, really becomes himself. "Man! Your entire life will become like an hourglass, always again turned over, and always running out."[34]

This individual can now be viewed, not as an identity which is part of a continuous order in the linear succession of time, but one which is part of a discontinuous order of repetitions in eternity. To the extent that the biography of each individual is the exact repetition of another series of instants which has already occurred an infinite number of times in an infinite number of cycles of the Eternal Recurrence, each individual, being different than he was in the previous instant and different than he will be in the moment which follows, is, nonetheless, in each moment, absolutely identical to himself. He is an infinite repetition of himself. Each individual biographical event is endowed with an individuality based on an eternal and unique model which becomes – absolutely – actualized within him. In this way, his individuality in each moment (that is, that which determines that each individual be precisely that individual in precisely that moment) is an eternal individuality which, in that moment of repetition, he embodies. That is because the individuality of the whole of his biography is a multiplicity of individualities which are made real in a multiplicity of "individuals" which comprise, in their succession, the biography of this same individual. "It is not enough to be an individuality," Nietzsche says, "but it is necessary to move from one individuality to another."[35]

Each individual's access to his own individuality occurs neither by stripping himself of his empirical conditions, so that he might become a transparent expression of his own timeless law, nor in the search for some individual model to constitute his sublime form. Individuality is not seen as something previous to the empirical existence of each individual, nor something beyond the individual: rather it is something within, mixed in with the individual, in an absolute sense, in each moment. To come into one's individuality, which is available in each moment to each individual as an original given, immanently conferred upon him from the beginnings of eternity, consists in responding positively to the question "Dost thou want this once more? and also for innumerable times?"[36] Individuality has the nature of an original given, and, simultaneously, of a task. It is that which we are and do in each instant, because in each instant we are simply repeating our existence exactly as it has been given once and for all from the beginning of eternity. On the other hand, it has to be mastered; it's not enough to simply be, you have to want to be what you are; to take yourself as an individual model to be realized, and to make this model coincide with what you are. "To live in such a way that we wish to live once more, and wish to live in eternity! Our task challenges us in every instant."[37]

The idea of the Eternal Recurrence provides a further basis for the individuality of each individual, a basis we can call, in Leibnizian terms, "radical." Even if the past is infinite, this does not mean that the number of individuals brought into existence by time is also infinite. Accordingly, the genesis of the individual, as distant as it may be, is far from being dissolved in the depths of time; it can only be prolonged up to the individual himself. The long chain of causation which originates in each individual terminates there as well. And it is there that the new genesis of his own repetition is likewise initiated, or rather the genesis of the infinite number of other individuals whom he repeats and announces, and who are only distinguished from him on the temporal plane, as different occurrences in time of the same individuality. This radical individuality is based on the fact that, within the same locus of concurrence, that is, in the same completed cycle of all possible individuals brought into being, no two indiscernible individuals can appear. Given the close interlinking of all causes, the implication would be that these two individuals had experienced the same genesis and that, in this case, they would not be two, but rather one in the same individual (either spatially or temporally identical as the single occurrence of the same individual, or merely temporally distinct, as different occurrences, in different cycles of recurrence, of yet the same individuality). "Whether indeed ... something identical has existed is entirely indemonstrable. ... Whether there can be something identical in one total state – two leaves, e.g.? I doubt it: it would presuppose that there were an absolutely identical generation, and for that we would have to assume that throughout all eternity something identical had endured despite all alterations to the total state and the creation of new properties – an impossible assumption!"[38] The idea of the Eternal Recurrence provides a "radical" basis for the principle of the identity of the indiscernible: because the roots of his genesis are plunged in eternity and even in himself, the individual becomes absolutely unique, a uniqueness which is confirmed by the eternal repetition of himself and of the entire chain of causes which lead to him.

Despite the fact that individuality is still thoroughly determined by its place in the order of temporal succession, it is certainly not annihilated there. On the contrary, new temporal determinations are found within it. This happens in two ways: within each cycle as a radically individualized and unique genesis, and within eternity as an infinite repetition of itself in each moment of its existence.

In developing his idea of the infinite repetition of all events, Nietzsche pushed his "anti-metaphysical" decision to remain on the plane of representation to its ultimate consequences, rejecting the categories of "reason," "beginning," and "finality." By eternally returning upon themselves, spatio-temporal relations become self-subsistent, conferring upon themselves, in a circular fashion, sufficient reason for being as they are, and not as they are not. In this universe, each individual consequently shares – by the mere fact of existing in a determined space and time – the privilege of being able to sport his *raison d' être* as the eternal basis of his instantaneous individuality.

And yet Nietzsche's notebooks of the period tell of the search for some other kind of cosmological justification for this new figure of individuality contained in the idea of the Eternal Recurrence. It is as though he had understood that the hypothesis, of all things being subject to repetition, still needed something to complement it. The Eternal Recurrence needed to be developed from the internal perspective of the individuality of each person and it had to go beyond the idea that one's temporal condition could be extended into infinity. It is precisely this perspective which Nietzsche would develop from 1885 on in his theory of the will to power.[39]

II. The Individual and Individuality in the Theory of the Will to Power

1. The return to metaphysics

The most important development in the theory of the will to power is in the abandonment of the plane of the visible as the only means of access to the world. Nietzsche needed to develop a principle to explain, on the contrary, all visual events on the basis of what in their visibility is manifested, and yet which remains unspent. The concept of the will to power (*Wille zur Macht*) reveals the interior plane of all appearance. Starting in 1885, then, Nietzsche – by precisely rejecting all meta-empirical categories – targets the mechanistic conception of the world:

> Of all the interpretations of the world attempted hitherto, the mechanistic one seems today to stand victorious in the foreground. It evidently has a good conscience on its side; and no science believes it can achieve progress and success except with the aid of mechanistic procedures. Everyone knows these procedures: one leaves 'reason' and 'purpose' out of the account as far as possible, one shows that given sufficient time, anything can evolve out of anything else, and one does not conceal a malicious chuckle when 'apparent intention' in the fate of a plant or an egg yolk is once again traced back to pressure and stress ... one has lost the belief in being able to explain at all.[40]

Because of its rejection of the categories of "reason" and "purpose," the mechanistic conception of the world limits itself to *describing* the visible and to formalizing its relations through the exclusive utilization of the categories of "stress" and "pressure." Nietzsche calls for an explicative perspective, which can be reached only via the interrogation of the internal processes of all phenomena. In his own words: "The victorious concept 'force,' by means of which physicists have created God and the world, still needs to be completed: an inner will must be ascribed to it, which I designate as 'will to power,' i.e., as an insatiable desire to manifest power, or as the employment and exercise of power, as a creative drive, etc. ... one is obliged to understand all motion, all 'appearances,' all 'laws,' only as symptoms of an inner event and to employ man as an analogy to this end."[41] Nietzsche radically inverts his way of interpreting the world. He abandons the decision to reject any kind of "intuition" beyond the plane of representation. Now it is precisely the interior, that which cannot be understood by any form of representation, which must construct the principle to explicate external and observable relations. All movements, all phenomena or laws must now be considered as a manifestation, a "symptom" of the processes of which they are merely an expression.

Nietzsche deliberately becomes a "metaphysician" in order to bring an explicative perspective to the plane of representation. What "intuition" can he now evoke in order to gain access to the interior dimension of force? Once again, he goes back to Schopenhauer. As with him, it is the analogy with man that constitutes the "secret passage" to the metaphysical world, to the "intelligible character" of all phenomena. This analogy will be explicitly invoked in *Beyond Good and Evil* when Nietzsche surmises:

> "Suppose nothing else were 'given' as real except our world of desires and passions, and we could not get down, or up, to any other 'reality' besides the reality of our drives – for thinking is merely a relation of these drives to each other; is it not permitted to make the experiment and to ask the question whether this 'given' would not be sufficient for also understanding on the basis of this kind of thing the so-called mechanistic (or 'material') world? ... then one would have gained the right to determine all efficient force univocally as – will to power. The world viewed from the inside, the world defined and determined according to its 'intelligible character' – it would be 'will to power' and nothing else."[42]

2. The discovery of the essence of the world within the individual

In this return to metaphysics the definition of the individual is called upon to play a double role. On the one hand, he becomes the analogous point of entry to the world seen from within; on the other, since there are no movements or phenomena which are not the result of relations between individual beings, explaining the world from within implies that we must describe individuals through their immanent dynamism.

Precisely because of the place it occupies, the concept of the individual becomes the object of two different descriptive procedures. The first starts with the individual as the subject of knowledge and proceeds to the world as it is named from within. The second attempts to elucidate the whole of the visible world, deriving it – as a symptom – from those internal processes revealed in the relationships between individuals.

Adopting man as an analogical principle does not reflect a simple methodological decision, but one based on a *de facto* observation. According to Nietzsche, man is condemned to being the primordial analogical referent of all interpretations of the world. The theory of the will to power is not distinguished from other interpretations of the world by the fact that it takes man as an analogy. The mechanistic perspective itself is nothing more than a consequence of this analogy – the concept of the atom, Nietzsche believes, is a projection of the concept of subject/ substance upon the smallest structure of the immaterial extension. For this very reason, the analogy is no longer a neutral procedure. Actually taking oneself as the first term of the analogy does not guarantee immediate access to the internal processes that preside over all phenomena. To start with man is to necessarily start from a particular interpretation.

So there is a need for a prior critique of systems for interpreting man and his fundamental stigmata before one can attempt to attain, through him, the internal perspective on the world.

Nietzsche believes that the fundamental error common to all interpretations of man – and that he, therefore, unjustifiably projects upon the world and upon the integers of his experience – is the error of the "individual." "The Individual [is] the more subtle error."[43] Does Nietzsche then deny the existence of particular beings, numerically distinct and temporally self-subsistent? Hardly. What he denies is a specific concept of the individual by which man can conceive of himself and, in consequence, the world. "In truth there are no individual truths, but rather mere individual errors – the Individual itself is an error. Everything that happens in us is in itself something other, that we do not know: we put intention and background and morality into nature in the first place. – I distinguish, however, the imagined individuals and the true 'systems of life' [*die eingebildeten Individuen und die wahren 'Lebens-systeme'*] of which each of us is one."[44] It is in the name of a new concept of the individual, as "system-of-life," that Nietzsche considers the concept of the "individual" as the most subtle of errors. This is why seeing the non-imaginary nature of every individual (as a "system-of-life"), which constitutes the analogical portal to the world's inner processes, presumes a critique of the "individual" (as an imaginary concept). Therein lies the error – man's false interpretation of himself leads him to a false interpretation of the world.

The theory of the will to power is above all geared toward the deconstruction of these false images of individuation. Nearly all of the notes dedicated to the subject of the individual which are to be found in the notebooks between 1885 and 1888 express this struggle. So it is understandable that Nietzsche's theory of the will to power has been seen as radical denial of the concept of the individual. Yet this denial is really only fully understood against the metaphysical backdrop of yet another concept of the individual which Nietzsche haphazardly worked out as the key to his new theory of the world and power.

3. Imaginary individuals and real individuals

Above all else, what Nietzsche rejects in the imaginary notion of the "individual" is the idea of a presumed unity. Against this he posits an idea of a plurality of individuals. Each organic being is "a plurality of animated beings which, partly struggling with one another, partly integrating and subordinating one another, in the affirmation of their individuality, also involuntarily affirm the whole."[45] For his part, Nietzsche denies the status of indivisible unity to each one of these animated beings which comprise this plurality that is the individual. "The very smallest 'individuals' cannot be understood in the sense of a 'metaphysical individuality,' and 'atom,' "[46]; "there are no durable ultimate units, no atoms, no monads: here, too, 'beings' are only introduced by us."[47] To accept the existence of such ultimate and simple units would, according to Nietzsche, be akin to transferring the unity and substantial identity which is denied individuals as composite wholes to the infinitely small.

Yet, since ultimate units do not exist, where might the roots of these "systems-of-life," which Nietzsche proposes as an alternative to the imaginary concept of the "individual," be planted? How can Nietzsche conceive of the nature of a being (as a multiplicity), while denying the existence of ultimate units? In the end, Nietzsche would be led to the plane of individuation, the plane of the continuous, of the homogenous, the plane of Schopenhauer's One. Will Nietzsche then deny, by some different route, the existence of authentic individuation?

What is also at stake here is not the absolute denial of particular beings, but a new form of contemplating the nature of the singular out of which the composite arises. The rejection of ultimate units has an essentially polemical effect; Nietzsche wants to condemn the concept of the atom as the final redoubt of the categories of subject and of substance, of that which lingers on in time beyond its own actions. "Whether as the fiction of a little clump of atom, or even as the abstraction of this, the dynamic atom, a thing that produces effects... Subject, object, a doer added to the doing, the doing separated from that which it does."[48] Nietzsche now opposes a new concept to that of the "atom," or the "thing": that of "dynamic quanta" (*dynamische Quanta*): "no things remain but only dynamic quanta, in a relation of tension to all other dynamic quanta: their essence lies in their relation to all other quanta, in their 'effect' upon the same."[49] The essence of these ultimate units lies in the fact that they are action, wherein it is impossible to distinguish agent and the effect of action. That is because action is always realized within a structure constituted by a multiplicity of equally active elements which arrange themselves simultaneously as object and obstacle.

These "dynamic *quanta*" find a fitting name in the will to power – they make up the primordial element of the universe, its homogeneous dynamic, that sea of forces from which individuation is realized. Having purged all illusory concepts of the individual, Nietzsche can now directly access the essence of the world, achieving once and for all a true understanding of its inner reality:

> And do you know what 'the world' is to me? ... This world, a monster of energy, without beginning, without end: a firm, iron magnitude of force that does not grow bigger or smaller; ... a sea of forces flowing and rushing together, eternally changing, eternally flooding back, with tremendous years of recurrence, with an ebb and flow of its forms; out of the simplest forms striving toward the most complex, out of the stillest, most rigid, coldest forms toward the hottest, most turbulent, most self-contradictory, and then again returning home to the simple out of this abundance, out of the play of contradictions back to the joy of concord. ... do you want the name for this world? A solution for all its riddles? ... This world is the will to power – and nothing besides! And you yourselves are also this will to power – and nothing besides![50]

4. Nomadic individualities

At this point, after having accompanied Nietzsche throughout this process that has brought him to the word's essence, to a world defined by its "intelligible character," it is crucial to try to understand how he conceives of the process of individuation from within this sea of forces which is the will to power. This will allow us, at a later point, to analyse the new notion of individuality to which he has been led.

Nietzsche posits the existence of an essential continuity in the universe of force between all of its forms, which lets them continually transform themselves from one into another. However, this continuum cannot be an undifferentiated whole. In Nietzsche's conception of it there are always differences of intensity, with at least two orders of relative potency (as force accumulates at one point, it dissolves at another). These differences in potency presuppose the existence of points, singularities that simultaneously constitute poles of condensation and principles of differentiation, as Nietzsche says: "Mere variations of power could not feel themselves to be such: there must be present something that wants to grow [*ein wachsenwollendes*] and interprets the value of whatever else wants to grow."[51] Differences in potency within a dynamic continuum would cancel each other out, were it not for "a certain something" (*ein Etwas*), a singularity capable of determining this difference and of interpreting it by relating it to its own value, to its power to grow, in order to exploit it. Therefore, in the universe of the will to power individuation precedes the right to differentiation.

What is this "certain something" that wants to grow, this minimal element of the universe of force? In the above-cited fragment, Nietzsche defines it according to two determinations: as *the will to grow* and as an *interpreting being*. This definition is completed by a spatial perspective: "when A acts upon B, then A is first localized, separated from B."[52] The minimum elements of force are always differently located, establishing among themselves a self-referencing system of co-localizations.[53] Nietzsche defines these localizations as centres of the will's movement: "I need initial points and centers of movement, from which the will propagates itself."[54]

In this way, minimal elements which compose the totality of force and which form the internal principle of its differentiation are based on four essential determinations: (a) they are differently located; (b) they are in a relation of tension with all other elements; (c) they are struggling to grow; and (d) they are interpreting systems of difference based on their own value.

The most important innovation in this conception of minimum singularities – those primal elements in a sea of force – is in the affirmation of *individuality* (at the expense of *individuation*) as the principle of the differentiation of force and, as such, the process of constituting individuals as "systems-of-life." If individuation precedes the right to differentiation, then individuation itself must be constituted by individuals endowed with individuality of an internal quality, based on which they will interpret differences of potency and set them up as oppositions. Since there is already a multiplicity of individualized singularities in the universe, each with its own individuality, the production of differences is possible, as well as the establishment of relations of tension between dynamic *quanta* and the constitution of individuals as organic totalities.

5. Individuality and spontaneity

But how does Nietzsche now conceive the basis of individuality for each one of these singularities? The fragments of this period, in which Nietzsche tries to construct a systematic vision of the concept of the will to power, are vague regarding the concept of individuality. Nietzsche seems to oscillate between an extrinsic definition, in which each individual appears as a simple expression of the system of relations in which he is found, and an intrinsic definition, in which the individual is endowed with immanent qualities which manifest themselves unconditionally in relations of conflict which he establishes with all other individuals. On the one hand, Nietzsche affirms: "The properties of a thing are effects on other 'things': if one removes other 'things', then a thing has no properties."[55] On the other hand, he has it that each being is that which it is, made up in an entirely individualized way which manifests itself in a particular fashion in each and every action before other individuals. With respect to this second sense, he says:

> That something always happens thus and thus is here interpreted as if a creature always acted thus and thus as a result of obedience to a law or to a lawgiver, while it would be free to act otherwise were it not for the 'law'. But precisely this thus-and-not-otherwise might be inherent in the creature, which might behave thus and thus, and not in response to a law, but because it is constituted thus and thus. All it would mean is: something cannot also be something else, cannot do now this and now something else, is neither free nor unfree but simply thus and thus.[56]

In this interpretation, all of the world's events are nothing more than the prolongation *ad infinitum* of each individual's being "thus and thus." It is his individuality in dynamic relation with all other individuals that explains each natural law, each organic form and each system of forces. How to then conciliate the intrinsic view of individuality (with its thesis on the structural condition of the qualities of each thing) with the thesis which states that the elimination of all other things would mean that one single thing would be without properties?

This hesitation over the basis of each individual's individuality leads to a strategic duality in Nietzsche's struggle against a mechanistic interpretation of causal processes. On the one hand, since he wants to endow the plane of dynamic relations with an explicative perspective, presuming those relations to be "symptoms" of internal processes, he looks for an immanent basis for the differentiation between dynamic singularities, which can be, by right, anterior to the system of causal relations and, because of this, stand as a principle of intelligibility. On the other hand, against the atomism that underlies that same interpretation (that which presumes the existence of extensive and indivisible elements endowed with internal properties that remain unconditioned by their actions and relations), Nietzsche tries to emphasize the essentially functional nature of each dynamic singularity and, consequently, tends to reduce his definition to an extrinsic point of view, as a simple pole of the converging relations it establishes with other singularities. The conflict is therefore linked to the ontological status of the concept of *relation* within the theory of the will to power. Which should, by right, come first: the universe of internally individualized singularities, or the system of relations from which its properties have been constituted? How can Nietzsche conceive of an immanent basis of each individual's individuality without reducing it to an isolated substance that subsists in time beyond its own properties or actions? And, conversely, how is it possible to affirm the functional nature of all individuals without conferring the status of ontological autonomy on very notion of *relation*?

While not pretending to be systematic in scope – which is certainly the case with Nietzsche's principal intuitions – we can see that the solution he adopts here toward the antinomy of the ontological status of *relation* is comprised of: (a) defining all dynamic relations as essentially perspectivist; and (b) affirming superiority of the internal dynamism of each singularity vis-à-vis its external relations.

6. The individual and its essential relations

For Nietzsche, *relation* is inherent to force; it derives from the fact that "a force can expend itself only on what resists it."[57] In its tendency to constantly increase in power, each force expands, not indefinitely, but by constantly modulating within a conflict with that which offers it resistance. Thus force can only exist in the context of a *field of forces*. How is this tension between forces established? Is their nature one of pressure, the chock of contiguity? How, in this case, should we understand their individuation and that they do not simply dissolve into some homogeneous mass? For Nietzsche, in order for one force to continuously act upon another they must be kept apart. As he says, "when A acts upon B, then A is first localized, separated from B."[58] Thus forces must necessarily act at a distance. But, if they are not contiguous, how can they capture the tensions between them and understand reciprocal differences of power?

In order to respond to this question, Nietzsche is led to adopt the thesis that the nature of all beings is essentially perceptual. "Do the various forces stand in relation, such that this relation is bound up with an optics of perception? That would be possible if all being were essentially perceptual."[59] Each force is related to all other forces because it perceives them: it is a prospect of that totality. Forces maintain equilibrium among themselves by preserving their co-localizations and the distance between them: "distant forces balance one another. Here is the kernel of perspectivism."[60] It is out of this game of multiple perspectives and constant inter-perception that a dynamic equilibrium is formed between forces.

"The 'effect at a distance' cannot be got rid of: something attracts something else, something feels itself attracted. This is the basic fact: in comparison, the mechanistic representation of pressure and impact is only a hypothesis on the grounds of appearance and the sense of touch ... In order that this will to power can manifest itself, it must perceive those [other] things."[61]

It is important to emphasize that the perception which Nietzsche has attributed to all forces and dynamic singularities is not figurative by nature, but purely intensive. Each force perceives only differences of power among the multiplicity of forces to which it is related. It is in this sense that Nietzsche concludes that there is more perceptual clarity and exactitude in the inorganic than in the organic world. "The transition from the inorganic world into the organic is a transition from fixed perceptions of force-values and power relations into perceptions which are uncertain and indeterminate – because a plurality of beings struggling against one another (the Protoplasma) feels itself as opposed to the external world."[62]

In the inorganic world the equilibrium between forces within a given system is stable, in the sense that differences of power have been crystallized. Because of this, the perception that each force has of these differences of value and of their relations is exact. By contrast, in the organic world, which is primarily distinguished by the fact that each individual being – no mere singularity, but, as Nietzsche says, "a plurality of beings struggling against one another (the Protoplasma) feels itself as opposed to the external world" – the relations which each individual establishes with another can never be stable. Differences of power are continually produced by the creation and destruction of internal relations of force and these differences modify power relations, on a hierarchically superior level, between the individual as plurality and the external world. Here, the perception of each individual is by now the result of a co-possibility of internal perceptions and the individual's perception of his own value – from which he determines differences of value between himself and other individuals – is uncertain and inexact.

Perception is not primarily an internal representation of an external given. If that were the case, clarity in the organic world would be more pervasive, endowed as it is with systems of resonance and evolution from without to within. Instead of this, Nietzsche conceives of perception as the regulated, dynamic relation between the totality of singularities in conflict and each one of those singularities. Perception exists because the multiplicity of elements of a structure are expressed in each one of its units. The more regulated this relation is, that is, the more stable are differences of power, the more clearly each singularity perceives, or better, the more it expresses in itself the multiplicity to which it is related. As such, if Nietzsche defines *relation* as the result of the perceptival character of each force, perception, in turn, exists only in function of its relational character: a disconnected and isolated force (in every sense impossible, due to its essentially functional nature) would be "blind."

7. Perspectivism

Even if, according to his thesis on the perceptual character of the relation between forces, Nietzsche consolidates the anteriority of the right of dynamic singularities and of their perceptions vis-à-vis the relations they establish through them, the perception that each force has of the system of power differences in which it is contained still does not allow for the internal determination of its individuality. Since perception is only possible at the heart of a dynamic structure, each force expresses, within itself, only differences of external power. Its uniqueness derives utterly from its status as a single pole of convergence for the multiplicity of perceptions that make up the field of forces within which it develops. Its definition is still exterior: that would require a knowledge of all of the perspectives that are directed its way. That is why Nietzsche says: "A thing would be defined once all creatures had asked 'what is that?' and had answered their question. Supposing one single creature, with its own relationships and perspectives for all things, were missing then the thing would not yet be 'defined'."[63]

It is not so much in the concept of *perception* (*Wahrnehmung*) as it is in *perspective* (*Perspektiv*) that it is necessary to look for the way in which Nietzsche conceived of the internal principle of individuality. This distinction between *perspective* and *perception* is not elaborated systematically in Nietzsche's oeuvre. And yet, it is only through it that we will understand other criteria for differentiating between the kinds of perceptions used by Nietzsche, that is, beyond those already established, between the inorganic and organic world. Indeed, a hierarchy of prolongation and accuracy of perspectives that each force exercises over the totality with which it relates corresponds, according to Nietzsche, to a hierarchy of the degrees of power various forces can claim. "You shall above all see with your own eyes the problem of *order of rank*, and how power and right and spaciousness of perspective grow into the heights together."[64]

While, from the point of view of the perception of external differences, the increase in internal structuring of each force – which corresponds to the passage from the inorganic to the organic world – amounts to a diminution of perspectival clarity and exactitude, by contrast, from the point of view of perspective, Nietzsche considers that an increase in power creates an enhanced sense of extensiveness and accuracy in the "vision" of each force. The clarity and exactitude of perception vary with the degree of external stability of power differences, while the extensiveness and precision of perspective are determined in function with each force's degree of internal power. The criterion of distinction between degrees of *perception* is therefore extrinsic to force, while the degree of perspective is intrinsic to it. In this way, *perception* and *perspective* are represented as the external and internal face, respectively, of the relation between forces; via perception each force will express in itself the point of view of the totality of forces and their differences in power and, via perspective, each force will express its own internal degree of power before that same totality.

It is the articulation between *force* and *perspective* that allows Nietzsche to affirm that all quantitative alterations are the translation of qualitative alterations and, in this way, to define the individuality of each singularity from an internal point of view. In terms of perspective, each force's degree of power will neither increase nor diminish without changing its nature: "Might all quantities not be signs of qualities? A greater power implies a different consciousness, feeling, desiring, a different perspective: growth itself is a desire to be more; the desire for an increase in *quantum* grows from *quale*."[65]

Any quantity of power is an expression of each forces's quality of perspective over other forces. Because of this, the will to power acquires an immanently intellective nature: the incessant transition of each dynamic singularity from one state to another superior state has as much to do with the struggle to increase power as it does with the struggle to extend perspective, with the combat for "consciousness."[66]

It is by virtue of the perceptual dimension of power that each dynamic singularity arises endowed with internal qualitative determinations. Its uniqueness no longer depends exclusively on its place in a hierarchy of power, or on its position in a system of perceptual relations. Perspective institutes a quality intrinsic to power. Via perspective, all differences, either qualitative or of nature, communicate with quantitative differences, or with those of degree. But how does this communication function?

Each dynamic singularity's increase in power, being quantitative, unfolds intensively, not extensively. This is to say that the power of each force is not the result of adding smaller units of power. Rather, it is simply a question of magnitude, or one of degree. This is why the increase of power happens on a continuous scale. Its numerically simple nature is guaranteed by the fact that it can be internally organized by a quality, by a perspective. For each degree of power there is a corresponding new perspective and not the addition of new perspectives. Because of this, each singularity's continuous increase of power happens within the parameters of an intensive internal restructuring beyond which discontinuities of power and qualitative discontinuities flourish. If a new perspective is able to completely organize the new *quantum* of power a real increase in degree will occur; the opposite scenario leads to a case in which the continuous increase of power reaches its internal breaking point and a consequent diminution of power entails. It is almost as if an internal wrinkle in the continuum of force were created, out of which two intensive poles will appear, both of a lesser degree and each one organized around its own perspective to create between them a simple relation of opposition: from one individual will come two. " 'Generation' is only derivative: originally, where one will is not sufficient to organize that which has been completely appropriated, a counter-will steps into force, and initiates the separating-off, a new centre of organization, after a struggle with the original will."[67] It is these points of discontinuity when there is a continuous intensification of force by a single perspective that constitute the points of communicaton between quantitative differences, or differences of degree, and qualitative differences, or differences of nature.

Each individual's higher degree of power does not, then, correspond to a maximum of extensive incorporation of forces, but rather to a more harmonious internal structuring, to a maximum intensification of force by a higher perspective. It is this internal intensification of power which, for Nietzsche, constitutes the interior quality of each singularity and the intrinsic principle of its differentiation, which is, by right, prior to all dynamic relations. Nietzsche offers a twofold designation for this: from the temporal point of view, he refers to "tonality" (*Stimmung*) – "what distinguishes men is the relatively lengthy amount of time they can maintain an elevated tonality."[68] From the point of view of the simple quantity of power, it is expressed as "value" (*Wert*) – "What is the objective measure of value? Solely the quantum of enhanced and organized power."[69]

8. Hierarchy as the principle of individuality

Individuality will never be static as long as it is seen to be the internal given of each singularity, which is, moreover, formally anterior to an inherent system of dynamic relations and dynamic perspectives. Within each individual and by virtue of the unending struggle that it wages with all other individuals, quantitative changes in power are being continuously manufactured that are transformed into qualitative changes in perspectives. Who owns the rights to the dynamic principle of these internal transformations? Once more we must ask: are they merely the result of structural changes, or is the opposite the case?

Nietzsche believes that, in sum, the amount of energy available in the universe is constant. This energy is harnessed, as though along vectors, by all those singularities which are part of the world and that turn this energy into an array of forces that exist in constant tension with each other. "Supposing that the world had a certain quantum of force at its disposal, then it is obvious that every displacement of power at any point would affect the whole system."⁷⁰ If the universe is a dynamic whole, does that mean that the rise and fall of each individual's relative power would be the result of general alterations in the system as a whole? If that were the case, individuality would have to transcend the individual, and the individual's internal viewpoint would be exclusively the reflection of his external relations. Nietzsche would then end up by conferring ontological primacy on the fact of the *relation*, to the detriment of the true multiplicity of individuals that make up the universe. This is the point at which the definition of the dynamic principle of force takes on a truly metaphysical significance, not as the struggle for self-preservation, but as the struggle for the continual increase of power. The fundamental principle of the theory of the will to power lies less in the thesis which sees the individual as a functioning whole, and more in his absolutely spontaneous nature. All transformations of power that happen within an individual are the result of his internal activity; general alterations of power in the force field or system in which he finds himself are an expression – a "symptom" – of that activity, and not the reverse. "The force within is infinitely superior; much that looks like external influence is merely its adaptation from within. Exactly identical means can be interpreted and used in ways diametrically opposed."⁷¹ Only the principle of the essential spontaneity of each individual, as will to power, lets Nietzsche arrive at a basis for his thesis on the anteriority of the right to individuation vis-à-vis differential relations of power. Likewise, it is only this principle that allows for the foundation of a thesis on the intrinsic nature of the individuality of each individual.

The external definition of individuality, as the unique expression of the multiplicity of differential relations of power, is, strictly speaking, a "symptom" of the internal definition, the degree of power and the quality of the perspective, just as all movements or events which occur on the plane of representation are "symptoms" of the internal processes in the conflict between absolutely individualized individuals. The opposition itself, between the interior and the exterior of each individual, is abolished – each individual is nothing more than interiority. If his interior force is infinitely superior to exterior influences, the latter being simply expressions of the interior forces of other individuals, what is left in each instant is the co-possibility between a multiplicity of absolutely spontaneous and individualized forces, within a finite and constant quantity of global energy.⁷²

9. Individuality and eternity

The model of an instantaneous co-possibility among the totality of individual actions in conflict confers upon individuality the nature of a given, and, at the same time, a task. From the internal viewpoint, individuality is the law of the series that already contains the totality of an individual's future actions within it by virtue of this individual's essential spontaneity. This is the sense in which "each one turns into that which he is ..., the beginning is simply a complex symptom of the what comes after."[73] From an external viewpoint, on the contrary, each action, since it is the result of the relation of co-possibility between individuals in conflict in the context of each event, has to be conquered through the instantaneous mediation of all other individualities. Co-possibility operates as though it were a natural selection among virtual beings, creating, in the end, the individuality of each individual. This is why the sphere of individuality is not cancelled, but rather truly realized in co-possibility. To this effect, Nietzsche states: "Every basic character trait that is encountered at the bottom of every event, that finds expression in every event, would have to lead every individual who experienced it as his own basic character trait to welcome every moment of universal existence with a sense of triumph."[74] Each instant of universal existence, each event, as co-possibility, is thus an expression of each one of these individuals in conflict, a disparate convergence of a multiplicity of virtual beings. There is a metaphysical correspondence between "every basic character trait that is encountered at the bottom of every event, that finds expression in every event" (*jeder Grundcharakterzug, der jedem Geschehen zu Grunde liegt*) and the basic character trait of each individual who takes part in this event. The individuality of the individual, his *Grundcharakterzug*, is the individuality of the event that, at each moment, is in the process of realizing his individual biography. Simultaneously, the basic character of each individual is the expression of the character of each event as the event, in turn, actualizes his virtual individuality.[75] In this metaphysical correspondence, Nietzsche discovers the basis for a new figure for the tragic *yes* to universal existence. The individual who discovers his individuality in the very fact of each of the events of his existence is led to experience "every moment of universal existence with a sense of triumph." As Nietzsche says in the following fragment from 1887: "It would need this fundamental characteristic in oneself to be felt precisely as good, valuable, with pleasure."[76] Only the one who validates himself as a unique being, in his absolute singularity, and who feels this singularity as good and valuable, only he can conceive of the totality of existence in that which is also unique and individual in existence. Only he has the right to judge existence in its entirety. And it is out of his judgment that the Dionysian "yes" to all things and the triumphal validation of all things will burst forth.

The theory of the will to power, in this way, disengages itself completely from the theory of the Eternal Return, upon which it was meant to confer it a metaphysical basis. The *Will to Power* not only contains a completely new concept of the individual and of his individuality, it lays the way for the conception of a new figure for the tragic "yes", a new metaphysical legitimization for the experience of affirming the universe in all its instantaneity and eternity. Since each event, each moment of universal existence is the result of a finite totality of individuals that in the twining of their perspectives and in the constant co-possibility of their actions, affirm and realize their individuality, to say "yes" to their own individual existence, and affirm it in its absolute difference, in its unicity, is, according to Nietzsche, to also say "yes" to the entire universe and to eternity. "If we affirm one single moment, we thus affirm not only ourselves but all existence. For nothing is self-sufficient, neither in us ourselves nor in things; and if our soul has trembled with happiness and sounded like a harp string just once, all eternity was needed to produce this one event – and in this single moment of affirmation all eternity was called good, redeemed, justified, and affirmed."[77]

It is because individuation and individuality are formally anterior to the universe of difference and relation, that Nietzsche can now conceive of the immanent basis for the Dionysiac "yes" to all existence. Yet now, within the theory of the will to power that "yes" no longer compromises individuation. This intuition – first formulated in *The Birth of Tragedy* – of a purely affirmative existence, of a "yes" to the world and everything in it, can now be conceived within a metaphysics of the individual. The Dionysiac experience no longer entails the dissolution of each initiate in the delirious experience of the mystical One. On the contrary, since each individual bases his individuality on the deepest essence of the world, or rather, on eternity itself, that eternity that was needed to give birth to every event of his existence, to say "yes" to the whole of the universe, is to say "yes" to oneself and to one's character as a unique event. It is to affirm our own individuality in the moment in which our soul vibrates with joy "like a harp string." In that moment, as Nietzsche writes, "all eternity was called good, redeemed, justified, and affirmed."

3

Necessity and Contingency in Nietzsche's Early Writings

Nietzsche's philosophy represents the last *metaphysics of necessity* of the modern period. It is true that his texts are loaded with symbols of contingency – like the throwing of the dice, the child's game, the labyrinth, and Zarathustra's dance. It is also true that the maxims, the imperatives, the heroic formulations with which Nietzsche punctuates each of his pages are always levelled at the philosopher-artist, at the *ex nihilo* creator, at a humanity in the midst of pure self-invention, in a word, at the indeterminate, at the unpredictable, at the absolutely free. Nevertheless, when he is pondering the world's mode of being, the condition of each natural occurrence, when he describes the structures of temporality, or when he seeks cosmological figures adequate to a vision of existence as innocence, and as the overcoming of all values, Nietzsche repeats the principal intuitions of a metaphysics of necessity. Herein lies yet another dimension of his work. Nietzsche is revealed as the true poet of the necessary, of that which can be none other than it is. This search for figures of necessity expresses perhaps what best defines Nietzsche's programme. He is seeking a cosmological representation that allows for the demonstration of the unique necessity in each event, for that event to be justified, inherently, as a univocal existence that contains and spends its singular essence as pure act. Like Spinoza, Nietzsche believes that only from the perspective of the *necessary* will we be able to conceive of a world beyond good and evil, only in the rejection of contingency will human existence be revealed in its true cruelty and exuberance, without reference to transcendent values.

The most paradoxical part of this programme is in its reformulation of the Stoic idea of the Eternal Recurrence. This is a more radical representation of the *necessary* than any other in the history of metaphysics. Since, contrary to Spinoza and the Stoics, Nietzsche's conception of the idea of necessity is inimical to all forms of monism and pantheism, the notion of necessity does not contain any index of perfection or of rationality. The modality of the necessary absorbs in itself alone all divinity and rationality in the form of pure facticity. But, it is precisely in this final figure of necessariness that the idea of necessity takes on new metaphysical determinations. It is transformed into the only adequate symbol of reality. This is why all of Nietzsche's concepts of physics converge in the idea of an immanent necessity and why all of his imperatives move in that direction. Nietzsche condenses this univocality of *being* and of *having-to-be*, this univocality of the physical and the ethical, into the Spinozan maxim of "amor fati," *love of what there is of the necessary in everything that happens*: "My formula for greatness in a human being is *amor fati*: that one wants nothing to be different, not forward, not backward, not in all eternity. Not merely bear what is necessary, still less conceal it – all idealism is mendaciousness in the face of what is necessary – but *love* it."[1]

Nietzsche inherits his disdain for systems that base freedom on theories of contingency from Schopenhauer. From the outset, he relates man's superiority to his appetite for necessity, to the power to be that which he is. His most beautiful poems are those that sing of this necessity. The dithyramb *Glory and Eternity* (*Ruhm und Ewigkeit*), written in December 1888, runs as follows: "my love is ignited / only by that which must be. / Image of what must be! / Highest star of being / what no longing attains / no denial defiles / eternal Yes of being / eternally am I thy yes / for I love thee, O Eternity."[2] Eternity is seen as a way for the world to desire itself, to say "yes" to itself, to love itself eternally. With this love, the world affirms its necessity as a univocality. Eternity itself becomes a mode of necessity. It becomes the symbol of necessity. This is why, in eternity, *being* and *necessity* become commutable. Everything that is, is necessary, and only the necessary is real.

In spite of the cosmological and ethical importance of the theses of necessity, there is no attempt in Nietzsche's work to formulate a physics or a metaphysics of necessity. Perhaps only concepts like *value* and *truth* are at once so central and so indeterminate. Yet, even though there are innumerable studies on the theory of *value* and *truth* in Nietzsche, the concept of *necessity* has yet to become the object of systematic elucidation. This does not mean that an atheology of the necessary has never been discussed in the nearly ten thousand titles that comprise the Nietzschean bibliography. On the contrary, the concept of *necessity* is a required topic, since it is impossible to understand the meaning of the idea of the Eternal Recurrence without considering the problems of modality, which are encompassed therein. What has hindered a systematic study of necessariness in Nietzsche is the fact that the concepts of *necessity* or of *amor fati* are always discussed in terms of their configuration in the cosmology of the Eternal Recurrence. It is as though Nietzsche's manner of orienting necessariness were derived exclusively from the cosmological and existential consequences of the idea of an infinite repetition of all events, above all as the idea is represented in *Thus Spoke Zarathustra*.

On the other hand, Nietzsche's theory of necessity is never studied as an autonomous problem; it is always seen as derivative of the (more poetical) Eternal Recurrence. Necessity thus gets confused with the idea of an exact repetition of all events and the paradoxes which run through that idea, which leads to the even graver neglect of the importance of formulations of necessariness that predate 1881, that is, precisely anterior to the inspiration, at Sils-Maria, of the idea of infinite repetition.

It becomes apparent in these early texts to what extent the idea of the Eternal Recurrence, instead of having dragged an implicit theory of the necessary in its wake, is itself the expression of a much earlier reflection of this same notion. So there is no doubt that attention should be given to the work that predates Nietzsche's discovery of *The World as Will and Representation* and, as well, to that period of six years in which Nietzsche published *The Birth of Tragedy* (1872) and, which is profoundly marked by the necessaryist metaphysics of Schopenhauer, *Human, All-too-Human* (1878). Indeed, it is an eventual rupture with the metaphysics of pessimism that will suggest the idea of the Eternal Recurrence. By concentrating on the works and the thinking that led up to *Human, All-too-Human* we will begin to understand how the most important difficulties that run through the ethic of repetition originate in Nietzsche's appropriation of Schopenhauer's metaphysics of modality.

I. Before Schopenhauer

It is particularly significant that the theme of necessity was given centre stage in Nietzsche's earliest substantial essays – *Fate and History* (*Fatum und Geschicht*) and *Freedom of Will and Fate* (*Willensfreiheit und Fatum*).[3] Nietzsche wrote them in April 1862 when he was just eighteen years old for his contribution to the Germania Society at the Pforta School. In both texts the concept of *necessity* is embodied in the Latin expression "*fatum.*" Nietzsche's insistence on the Latin is more than a simple affectation of style. In the indetermination of this term Nietzsche is able to condense a great variety of meanings without having to confront the theoretic problems which the concept perforce implies. Because *fatum* designates, simultaneously, both a physical determinism and the teleological category of "fate," as well as the facticity of existing, Nietzsche can employ these three meanings as though univocal relationships between them were a given. Certainly his exploitation of the ambivalence of the concept of *fatum* is what makes these essays so fecund. They condense the great metaphysical and ethical questions that will run through the whole of Nietzsche's work into this one concept.

The two essays are conceived as a whole. They explore the collective and individual spheres of the conflict between *necessity* and *freedom,* through the figures of *history* and free *will*. What is so impressive about the questions that Nietzsche raises in these essays is how they anticipate his later work. "We hardly know whether mankind itself is only a stage, a phase in the universal, in becoming; whether it is not merely an arbitrary appearance of God. Is man not perhaps the development of stone through the medium of plant or animal? Could it be that perfection is already attained here, that herein lies history? Has this eternal becoming no end? What are the mainsprings that drive this great clockwork? They are hidden. But they are the same in the great clock we call history."[4] Some of the themes that will come to characterize Nietzsche's philosophical style are already present here. Among them are the questioning of man's place in nature, the search for the immanent meaning of history, the inconceivability of an interminable becoming and, finally, the link between history and eternity. The fundamental question is whether it is possible to create a moral order for the world that would go beyond intelligibility, beyond the metaphysical justification that the world is an "arbitrary appearance of God." The world is justified as order, regularity. Chance, which in *Thus Spoke Zarathustra* will be the principle of the innocence of becoming, is just the opposite here, clearly synonymous with the arbitrary. And God manifests himself arbitrarily. In the search for a moral order for the world, Nietzsche must respond to the theological imperative: that of immanence. God is pure will, the arbitrary. The world is the reciprocal conditioning of its parts, that which is determined. This incommunicability between God and the world, which serves to organize the way in which Nietzsche takes up the classic question of theodicy, is also manifested in each one of his responses. Transcendence is not rejected via the figure of the arbitrary alone. In the hypotheses that he advances for the ordering of the universe, Nietzsche above all rejects the theological perspective. The interminable prolongation of becoming cannot be an expression of any totalizing finality which is yet unrealized. As a finalized process, the world renounces effectivity unjustifiably, becoming the eternal deferral of itself. Nietzsche confronts theology with a general archaeology, which he calls "the common center of all oscillations" (*das gemeinsame Centrum aller Schwingungen*).[5] The obvious contingency and multiformity of history is the manifestation of an immutable form, the ahistorical groundwork that maintains itself as the unifying principle of diversity. Only as "essence," as the expression of an archetype, can humanity be seen as an immanent end. In order to deny the transcendence of a "telos," Nietzsche adopts a Platonism of general forms.

But this Platonism does not adequately meet the requirements of his anti-transcendentalism. It is precisely the idea of "a common center of all oscillations" that Nietzsche designates as the concept of *fatum*. In this way he can get around the realist interpretation of universal form and of the archetypal plane of all variations. *Fatum* is homogeneous with respect to the totality of existents, of which it is a form. It has the nature of the given, of that which exists only when realized through action. It is the mode of being of each event, the crystallization, in the present, of the whole series of events which, in their turn, have made it possible.

Nietzsche distinguishes three planes of *fatum*: humanity as a whole, a particular people and each unique individual. On the first plane *fatum* is designated as man's biological dimension, as that which constitutes his natural specificity, which, Nietzsche concludes, derives from "a fatalistic structure of skull and spine."[6] On the second, *fatum* signifies the spiritual legacy of a people, their cultural identity. On the third, *fatum* is ascribed to individual characters. It expresses "the condition and the nature of their parents; the triviality of their relationships."[7] Nietzsche also designates it as "temperament." The first plane of *fatum* is the object of the natural sciences, the second that of history. The third belongs to the dominion of the ethical: only in experience of being himself can each individual accede to his individuality.

There is nothing original in this architectonic of the planes representing the constraints against individual existence, in which History functions as the middle term connecting Nature's mechanical will to the biography of each singular will. What is important to underline is the way in which Nietzsche rejects a merely negative understanding of necessity. Certainly *fatum* is maintained as that sphere of action which manages to escape the power of the adaptive processes of specific man, or the historicity of collective man and the free will of the singular man. But it is, above all, in the fact of its being primordial and immutable that the possibility of acting freely can become the basis of human will. In like manner, free will does not signify the unconditional. The sphere of action is not necessarily opposed to *fatum*. The possibilities which each individuality creates are actuated on the level of the will. This allows Nietzsche to emphasize the link between *fatum* and history, and between *fatum* and free will. This is because there is no opposition between them, they are not even parallel spheres. The will and history do not constitute autonomous realms in confrontation with the biological, the historical or the individual reality of each man and each people; in no way are we speaking of a realm of freedom and possibility which is opposed to a realm of necessity and effectivity. *Fatum* is the given, the condition for the possibility of History and free will, which are its realizations in time. It is only as a condition that it limits the conditioned, that it circumscribes the world of free will. There is an essential continuity between *fatum* and free will. The distance between them is only a matter of degree. The exercising of free will is akin to effecting *fatum*, of raising it to its maximum power, in the same way that the spirit, in its freedom, is nothing more than the subtle realization of the material. In Nietzsche's words, "as spirit is only the smallest infinitesimal substance, the good is only the most subtle evolution of evil, so, perhaps, free will is nothing but the highest potency of fate."[8]

On the plane of individual will (the theme of Nietzsche's essay "Freedom of the Will and Fate") the univocality of *fatum* and of its manifestations is explored through the figure of the duality between the conscious and the unconscious: "free will is only an abstraction indicating the capacity to act consciously; whereas by fate we understand the principle that we are under the sway of unconscious acts."[9] Here the concept of "unconsciousness" carries a lot of the baggage of naturalism and is delimited as a conjunction of the conditions behind the act which evade conscious decision. Among these he includes biological, historical, and biographical factors. For this reason, the duality between the conscious and the unconscious simply reproduces this strange modal state of the human will which links the conditional necessity of facticity with all of those possibilities over which it deliberates. The metaphor that describes man as something that is half way between automaton and God is indeed eloquent. "Absolute freedom of will, absent fate, would make man into a god; the fatalistic principle would make him an automaton."[10] It is the nature of the will – at once necessary and contingent – that marks man for what he is. We belong simultaneously to the world of the past and the present, the world of the possible and the necessary. This duality is the essence of our humanity. Yet because the general form only exists in each individual man, it is the concept of "individuality" (*Individualität*) that contains the central plot of this conflict: "if the concept of unconscious action is not merely taken as a submission to earlier impressions, then the strict distinction between fate and free will disappears and both concepts fuse with the idea of individuality."[11]

II. A Fragile Necessity

In the tension between the *automaton* and *God* two distinctive perspectives of the idea of necessity emerge: one which belongs to the metaphysics of nature and another which returns to the modal plots of temporality. In the first, as we can see, the necessary is the anatomical structure of the species, the spirit of the people, or the unique individuality of each singular being. In this case, the collective and singular existence of each individual is the expression of an *essence* – biological and historical. It is that essence which constitutes *fatum*. A pure existence, or rather a free will that was not the expression of a predetermined essence, would be nothing more than pure spirit. "Free will appears as unfettered, deliberate; it is boundlessly free, wandering, the spirit. But fate is a necessity ... Fate is the boundless force of opposition against free will. Free will without fate is just as unthinkable as spirit without reality."[12]

On the other hand (and from the perspective of modalities created by the structure of time), *fatum* alone is conceived as a figure of the past. The past, because it is irrevocable, is necessary and limits the freedom of will: the will can do everything except re-do what is already done. If this were not the case, the will would cancel its own link with the real. Altering the past would annul the will's condition of possibility, which would cause it to destroy itself. The possible, in and of itself, cannot become action if there is not already something real and present. And something real and present, when it is an act, necessarily participates in the past and in its irrevocability. It is the necessary condition of the *effectivization* of the possible, in short, its *fatum*. The total freedom of the will would lead to a merely virtual universe, where all possibilities would be waiting to be realized because of a failure to commit to the *effective*. Man would be a pure god, but a god without a nature. In this sense, "If it became possible completely to demolish the entire past through a strong will, we would immediately be transported into the realm of autonomous gods, and world history would suddenly be for us nothing but a dreamy self-deception."[13] Nietzsche still lacks a modal understanding of the difference between the past and the future. He likens the irrevocability of the past to the finitude of the will. It is not the metaphysical impossibility of realizing the possible in the past that explains why the past is immutable. For Nietzsche the past is an object of wanting, just as the future is. If the past cannot be revoked, that is only due to a determination of the will. The will is not sufficiently "strong" to alter it. This confusion between two meanings of "impossibility" – the modal and the anthropological – will be repeated in *Thus Spoke Zarathustra*, when Nietzsche equates the irreversibility of time with the irrevocability of the past. The revolt against the "already was" which in *Thus Spoke Zarathustra* defines the "spirit or revenge," the rage of the will when confronted with its powerlessness to change what has already happened, is redeemed in the idea of the Eternal Recurrence.[14] The presumption is that the recurrence of a series of events can change the irrevocability of the past, as though repetition would influence time whilst leaving the contents of time untouched.

Nietzsche could not come to terms with the problem of articulating both the metaphysical and the temporal perspective of the concept of *fatum*. To base the immutability of human essence on the irrevocability of his biological and spiritual history is to transform man into a contingent reality, to make him the consequence of the sedimentation of free action. Inversely, to infer the immutability of the past based on man's atemporal essence, as though he were a manifestation of time, would be to deny his free will.

Nietzsche is anticipating certain modal problems in this conflict between the metaphysical and temporal perspectives of *fatum*. These problems will run through the whole of his oeuvre. And they will surface anew, most notably, with the idea of the Eternal Recurrence. At that point he will give primacy to the temporal interpretation of necessity. The essence of each individual is the consequence of his temporal existence as an exact and immutable repetition of a series of prior voluntary acts. And will itself can be freed from the fetters of the irreversible, from the limits of the "already was." Yet, the great paradox will persist: if the past returns, that is, if it takes on the temporal status of the future, this does not mean that it will acquire the future's modal status. Instead, it will become, like the future, the object of will – even though it would be an "already completed" future, immutable in its modal condition as a past.

This same conflict, which will bring two conceptions of necessity into confrontation within the cosmology of the Eternal Recurrence, is already present in the connection between *fatum* and free will. In both of the 1862 texts, Nietzsche finds a compromise. He defines man as a tensional being hovering between the unconscious and the conscious, between automaton and God. But this mixing of contents, this indetermination, is a way to avoid being explicit about the profound incompatibility between what we can consider to be the *nominal definition* and the *real definition* of freedom. From the point of view of the nominal, Nietzsche defines freedom negatively: it is the non-conditioning of the will, and his anchor here is action and the creation of the new. But when he wants to formulate its real definition, that is, the condition of the possibility for this autonomy, he refers to the necessary expression of an immutable essence. This has to do with the individual essence of the subject who acts and not with the mode of acting. Action is free, but it is grounded in the unfree. Only in this way is it guaranteed that the "conditioned" will not alter its own condition.

This concurrence of difficulties, regarding firstly the definition of necessity, then the understanding of the link between *fatum* and free will, and finally the incompatibility between a definition *for* and a basis *of* freedom, will eventually undergo a significant reformulation after 1865, with the discovery of Schopenhauer's *The World as Will and Representation*. Yet, as we will see, even if these metaphysical and ethical antinomies would eventually be overcome, it was only to open the way to new antinomies: those which Nietzsche inherited from Schopenhauer himself, and which are configured in the anthropological schism, which Schopenhauer inherits from Kant, between a human dimension *in itself* and its *phenomenal* dimension. Nietzsche will identify the meaning of the individual essence of *fatum* as the *thing-in-itself* based on an upgrade of the Kantian theory of "intelligible character," which attributes the condition of a reality that is independent of the forms of space and time to the individual essence of each subject. Like Kant, Nietzsche will theorize human existence according to the series of phenomenal, spatio-temporally determined manifestations of this individual *fatum*.

III. The Schopenhauerean Model of Necessity

In 1865, following his reading of *The World as Will and Representation*, Nietzsche was now in possession of a systematic "Metaphysics" over which he will trace his own tenuous theory of necessity. The influence which Schopenhauer's book will come to exercise is at least partly due to the fact that it responded quite nicely to those questions whose most significant contours appear in the two 1862 essays on the concept of *fatum*. Beneath the appearance of their simple speculative basis, it is, however, possible to detect in Nietzsche's two youthful dissertations a profound reformulation in the way he conceives of the figures of *necessity* and *freedom*.

For Schopenhauer the centrepiece of ethical reflection is precisely the conflict between necessity and liberty. He considers that Kant's great contribution was to have found a metaphysical solution for this conflict. Schopenhauer does not tire in affirming that the Archimedean point of critical philosophy is found precisely in the way in which it resolves the Third Antinomy of pure reason, that is, the conflict between the determinism which reason discovers in natural phenomena and the freedom which it demands of human action as the basis of morality.[15] According to Schopenhauer, critical philosophy really had, via this resolution, found a point of immediate access to the *thing-in-itself*, which had been deliberately preserved in the Transcendental Aesthetic and the Transcendental Analytic as a problematic concept.[16]

It will be recalled that, according to Kant, from the dynamic point of view, phenomena are not uniquely determined as successive in a series of time, but fixed laws preside over this succession, that is, the relation between the antecedent and the consequent is a relation of irreversible and perfectly determined succession. The mathematical relation of succession is accompanied by a dynamic relation of causality. In the search for "an unconditioned" in this series of causality, reason is faced with a dilemma: the complete determination of a series of causes demands an ultimate term, a first cause that would be pure antecedent, a term which, by virtue of the general conditions of experience, cannot be conceived as an empirical object, but which has to be a meta-empirical term, causally independent, and endowed with absolute spontaneity. It is important to stress that reason's interest in this conflict is not merely speculative. There is also a practical interest in which the condition of the transcendental possibility is at stake, the *ratio essendi* of moral law. The solution to the conflict between the dynamic regularity of phenomena and the demand for free causality was shifted to the introduction of the concept of "character," precisely the meta-empirical term, exterior to relationships of cause and effect, that was required.[17] In another passage from the *Critique of Pure Reason*, the concept of "character" acquires the condition of spontaneity, the ability to initiate alone a series of events in time, independent of all anterior events, not according to time but according to causality.[18] From an empirical point of view, voluntary acts are all a consequence of an empirical law, of an "empirical character," because they are always determined by rational motives and representations derived from phenomena and their rules. Yet, Kant affirms that beyond "empirical character," there is an "intelligible character" which is truly the unconditional basis of voluntary action. The causality of "intelligible character" is the condition of a successive series of events, it itself being empirically unconditioned since, because it is causality, that is, being a real determination of action, it does not originate in time, it does not begin in a given moment to produce an effect. "Intelligible character" does not depend on a series of anterior phenomena but, as pure spontaneity, it has the ability to initiate by itself a series of happenings in such a way that, in it, nothing actually begins.

This is its positive dimension – the capacity to unconditionally initiate a series of happenings in time – which Schopenhauer will highlight in Kant's concept of *thing-in-itself*. This is why the *thing-in-itself* can emerge from Schopenhauer primarily as a synonym for spontaneity, that is, for the will, as it manifests itself in each singular existent. Such a reification of the concept of "character," as unconditioned spontaneity, not only founds a basis for the ethics of pessimism, but, also, for his metaphysics of the will. The freedom demanded by reason as a basis of the ethicalness of acting loses its existential purpose, it ceases to be a determination exclusive to action, in order to be reduced to a determination of the being that acts. For Schopenhauer, the "intelligible character" designates at once the atemporal individuality of the subject that acts and his individual will as a force for beginning to act unconditionally.

Schopenhauer identifies himself with the Romantic movement in an attempt to break the finitude of the Kantian subject. He reclaims Kant's own anthropology, conceiving the ethical agent as not only formal subject, author of universal axioms, but as effective will, the basis of the spontaneity to act. Nevertheless, that real subjectivity remains petrified within the confines of its own foundation. Schopenhauer's ethic of pessimism was certainly victimized by his reading of Kant. Each moral individual is endowed with the attributes that Kant recognized in the *thing-in-itself*. Negatively, he is unknowable. The individual will is radically unfathomable – it becomes the very emblem of the irrational. When the individual is configured positively, as intelligible character, that is, as immutable individuality, unconditioned when faced with empirical motives, he is unable to freely project himself into the dimension of action. Freedom is the moral subject's property of being, it is the fundamental attribute of its individuality as it presents itself as a pure given, primordial and immutable. In other words, freedom is a metaphysical given and not a virtual form that only comes into being by playing a role in the time of individual essence. Man is irremediably free because he is an "intelligible character," an atemporal, individual law that stipulates that he will act in a particular way. The foundation for the legality of this action is constituted solely by freedom. As Schopenhauer says in *On the Basis of Morality*: "Freedom appertains not to the empirical character but only to the intelligible. The *operari* of a given person (what he does) is necessarily determined from without by motives, and from within by his character; hence everything he does necessarily takes place. In his *esse* (what he is), however, freedom lies. He could have *been* a different man, and guilt or merit lies in what he is."[19]

The tension between *necessity* and *freedom* disappears in Schopenhauer. Each individual is free because his individuality is necessary. And it is that metaphysical necessity which at once establishes and absorbs the individual's freedom. Contrary to Kant, the unconditioned in Schopenhauer, the undetermined, is not that which in the moral decision is conditioned by something else – the respect for moral law – but solely that which is immutable, the necessary. Human acts are doubly necessary: in the phenomenal order, everything is determined as a regulated linking of the series of motivations in time. In the order of the *thing-in-itself*, of the intelligible character which these acts empirically express, everything is immutable since it is atemporal. Man is free according to Schopenhauer, yet, paradoxically, "condemned" to his freedom, that is, to his immutable individuality.

IV. Necessity as *Eternity* in the Basel Texts

The absorption of the *"operari"* into the sphere of the *"esse,"* which Schopenhauer achieved in his metaphysics of the will, could hardly not have left its mark on Nietzsche's conceptions of necessity. In the works which he published during the period when he was professor of philology at the University of Basel (1872–8), the connection between *fatum* and free will ceased to be conceived from a monist perspective. As a model for his "individual *fatum*," Nietzsche adopts – just as Schopenhauer had dogmatically done before him – the Kantian concept of "intelligible character." He counters the concepts of *fatum* and free will with those of *thing-in-itself* and *phenomenon*, reconceiving them as the *intelligible* and *empirical* dimensions of action. The immutability of individual *fatum* is now the result of its atemporal nature. In Kantian/Schopenhauerean language, such immutability is the expression of the unconditioned in the presence of space and time. *Individuality*, or *temperament*, is unalterable. But now, contrary to what Nietzsche had espoused in the 1862 texts, the immutable condition of individuality is not a condensed expression of the totality of time which materializes biological evolution, the history of a people, and the biography of an individual. After his reading of Schopenhauer, the necessary is what is beyond any species of temporality, any species of causality. For this reason, the concept of individuality loses its status as principle of the synthesis of necessity and free will which in itself harmonized the unconscious and conscious dimension of action. Individuality, traced, as it were, over the Kantian concept of "intelligible character," is now defined solely as the mark of the ethical subject's uniqueness, the basis of the identity of its existence in time beyond the diversity of its historical manifestations, and shifted to the plane of immutability, of individual *fatum*.

In this way Nietzsche establishes a hierarchy between these perspectives – the metaphysical perspective and the temporal perspective of necessity, that is, between the plane of individual essence and that of the role it plays in time – whose tension oriented the 1862 texts. This same hierarchy is very much present in his most Schopenhauerean essay. Indeed, in the third *Untimely Meditation*, expressively subtitled "Schopenhauer as Educator," he writes: "That heroism of truthfulness consists in one day ceasing to be the toy it plays with. In becoming, everything is hollow, deceptive, shallow and worthy of our contempt; the enigma which man is to resolve he can resolve only in being, in being thus and not otherwise, in the imperishable. Now he starts to test how deeply he is entwined with becoming, how deeply with being – a tremendous task rises before his soul: to destroy all that is becoming."[20] Nietzsche is guided here by idealism. From paradoxical terms he creates a metaphysical hierarchy. *Fatum* continues to be conceived as the essence, the individual's, or a people's, mode for being unique. But now essence finds its character in the atemporal, in the imperishable. As individual intelligible character, it is outside of time. The whole of an individual's biography comes down on the side of appearance. It is not what each one does, thinks or desires that represents his individuality. That is left up to the conditioned, that which is realized in time. From whence Nietzsche's appeal: "Be your self! All you are now doing, thinking, desiring, is not yourself!"[21] Individuality is immutable not because it is irreversible. That would imply defining it, as Nietzsche did in the 1862 essays, as identical to the past. It is immutable because it is not conditioned by time.

The dimension of the will itself, as it was conceived in the 1862 essays as an exploration of the world of possibilities opened by *fatum* (biological, historical, and individual) as its protaganist in time, is expunged in later writings. As in Schopenhauer, free will is the exclusive result of the immutability of *fatum* – of which it is the expression. And between *fatum* and historical atemporality a true metaphysical abyss originates. *Fatum* does not require any kind of role to reach its pure state of contemplation or perfection. The will does not raise it to its maximum power because as long as it is immutable, as long as it is necessary, it contains no dimension to make present and real. In *The Birth of Tragedy*, Dionysian ecstasy – as the means to get beyond the forms of time, to the World's eternal essence – leads to this negation of the practical dimension of human existence. "In this sense the Dionysian man resembles Hamlet: both have once looked truly into the essences of things, they have *gained knowledge*, and nausea inhibits action; for their action could not change anything in the eternal nature of things."[22] Action unbinds itself from the immutable being that expresses itself insofar as it is an ephemeral manifestation in time, of an atemporal reality.

Because it presupposes the dimension of time – which is the exclusive determination of phenomena – action is suddenly metaphysically baseless. It can only be justified as appearance. This is why Apollo, the god of appearances, is also presented as an "ethical divinity." Only in the belief in the reality of space and time does he push men to act. Buried in the Dionysus/Apollo duality is another, more primordial duality, between *fatum* and free will, now seen in the light of the Schopenhauerean reification of the Kantian concepts of intelligible and empirical character.

V. A History of the Nonhistorical

The second *Untimely Meditation*, entitled "The Utility and Disadvantage of History for Life," once again takes up this metaphysical duality between atemporal essence and existence in time, and it does so by creating an opposition between *life* and *history*. The essay can actually be read as a rewriting of the 1862 *Fate and History*, recast now in the light of Schopenhauer's works. As in 1862, Nietzsche now (in 1874) discusses the possibility of finding some meaning for "this great movement of the clock called History." In both essays the teleological response is rejected in favour of an archetypal conception of meaning. The intelligibility *of*, and the metaphysical justification *for*, history can be achieved only in the revelation of the immutable form which is, itself, a contingent manifestation of history – in this case *life*. In their spontaneity, the eternal and the necessary of life provide the basis for the ephemeral and the contingent. Just as the concept of biological, historical, and individual *fatum* had provided the content for this idea in 1862, so unconditioned *life* does now in 1874. But this occurs in a diversity of ways, because the models of necessity adopted are now different. While in the concept of *fatum* the necessary is the past, the irreversible that, in its immutability, constitutes the condition of the possibility of the present and the contingent, now, in the concept of life, the necessary is the atemporal, that which is outside of time, because it is absolute spontaneity and free causality. Thus, the essential tension between the mode of being, the "character" of a people and its role in time as history, disappears. Not only does the being of each people lose its status as materialization, as the sedimentation of the whole of the past, but history itself can no longer empower a collective *fatum*. History has now become that which manifests itself temporally in a reality that is truly atemporal and nonhistorical.

The metaphysical abyss between life, as an essentially ahistorical reality, and history, as a mere ephemeral manifestation in the temporal sphere of this atemporal life, has enormous consequences for the status of History, that is, for the condition of the possibility of a knowledge whose end is the visible configurations of the life of peoples and individuals. Nietzsche wants History to respect its metaphysical dependence vis-à-vis life, vis-à-vis this unfathomable sphere of pure creation outside of time. Nietzsche bases his denunciation of the pretension of historical discourse in constituting itself as a science on this metaphysical subordination. "Insofar as it stands in the service of life, history stands in the service of an unhistorical power, and, thus subordinate, it can and should never become a pure science such as, for instance, mathematics is."[23] He is essentially proposing a different ethical posture for dealing with historical phenomena in general. This *Untimely Meditation* interrogates, precisely as the title indicates, "the advantage and disadvantage of history for life." The questions asked therein are directed at the possibility that historical knowledge could strengthen life as a nonhistorical reality.

Early on in the preface to this "meditation," Nietzsche, citing Goethe, underlines the following absolute primacy of life. "In any case, I hate everything that merely instructs me without augmenting or directly invigorating my activity."[24] Knowledge is only justifiable when it enlivens, when it fortifies the individual's vitality, his ability to play a role in time. Historical knowledge, the subject of the essay, which takes the action of man in time as its object, is thus seen to have an ambivalent relationship with life. To act is to act in time, it is to anticipate the future from a consciousness that is founded on the unveiling of itself as law of the past; it is through the past that man understands the meaning of his existence in the present and is able to project it into the future – where it can be realized. This whole – past-present-future – is condensed in each act. This means that every act has a historical texture. So, to the extent that this historicity of action constitutes the object of knowledge, life itself, with its role to play in time, becomes an object of knowledge. In other words, if history, as knowledge, is opposed to life, to the extent that it takes life and its role as an object, history can create a life-instilling force. Through knowledge of the past, history roots man in the present, establishing reference points, paradigmatic moments in which the present can be recognized. But, simultaneously, given that it exposes the ephemeral nature of events and the ruin of everything, history also leads to the weakening of our confidence in the process of eternalization, which animates the activity of peoples. "We want to serve history only to the extent that history serves life: for it is possible to value the study of history to such a degree that life becomes stunted and degenerate."[25] Through the intermediary of history, Nietzsche makes his first attempt to overcome the opposition between spontaneous life and life which knows the laws that condition action. Knowledge is no longer absolutely separated from life and its activity; the attempt to know something can be converted into an affirmation of the will to live. Nevertheless, the structure of the original opposition is maintained. In the subordination of history to the imperatives of life there is no metaphysical continuity between the unconditioned and the series of events in time. The subject of knowledge that learns how to act in time and the ethical subject, the subject of life, run on parallel tracks, even if their interests converge. The persistence of this schism causes Nietzsche's meditation to swing between two extremes: it moves between using history as a way of looking at life, questioning which types of history most serve it, and life, as a way of looking at history, to question its existential limits. The intersection of these perspectives comes to bear around a new determination of life's essential temporality, based as it is on the temporality of being an immutable single being.

In terms of the historical point of view, Nietzsche breaks with diverse extant historiographies, seeing them as symptoms of various types of life, or as a way of understanding the extent of a people's historical knowledge of life, or of an individual. "History pertains to the living man in three respects: it pertains to him as a being who acts and strives, as a being who preserves and reveres, as a being who suffers and seeks deliverance. This threefold relationship corresponds to three species of history – insofar as it is permissible to distinguish between a *monumental,* an *antiquarian* and a *critical* species of history."[26] *Monumental History* interests the active man because of the necessity that he has for models and for heroes. To believe in the possibility of repeating in the present great moments that have already occurred in the past gives him courage, frees him from the doubt which assaults him in moments of weakness.[27] From this perspective, the totality of the process of humanity is seen as an atemporal chain of paradigmatic events which, once they have become real, are proof of the atemporality of their *possibility*. Greatness acquires the condition of *pure possibility*. Nietzsche nevertheless alerts us to this historiography's groundlessness when it is carried to the limit: namely that it would presuppose that an exact replication of events could occur in the first place, as though the *possibility* of an absolutely determined mode could exist.

> At bottom, indeed, that which was once possible could present itself as a possibility for a second time only if the Pythagoreans were right in believing that when the constellation of the heavenly bodies is repeated the same things, down to the smallest event, must also be repeated on earth. ... Only if, when the fifth act of the earth's drama ended, the whole play every time began again from the beginning, if it was certain that the same complex of motives, the same *deus ex machina*, the same catastrophe were repeated at definite intervals, could the man of power venture to desire monumental history in full icon-like *veracity*, that is to say with every individual peculiarity depicted in precise detail ... but it is not the truly historical *connexus* of causes and effect – which, fully understood, would only demonstrate that the dice-game of chance and the future could never again produce anything exactly similar to what it produced in the past.[28]

This rejection of the hypothesis that there is repetition of all happenings impresses one, by contrast, because of its prescience: seven years later, in 1881, employing exactly the same elements utilized in this argument as a basis (the linking of causes, the throwing of the dice, the regular intervals of cosmic repetition), Nietzsche will advance the hypothesis of the eternal recurrence.

It is important to emphasize that Nietzsche's rejection here does not refer simply to the impossibility of such a hypothesis as a cosmological conception. It is aimed as well at fighting against its influence over life. The possible repetition of historic happenings can bring the courageous man, who needs this repetition, to hold the circumstances of his own actions in contempt. As far as the enthusiast is concerned, the one who is looking for a justification of events, he can be carried to fanaticism, passive before the immanent power of his own actions.

The second way the experience of time is inscribed in the atemporal spontaneity of life is through *antiquarian History*, which offers one the sensation of being rooted in time and the pleasure of knowing that one is not simply a purely arbitrary and fortuitous being. "The contentment of the tree in its roots, the happiness of knowing that one is not wholly accidental and arbitrary but grown out of a past as its heir, flower and fruit, and that one's existence is thus excused and, indeed, justified."[29] In *antiquarian History* the categories of collective *fatum* from the 1862 essay on

History remain. In its immutability and as the place where the essence of a people is constituted, the past forms a people's basis, confers upon them the status of the necessary and thus justifies them in what they are.

The third form of historiography, *critical History*, is the antidote to the first two forms. Its job is to animate the past by questioning the advantages it has for life.

> Here it becomes clear how necessary it is to mankind to have, besides the monumental and antiquarian modes of regarding the past, a *third* mode, the *critical*: and this, too, in the service of life ... he does this by bringing it before the tribunal, scrupulously examining it and finally condemning it; every past, however, is worthy to be condemned – for that is the nature of human things: human violence and weakness have always played a mighty role in them. It is not justice which here sits in judgment; it is even less mercy which pronounces the verdict: it is life alone, that dark, driving power that insatiably thirsts for itself.[30]

It is not in the past that c*ritical History* seeks its condition as past, which is, in fact, irrevocable. Instead, it would look for a living force within the past, that of the anticipated and eternal present. That is why this form of historiography would forget the ephemerality of all events and reconstrue the past *a posteriori* in a way that it would like the past to have been. Judging the past and condemning it in the name of life is a true reformulation of the resulting essence, that essence whose only mode is irrevocability, the immutability that has passed. "For since we are the outcome of earlier generations, we are also the outcome of their aberrations, passions and errors, and indeed of their crimes; ... The best we can do is to confront our inherited and hereditary nature with our knowledge, and through a new, stern discipline, combat our inborn heritage and implant in ourselves a new habit, a new instinct, a second nature, so that our first nature withers away. It is an attempt to give oneself, as it were *a posteriori*, a past in which one would like to originate in opposition to that in which one did originate."[31] Through *critical History* man raises himself to nearly the condition that, in 1862, Nietzsche attributed to the gods. *Critical History* modifies man's nature because it modifies that past form whence this nature emerged, substituting its first *fatum* with a second one founded on a past reconstructed *a posteriori*. If this reformulation is not in itself reasonable, since the past is immutable, it is still within the reach of History, or rather, of a certain use of History, that is within the reach of *critical* historiography. Through the fiction of a desirable past, life moulds its second *fatum*, a second nature, a second necessity.

Through these three approaches of creating History, Nietzsche discovers a common line – vis-à-vis the past all of them are unjust; all of them seek to wrest it from its state of inertia and petrification; all of them would like to reinscribe it in the dynamism of the present so that it might serve life in its incessant search to justify its spontaneity, its atemporality. Because in and of itself life has no reason for being, it has no immanent nature that would justify its spontaneous reality, but rather invariably depends on its sedimentations in the past which channels back to it the nature it lacks, the essence which it is incapable of constituting, life needs to be unjust with the past. Life is forced to decry knowledge.

Yet, in this seeming subordination of the epistemological to the ethical, what is effectively in play is the cancellation of ethics from the metaphysics of life. If life is autonomous in its ahistoricity, and necessary as pure actuality, then History would be unable to alter its eternal nature. No longer is History a dimension of free will, since freedom is not a mode of *acting* but of *being*. History is reduced to a mere manifestation of the will and plays no role in its workings. To finally understand the nonhistorical content of existence is to discover one's nonteleology, that is, to discover one's completeness in each instant. Nietzsche defines this new awareness as "supra-historical." The "supra-historical man, who sees no salvation in the process and for whom, rather, the world is complete and reaches its finality at each and every moment."[32] The Schopenhauerean philosopher's true way of seeing time is "supra-historical." Here Nietzsche repeats, almost word for word one of Schopenhauer's fundamental theses: time is a pure irreality. "He will not believe with the general public that time may produce something actually new and significant; that through it or in it something positively real may attain to existence, or indeed that time itself as a whole has beginning and end, plan and development, and in some way has for its final goal the highest perfection (according to their conceptions) of the latest generation that lives for thirty years."[33] Just as in Schopenhauer, Nietzsche's "supra-historical man" understands that the world, in its unconditioned totality, is a pure act; in each moment it achieves perfection.

Present also in the figure of the "supra-historical man" is that other experience of the atemporal, which has occupied the centre of *The Birth of Tragedy*: Dionysian ecstasy. Just as the members of the tragic chorus become aware of the dissolution of their condition as subjects of knowledge, which affects them at the moment they are raised beyond the temporal, after having torn their veils of representation away, so what is important to the "supra-historical man" is the revelation that there is something unconditional and immutable underlying his own "becoming" and that is what gives him his eternal character. Both express the mode in which, just as in the Kantian/Schopenhauerean conception of the unconditioned, Nietzsche bases the necessary on the eternal. The metaphysical concepts of "Life" and "the primordial One" – where this identification occurs – propose a representation of the world wherein this is justified immanently in the convergence of those two modes of the necessary that, in Kant and Schopenhauer, define human freedom: actuality and immutability.

Nietzsche will attempt this same convergence of the actual and the immutable following his rupture with Schopenhauer. It is a convergence which will be found in the idea of the Eternal Recurrence. But there, as we shall see, the necessary is not outside of time. It is created within time as infinite repetition of each instant inside eternity.

4
Nietzsche and Stoicism

We know how Nietzsche had a need to create enemies, to dispute theses, philosophical systems, and values. Socrates, Kant, Hegel, Schopenhauer, and Plato, all became his privileged targets in this "practice of war," as he referred to his own philosophical aggressiveness in *Ecce Homo*.[1] So it was inevitable that once Nietzsche had a philosopher in his sights he would use him as a kind of "strong magnifying glass,"[2] which he then trained upon a set of philosophical idiosyncrasies to construct a series of caricatures which are often difficult to recognize.

Such images, because they are distorted, call for a symptomological reading, as though we were scrutinizing a photographic negative to uncover its positive values. It is best to hold Nietzsche's lens in the same way that he did, that is, backwards. If Nietzsche is to be understood, we must once again tour his philosophical gallery, questioning why he chose to hang this or that portrait and why he chose to reveal them in the way he did. This is especially pertinent since many of his philosophical duels are nothing other than the visible expression of internal conflicts, of crises in the growth of his own theoretical programmes. The "Wagner case," or the "Schopenhauer case," even if they are the most paradigmatic, are not the only ones.

Nietzsche also fought a pitched battle with Stoicism. That it was a less visible confrontation, nearly secretive, does not mean that it was any less important for his work. One of the central problems in Nietzsche's philosophical programme is played out in his confrontation with Stoic ethics and Stoic physics, namely in his attempt to absorb ethics into a philosophy of nature. Nietzsche attempted to create this ethic of immanence through the Spinozan formula of *amor fati* – the love of destiny, or the love of the necessary as it exists in nature. For Nietzsche this means wanting yourself and the world in each happening such as it is and to see in such necessity the beauty of things, their own meaning and their own "logos." Nietzsche knew that this *wanting what is necessary in each happening* was the central pillar of the ethical programme of the philosophy of the Portico and that it was embodied in the maxim "live in accordance with nature."[3] And yet, in aphorism 9 in *Beyond Good and Evil*,[4] his most widely read critique of Stoicism, he condemns one of Zeno's maxims, in which the Stoic expresses precisely this same idea: that is, that Ethics is absorbed in Physics, or in other words, the human will is absorbed in natural necessity. The only explanation for Nietzsche's response is that what he is really doing is taking issue with himself, since, in the moment that he jeers at the Stoic ideal of the complete absorption of human will in the cosmic dynamism of each happening, he betrays the basis of his own ethic of immanence.

Unfortunately, whether in studies of the Stoics, or in those dedicated to Nietzsche himself, we only occasionally find references to Nietzsche's problematic relationship with the Portico. Yet, to really understand the Stoic resonance in the history of Western philosophy, we are obliged to take Nietzsche into consideration. His idea of the Eternal Recurrence gives new life to the Stoic cosmology and once again places the heroic figures of destiny at the centre of ethical theory.[5] One scholar who does discuss Nietzsche's relationship with the Stoics is Charles Andler. He is most concerned with the Roman Stoics and their influence on Nietzsche's ethics, frequently underlining the Stoic roots of the idea of the Eternal Recurrence and the importance of Epictetus's maxims on the autonomy of the will in the critique of the ethics of duty. But his estimation is that the influence of Stoic morality is restricted to Nietzsche's so-called "intellectualist period," that is, to that period which corresponds to the composition of *Human, All-too-Human*, in which the Stoics crop up mostly as symbols of a rational serenity against the fictions of the metaphysical and the moral.[6] Georges Morel, in *Nietzsche: Introduction à Une Première Lecture*, in the chapter on the decisive moments in the history of nihilism according to Nietzsche, dedicates two pages to Stoicism. Based on certain stray comments Nietzsche made on the Stoics, Morel concludes that Stoicism in Nietzsche's eyes was nothing more than a simple prolongation of Socratic decadence.[7] Jean Granier tries to distinguish between *inner* and *outer finality* in the concept of the will to power (*Wille zur Macht*) based on the Stoic distinction between *skopos* and *telos*, though he never discusses any of the influences of the Portico's physics on the Nietzschean theory of the will.[8] It was Deleuze who got closer to the nucleus of the relationship between Nietzsche and the Stoics. And, in spite of the fact that he contributed greatly to the rebirth of Stoicism in contemporary thought,[9] in *Nietzsche et la Philosophie*, Deleuze highlights Nietzsche's reductive interpretation of the Stoics in the ninth aphorism of *Beyond Good and Evil*. For this reason, even if he correctly establishes the parallel between the Stoic maxim "Live according to Nature" and the Dionysian "yes" to life, as proof of Nietzsche's original approach to the tradition of the necessary, Deleuze nevertheless cites the basic difference being between the physics of the Stoics and Zarathustra's nature metaphors, declaring that there is an utter opposition between the acquiescence to Epictetus's notion of destiny and the Nietzschean *amor fati*. Yet nowhere does he attempt to determine the real lines of confrontation between Nietzsche and Stoic ethics.[10] In the end, all that we get from Nietzschean studies are casual intersections, parallels drawn, resonances and radical oppositions. There is no systematic study of Nietzsche's relationship with Stoicism.

The urgent need for such a study goes beyond just Nietzsche's oeuvre. What is at stake is not only an elucidation of Nietzsche's contradictions (that is to say the mechanism which allowed him to move, without any principles of continuity in place, from a highly elaborate and pedantic identification with the thinkers of the Portico, to insulting their ideal of the sage and crudely caricaturing their maxims) but our ability to conceptualize our own ties to the Stoics. For it is in these contradictions, in these often vague and disconnected evaluations of Stoicism that punctuate Nietzsche's texts throughout, that our perspectives about the ethical experiments of Antiquity come into play. If much of our knowledge of Greek culture is marked by Nietzsche, this is not only due to his interpretation of the place of Dionysian cults in the birth of tragedy, or to his turning away from Platonism and his return to the tragic experience of the Presocratics, against the formalism of Kantian morality and against its epigones in Hegel's theory of law, in Schopenhauer's morality of compassion, and in the utilitarianism of Mill and Spencer, Nietzsche revives the major components of the ethics of Antiquity. His programme for a tragic anti-morality and his thousand metamorphoses of the Promethean hero, who dares to face down the gods and who dwells beyond good and evil, open to contemporary thought a unique road back to the ethical world of the pre-Christians, oriented as they are toward the question of how to achieve a happy life, toward the ontologies of pleasure, the practices of caring for oneself, in a word, toward the "aesthetics of existence," to use Michel Foucault's expression.

Nietzsche was one of the great interpreters of those aesthetics of existence. To ignore his confrontation with the Stoics would hamper our ability to understand not only Nietzsche himself, but also our ability to properly discuss the full evolution of ethical systems. The maxim "Live according to Nature," was formulated for the first time in the fourth century BC by Zeno of Citium and then six centuries later, by Epictetus, from whom Nietzsche would wrest it for the purposes of debate. Its proximity to the *amor fati* of the revaluation of all values is what concerns us here.

I. Stoicism as a Philological Problem
[Let us remain *hard*, we last Stoics! *Beyond Good and Evil*]

It is almost certain that on 1 August, 1867, at the age of just twenty-two, when Nietzsche arrived at the University of Leipzig with the manuscript of his essay for that year's university Latin prize (on the sources of Diogenes Laertius), he hardly suspected that this would be the beginning of an immense dialogue with the philosophy of the Portico, which would only deepen as time went by.

In this, his first philological essay, Nietzsche shows how all of the information contained in *Lives and Opinions of Eminent Philosophers* about the school of Zeno of Citium, calls for serious philological reservations. According to Nietzsche, the lost work of Diocles of Magnesia, *Cursory Notice of Philosophers*, did not simply constitute, as Diogenes would have it, the source of paragraphs 49 to 82 (on logic), but all of book VII dedicated to Stoicism.[11] Nietzsche also shows that Diocles of Magnesia was a partisan of Epicurus and, as such, would have been an unreliable witness of a rival school.[12] Nietzsche is calling into question one of the most important doxographical sources for ancient Stoicism, and nearly the only one on its logic.

It is interesting to highlight the research methods employed in this essay. Nietzsche's work did not consist in discovering or presenting new doxographical data. It was not in the name of some more credible source, but simply through a well-founded internal critique of the sources of Diogenes Laertius that Nietzsche dared to call the credibility of his image of Stoicism into question. Thus, Nietzsche's essay – the first in the history of classical philology dedicated to this important source of ancient thought – ends up by paradoxically casting the original members of the school that occupied the centre of the philosophical debate in the third century BC into even greater obscurity. Nietzsche, we can say, in addressing the doxographical tradition of Stoicism, had already fallen upon that which would be the fundamental experience of his philosophical style: the truth is essentially the denunciation of a palimpsest.

On the frontispiece of this essay, Nietzsche inscribes, through the voice of Pindar, the maxim which would punctuate the whole of his oeuvre: "Become who you are!"[13] Just as the singularity which we are does not necessarily directly manifest itself as identity via some thetic judgment, but is rather the difficult goal of an ethical experience, so, with Nietzsche's essay, our understanding of Stoicism emerges looking less like a philologically acquired given and increasingly like a philological and philosophical task. As we will try to show, the combat that Nietzsche wages in support of the truth of Stoicism against the Epicurean deformations of Diogenes Laertius's sources will reveal what is more truly a combat with himself, and a precedent for his own philosophical project. As an ethical model, as inspirer of the most beautiful metaphors for *nature* and *necessity*, the philosophy of Zeno and Chrysippus will provide a constant and decisive reference for an oeuvre that will culminate in Nietzsche's *Ecce Homo* – his philosophical autobiography, written a few months before he descended into delirium – the subtitle of which is precisely "how one becomes what one is" (*wie man wird, was man ist*).

II. The Stoic Ethic as Opposed to Christian Morality

After the essay on the sources of Diogenes Laertius, the Stoics disappeared from Nietzsche's research. It is still surprising that in *The Birth of Tragedy* (1872), the work that is most specifically dedicated to classical civilization, there is not a single reference to Stoicism. This absence becomes more understandable once we understand what Nietzsche wants to deliberate upon here is the conflict between the intuitive man (*der intuitive Mensch*) and the rational man (*der vernunftige Mensch*), based on which he will explain the death of tragedy. In Nietzsche's version, the model of the Stoic wise man is subsumed by the figure of the "rational man," or the "Alexandrian man." The figure of the Stoic appears in name a year later in an 1873 text, as the one who protects himself from the essential suffering of the tragic vision of a world by isolating himself in the imperturbability of reason, in an abstract universe of concepts.[14]

Nevertheless, in the period which begins in 1876 with the publication of *Human, All-too-Human*, the school of the Portico will be reappraised. With Greek culture and its decline as a backdrop to his thinking, Nietzsche abandons the polarity between the tragic man and the Socratic man, substituting it with another one: the Romantic opposition between Hellenism and Christianity. This shift in his diagnosis of the structuring antagonisms of classical culture leads to a profound reversal of Nietzsche's central positions. It is no longer the conflict between art and knowledge, or between intuition and reason that reveal what is essential in the Greek spirit. After his rupture with the pessimist metaphysics of Schopenhauer, it is the conflict between *knowledge* and *illusion* (whether religious, metaphysical or moral) which constitutes for Nietzsche the basis of all civilizations. Thus, while in *The Birth of Tragedy* the praise of the tragic man reflects the absolute privilege which Nietzsche confers upon art and religion (which he views as means of intuitive access to the "metaphysical world," just as Schopenhauer had considered them to be),[15] with *Human, All-too-Human* we find a reduction of all ideas to that which Nietzsche designates as an "aberration of reason and imagination" (*Verirrung der Vernunft und Phantasie*).[16] At this point Nietzsche has become the inheritor of that same Socratism which he had so vehemently criticized in his work on tragedy.[17] The only imperative which governs his meditation is the rational knowledge of the world and of man.[18]

The figure of the religious man, especially that of the Christian, suddenly becomes one of Nietzsche's preferred targets. Nietzsche sees in him the final expression of what he considers to be one of the great delusions of the all-too-human man: the contempt for reason in the name of some expectation of a superterrestrial world, together with the annihilation of the Hellenic ideal of the autonomy of the individual in favour of a gregarious morality, a morality of compassion.[19]

It is in this context that, in 1878, Nietzsche begins to recognize himself in the philosophy of the *Stoa*, in the model of an existence governed by reason in its search for an absolute autonomy of the "I". "How the overall moral judgments have shifted! The great men of antique morality, Epictetus for instance, knew nothing of the now normal glorification of thinking of others, of living for others; in the light of our moral fashion they would have to be called downright immoral, for they strove with all their might *for* their *ego* and *against* feeling with others (that is to say, with the sufferings and moral frailties of others.) Perhaps they would reply to us: 'If you are so boring or ugly an object to yourself, by all means think of others more than of yourself! It is right you should!' "[20] Nietzsche will gradually adopt the Ethic of the Portico as a counterpoint to Christian morality. "Stoicism or Christianity, Aristocracy of Individuum or herd goods" (*Stoicismus oder Christenthum, Aristokratie des Individuums oder Heerden-Güte*)[21] is how Nietzsche expresses the new archetypal polarity that organizes his works of this period.

Clearly Nietzsche could not fail to be conscious of the difficulty of marking a boundary between Stoicism and Christianity. He had to be aware of the hierarchy of values which necessarily lies behind this demarcation. "You say that the morality of pity is a higher morality than that of stoicism? Prove it! But note that 'higher' and 'lower' in morality is not to be measured by a moral yardstick."[22] Nietzsche seeks to make this difference evident where it is most thoroughly concealed. For example, if Christianity found fertile terrain in the slaves of the Roman Empire, Nietzsche will find the exception in Epictetus, whom he takes as an ostensible demonstration that Christianity is, as he would say, "one morality of slaves," not *the* morality of slaves.[23]

> Epictetus was a slave: his ideal human being is without class and possible in every class, but is to be sought above all in the depths of the masses as the silent, self-sufficient man within a universal enslavement who defends himself against the outside world and lives in a constant state of supreme bravery. He differs from the *Christian*, above all in that the Christian lives in hope, in the promise of 'inexpressible glories,' in that he accepts gifts and expects and receives the best he knows at the hands of divine love and grace and not at his own hands: while Epictetus does not hope and does not accept the best he knows as a gift – he possesses it, he holds it bravely in his own hand, he defends it against the whole

world if the world wants to rob him of it. Christianity was made for a different species of antique slave, for those weak in will and mind, that is to say for the great mass of slaves.[24]

Ten years after his essay on the sources of Diogenes Laertius, Nietzsche is once again fighting for the truth of Stoicism. It is no longer a philological combat, but philosophical. What is at stake in terms of the Stoicism of the imperial period is not the credibility of the sources, but the interpretations, since the texts, in this case, constitute an irrefutable philological given.[25]

One question, however, is whether or not the struggle for the Hellenic purity of Stoicism is spent in the polemic Nietzsche conducts – via this very struggle – with Christianity? Is he not playing the part of some latter-day Hellenist looking for the whys and wherefores of the decline of Greek civilization? Something more decisive seems to be at stake. Nietzsche's affinity with the ethical ideal of the Portico is an expression of a real programmatic similarity, which is to separate human action from the moral universe and thus demonstrate the essential necessity of all of that which does not depend on us and upon which the infinite power of our will is exercised.

Among the posthumous fragments of this period, there is one which, because of the rare clarity with which it defines Nietzsche's philosophical programme and for the similarity between it and the philosophy of the Portico, allows us to highlight this subterranean affinity. Here is what Nietzsche has to say in the fragment, which is contemporaneous with the publication of *Daybreak*. "To not acknowledge false necessity – which would mean useless submission and would be servile. Therefore, knowledge of nature! But also want nothing that goes against necessity! That would mean a waste of strength and weakening our ideal and, as well, to want deception more than success."[26] Here we find, in condensed form, arguably the two most cardinal imperatives in Nietzsche's philosophy: the first, theoretical in character, calls for a knowledge of Nature and of its true Necessity, and orients Nietzsche's research into physics, which will lead him to the idea of the Eternal Recurrence in 1881, as well as to the theory of the Will to Power in 1885;[27] the second imperative, this time ethical, is stated, unusually so, in negative terms: "want nothing that goes against necessity!" (*nichts gegen die Notwendigkeit wollen*), but which, in the maxim *amor fati*, love of the necessary – its positive formulation – will be considered by Nietzsche to be the supreme expression of his morality.[28] The philosophy of Stoicism resonates clearly through these two imperatives and in the way in which they are articulated, that is, to use the language of the Portico, in the way they link Physics to Ethics. It is the need to contain the will within its limits, while preventing it from being stripped of force, which obliges us to know Nature and its dynamic. But, if a knowledge of Nature stems from an Ethical demand – in conformity with Nature itself – this does not imply that Ethics is simply subordinated to Nature. Knowledge orients action, as it is only through knowledge, that is, only if we start with a knowledge of true physical necessity, that love of the necessary will not be reduced to a useless and servile submission, to a falsely construed Nature. On the other hand, because this knowledge does not refer to realities from which precepts will have to be derived, but to Nature in its immanence, as a fusion of actions – of its goals and its circumstances – the subordination of action to knowledge is not like that which is established between a copy and its model, but rather one which is in agreement, a homology, as it were: the dynamism of action and the dynamism of Nature. It is for this reason that the knowledge of Nature will finally strengthen the harmony with the Necessary, which was demanded by Ethics. Likewise, the love of the Necessary is aimed not exclusively at empowering the will; it also has a theoretical value. By demonstrating the absolutely necessary and unfinished character of all events, the love of the Necessary refines our ability to interpret whatever is seen as moral by showing the world and human action in all its innocence. "Everything is necessity – thus says the new knowledge.... Everything is innocence: and knowledge is the path to insight into this innocence."[29] It is not surprising that Nietzsche wanted to express such innocence through the solitary voice of Epictetus, citing a passage from his *Manual*:

'So long as one always lays blame on others one still belongs to the mob, when one always assumes responsibility oneself one is on the path of wisdom; but the wise man blames no one, neither himself nor others.' – Who says this? – Epictetus, eighteen hundred years ago. – It was heard but forgotten. – No, it was not heard and forgotten: not everything gets forgotten. But there was lacking an ear for it, the ear of Epictetus. – So did he say it into his own ear? – Yes, that is how it is: wisdom is the whispering of the solitary to himself in the crowded marketplace.[30]

Nietzsche's use of the morality of the *Stoa* to critique Christian morality is not then a simple rhetorical and circumstantial expedient, but expresses a real (however undeveloped) affinity between Nietzsche's programme and that of the Stoics. As we will see, it is upon this radical innocence of the universe and all the acts contained therein that Nietzsche will base his critique of what he will come to consider the nihilistic theses of Christianity.[31] What's more, it will be this same programme (which calls for both a knowledge and a love of Nature) from which the idea of the Eternal Recurrence will emerge – the idea in which the philosophy of the Portico will resonate most clearly and which Nietzsche will consider in 1887 to be the experience that spells the definitive end of Christian morality.

III. Physics as a Basis for Ethics: The Stoic Idea of the Eternal Recurrence

The Eternal Recurrence effectively emerges from Nietzsche's *Stoic* programme in the summer of 1881, the result of a sudden inspiration at Sils-Maria. It will point the way toward ridding human action of its servile dependence on the natural causality that Nietzsche so condemns. Conceiving all happenings as the exact and infinite repetition of themselves, each individual, to the extent that he acts in the desire to repeat each and every instant of his life, does not alienate his will, but rather, in saying "yes" to Nature, he says "yes" to himself, to this absolutely necessary individual who returns to himself in each instant as the repetition of himself.[32] The love of necessity, now identical to the love of eternity which is manifest in each happening, is thus converted into the condition for the possibility of the empowerment of the will – self-will mediated by the will of the totality of the Universe's happenings.[33] The idea of the Eternal Recurrence will unify the maxim which tells us to know and to love the necessary, which orients Nietzsche's meditation after 1878, with the other one which, ten years earlier, he had pronounced in his essay on Diogenes Laertius: to want the necessary (which, in the terms of a temporal cycle, means to want the infinite repetition of oneself), that is, in fact, to become truly what one is.

But there is something still more decisive to underline in this new physical/ethical model. If the imperative "want nothing that goes against necessity," from which the knowledge of nature unfolded as a task, was already clearly Stoic, the cosmological solution which this imperative implies is even more so. As Nietzsche will recognize in *Ecce Homo*, the idea of the Eternal Recurrence was already envisaged in Antiquity, by none other than the school of the Portico.[34] Thus we can say that what Nietzsche had considered his supreme idea can be understood not only as the conclusion of a "Stoic Programme," but in the way it converts into a visible expression, the manifest symptom of an affinity that he himself is forced to recognize. Even though Émile Bréhier, emphasizing the providential character that the idea of a cosmic cycle had for the *Stoa* – a characteristic that Nietzsche rejects – points to a fundamental difference between the way Nietzsche and the Stoics conceive of this idea,[35] a detailed analysis of both conceptions will, on the contrary, reveal how similar they actually are, not only on the cosmological plane, but on the ethical plane as well.[36]

But this nearly perfect symbiosis between Nietzsche and the Stoics will lead Nietzsche, paradoxically, into a desperate search for differences. In that very moment in which his greatest affinity with the physics of the Stoics and with their ethic based on love of one's own destiny is reached, Nietzsche suddenly becomes their fiercest critic. The sudden change becomes apparent in the autumn of 1881. Look, for example, at the following passage from his notebooks: "Stoicism in its resolute patience is a sign of paralyzed strength, counterbalancing suffering by its own inertia – lack of heroism, which is to always fight (and not suffer), the stoic 'voluntarily seeks' suffering."[37] How to explain such a change of mind? Nietzsche seems to be almost desperately trying to mark out his differences with the Stoa, and at the precise moment in which those differences had all but dissolved. We need look no further than *The Gay Science*, published in 1883, for examples. It is here that those central ideas that owe so much to the Ethics and the Physics of Stoics first appear – *amor fati*[38] and the idea of the Eternal Recurrence.[39] But this is also the book in which Nietzsche endeavours – also for the first time – to denounce Stoic morality. And yet, significantly, at issue is neither the egoism nor the probity of the Stoic wise man, whom Nietzsche had previously praised as a counterpoint to the morality of piety. Nor are the innocence and the amorality of human existence as they were proclaimed by the solitary voice of Epictetus at issue. On the line now is the very foundation of his whole affinity with Stoics – with the sage's notion as to the necessity of nature. "The Stoic, on the other hand, trains himself to swallow stones and worms, slivers of glass and scorpions without nausea; he wants his stomach to become ultimately indifferent to whatever the accidents of existence might pour into it...."[40] When it comes to love of necessity (accepting what happens in a manner that befits its happening), Zarathustra's creator will beg to differ from the Stoic wise man. Yet Nietzsche's criticism is directed beyond the trivial and superficial image of this ideal of the Portico, the sage. This is obvious when he comments: "At least the Stoics believed that this was how things were, and they were consistent when they also desired as little pleasure as possible, in order to get as little displeasure as possible out of life."[41] That which is an essentially active morality – permanently geared toward action, toward the actualization of reason and of passion, in the presence of happenings whose necessity must be understood in order to be accepted[42] – is interpreted by Nietzsche as a flight from the real, as an incapacity to accept the unforeseen amidst the hypothetical imperturbability of permanence and its anaesthetizing quietism.

Because Nietzsche at this point only views the sage at his tritest, the basis of that secret resonance between the two will remain unquestioned. We will have to wait until 1886, the year which coincides with the first formulations of the doctrine of the will to power, to witness the crucial experience in this affinity.

IV. A New Basis of Ethics in Physics: The Stoics and Nietzsche Before Nature as Will

We can situate Nietzsche's final confrontation with the Stoics' ethics and physics in the work *Beyond Good and Evil*, published in 1886. It is here that Nietzsche goes further than he has ever done in affirming his affinity with the *Stoa* when, in one exhortation to "free spirits" he concludes: "... let us remain *hard*, we last Stoics!"[43] But it is also in this work that he dares to explicitly confront that which we will try to show is the real basis for this affinity – the imperative that he shares with the Stoics, the desire to love the necessary through a knowledge of Nature. The whole of the ninth aphorism confronts the way in which the Stoics formulated this imperative in the maxim "Live according to Nature."[44] The structure of the aphorism mimics the very ambiguity that the maxim induces in him. That is, it begins by condemning what would seem to be its ethical paradoxes and concludes with a denunciation of its metaphysical presuppositions. We will trace these two moments in our commentary, but first we must cite at length from the text.

> 'According to nature' you want to *live*? (*gemaas der Natur' wollt ihr leben?*). O you noble Stoics, what deceptive words these are! Imagine a being like nature, wasteful beyond measure (*verschwenderisch ohne Maas*), indifferent beyond measure (*gleichgultig ohne Maass*), without purposes and consideration, without mercy and justice, fertile and desolate and uncertain at the same time; imagine indifference itself as a power – how *could* you live according to this indifference? Living – is that not precisely wanting to be other than this nature? Is not living – estimating, preferring, being unjust, being limited, wanting to be different? And supposing that your imperative 'Live according to Nature' meant at bottom as much as 'Live according to life' (*gemaas dem Leben leben*) – how could you *not* do that? Why make a principle out of what you yourselves are and must be?[45]

More than a real discussion of the Stoic maxim, what we have here is rather a subtle mechanism of rhetorical distortion, accompanied by a double plea for principle.

Nietzsche begins by translating the maxim with the expression "*gemaas der Natur leben*" (live to the measure of Nature). We know that the original formulation of this maxim hardly justifies this translation. In none of its various versions does the meaning "measure" appear. Indeed, both in Diogenes Laertius's text, which states "live in agreement with nature" (*tôn phúsei sumbainónton zên*),[46] or in another version attributed to Chrysippus, "*ómologouménos tê phúsei zên*" and translated in Latin as "*congruenter naturae vivere*" (live in congruence with nature),[47] what is at stake is a homology, a harmony with nature. The same occurs in the expression, cited by Cicero, "*convenienter naturae vivere*" (live in a way that is suitable to nature),[48] or another one, "*convenienter congruenterque naturae vivere*"[49] (live in a way that is suitable to and congruent with nature). We can also refer to the expression "*vivam secundum naturam*,"[50] which is the Latin translation of the formula "*tà katà phúsin*" (according to nature).[51] It is only by this distortion of the original that Nietzsche can consider the maxim to be a contradiction in terms when faced with the immeasurable [*ohne Mass*] character which he considers the essence of Nature. Avoiding, for the moment, a discussion of the solid basis of this thesis, we can conclude that such an opposition only makes sense in light of yet another distortion, in this case the meaning of "gemaas." Since Nietzsche emphasizes the component "maas" (measure), conceiving Nature as without measure (*ohne Maas*), the Stoic imperative becomes self-contradicting; indeed, how to *live to the measure* of something that has no measure?

Nietzsche so extends this process of distortion that he himself finally becomes a victim of it as well. Imagining the absence of measure in a qualitative physical determination implies the cancellation of any real difference vis-à-vis other determinations, forcing Nature to become "indifferent," that is, simultaneously fecund, sterile, and indefinite. Against this "indifference," Nietzsche pits Life, which he defines as the struggle for difference. This is why he wonders: "how *could* you live according to this indifference? Living – is that not precisely wanting to be other than this nature?" In itself, this distinction between Nature (*Natur*) and Life (*Leben*) seems strange. Does Nietzsche not postulate, in aphorism 36 of this same work, an essential likeness between all of the modes of existence – mechanical, organic, instinctive, reflexive, etc. – as the expression of a single fundamental form of life, as will to power (*Will zur Macht*)?[52] Does Nietzsche not conceive of Nature precisely as Life? And, since Nature is will to power, is it not Nature that struggles for an infinite self-overcoming, and thus an infinite production of difference within itself? Nietzsche's thesis cancels itself in its very formulation. Life's struggle for a differentiation vis-à-vis Nature is, itself, an expression of Nature, as Nietzsche will have to recognize at the end of this aphorism. But let us linger with the passage already cited.

After having established a complete abyss between Nature and Life, in utterly solipsistic fashion, Nietzsche then endeavours to reduce the maxim of the Portico to a pure tautology: "And supposing that your imperative 'live according to nature' meant at bottom as much as 'live according to life' – how could you *not* do that? Why make a principle out of what you yourselves are and must be?" It is important to ask: even interpreting the Stoic maxim as an appeal to live *to your own measure,* to the measure of that which each individual is, can we reduce such an appeal to an abstract, thetic judgment, to the affirmation of a simple likeness between the subject of the action and his own self? What is more: doesn't seeing oneself as "an ethical task," or (in Nietzsche's words) making "a principle out of what you are" mean the same thing as Pindar's "become what you are"? And is this not the meaning of *amor fati*, that is, "consider yourself as a *fatum*, don't want to be 'other'," as Nietzsche wrote in *Ecce Homo*? We are forced to recognize that, in his criticism of Stoicism (as much in his view of its physics as its ethics), Nietzsche is criticizing his very own foundations, betraying himself in order to abjure what, at the most profoundest point of his programme for an ethic of immanence, still resonates with his secret dialogue with the Stoic doctrine.

The second part of the ninth aphorism of *Beyond Good and Evil* leads Nietzsche toward equally unavoidable paradoxes. After having reduced the Stoic maxim to the status of tautology, or so he believes, he then endeavours to denounce what he considers to be its suppositions. He is then faced with a pivotal problem, both in terms of his programme for a metaphysic of the will to power, and in terms of the philosophy of the Portico. This problem has to do, precisely, with the very possibility of an Ethic of immanence, that is, one that is founded not on Morality, but on Physics. Does not rejecting all autonomy of the *ought-to-be*, in the name of unalloyed fidelity to the facticity of the *being*, reduce this *being* to an unconscious *ought-to-be*? It is precisely because of this suspicion that Nietzsche denounces Stoicism. Nevertheless, as we have ascertained, Nietzsche himself will become ensnared in this same suspicion.

> In truth, the matter is altogether different: while you pretend rapturously to read the canon of your law in nature, you want something opposite, you strange actors and self-deceivers! Your pride wants to impose your morality, your ideal, on nature – even on nature – and incorporate them in her; you demand that she should be nature 'according to the Stoa,' (*der Stoa gemaas*) ... For all your love of truth, you have forced yourselves so long, so persistently, so rigidly-hypnotically to see nature the wrong way, namely Stoically, that you are no longer able to see her differently.... is not the Stoic – a *piece* of nature? ... But this is an ancient, eternal story: what formerly happened with the Stoics still happens today, too, as soon as any philosophy begins to believe in itself. It always creates the world in its own image; it cannot do otherwise. Philosophy is this tyrannical drive itself, the most spiritual will to power, to the 'creation of the world,' to the *causa prima*.[53]

Nietzsche recognizes that the circularity which he denounces in the Stoic maxim to "live to the measure of Nature" is not confined to

Stoicism, but is part of all "philosophy," of any interpretation of the world. This means that the truth of each "philosophical system" is symptomological; it is the expression of an essential tie between each perspective and the world viewed from that perspective. Each moral interpretation of the world presents itself as intrinsic to this same world which, via this interpretation, is falsified, to the extent that the act itself of morally knowing the world, as will to power in its paramount degree of spiritualization (which aims to impose the Ought-to-Be of its will on Being), is nothing more than a manifestation of the world's way of being as it is, spiritualized in the totality of its interpretations. It is the world itself, as will to power, which is known to itself through the different "philosophies" which it engenders. In this case, therefore, also known to itself through the philosophy of the Portico (now unexpectedly and involuntarily revalorized). What then distinguishes between two interpretations of the world? What hierarchy or principle of differentiation distinguishes the philosophy of Nietzsche from that of the *Stoa*? For Nietzsche the difference is exclusively typological, no longer deriving simply from a distinction between truth and falsehood, but in the type of images of the world which goes into their construction. The difference between Nietzsche and Stoicism is now shifted completely to their respective theories of physics. Yet, what is most surprising is that between the theory of the will to power, which Nietzsche began to chart precisely in the year in which he published *Beyond Good and Evil*, and the Stoic cosmology, there is a similarity which Nietzsche never suspected. What's more, we can even ask to what extent this world created "to the measure of the *Stoa*" (*der Stoa gemaas*), with its materialist physics, its conception of the world as will and its notion of the eternal recurrence of all events, is not – of all the different images of the world produced by the history of philosophy – that which has come closest to the world as will to power, created "to the measure of Nietzsche"?[54]

Nietzsche's similarity with the Stoics increases in proportion to the ferocity with which he debates them. The more fundamental are the aspects of the Stoic system he targets, the more he makes them his own, until finally he becomes ensnared in the system, as much at the level of imperatives as at that of images of the world. It is almost as though, during this whole long and immense dialogue with the Portico, an authentic process of "becoming stoic" had occurred. It is a process that began in his youth, when he inscribed Pindar's maxim "become what you are" on the frontispiece of his essay on the sources of Diogenes Laertius – that essay which revealed to the world how little it actually knew about the Stoics.

5

The Role of the Idea of the Eternal Recurrence in the Genesis of the Project for the Revaluation of All Values

I. Small Chronology of a Project

The "revaluation of all values" (*Umwerthung aller Werthe*) would have to wait until 1886 for its first appearance in Nietzsche's writings. It is mentioned for the first time in the summer of that year in one of his notebooks as the subtitle of a work which, at the time, he was beginning to imagine to be called *The Will to Power (Der Wille zur Macht)*.[1] The expression would persist as the book's subtitle until August 1888, by which time thousands of pages had been written. This material was later misleadingly reorganized by Nietzsche's sister in a posthumously published book under the same title. And yet, by 1888 Nietzsche had in fact abandoned his attempt to systematize all of his theoretical positions in a single work to be called *The Will to Power*. He then began to fill his notebooks with plans for four distinct books. These took on the titles *The Antichrist, The Immoralist, We That Say Yes* and *Dionysus*. Most significantly, this tetralogy was no longer called *The Will to Power* but was unified under the generalizing title of *The Attempt at the Revaluation of All Values*.[2]

We know that in the end only the first of these books – *The Antichrist* – was actually written. It was finished on 30 September of this same year, 1888.[3] It was thought that Nietzsche would then turn to the other works, which were intended to complete the tetralogy. This was not to happen. During the month of October and the first weeks of November, he wrote *Ecce Homo* and, when on 20 November, in a letter to Georg Brandes announcing the conclusion of his philosophical autobiography, he defined *The Antichrist* as "the prelude to the 'Revaluation of all Values'" and, surprisingly, added "that work that I now have concluded before me."[4] Colli and Montinari, the editors of the most recent critical edition of the works of Nietzsche, point to this letter as decisive. It is the first bit of evidence we have that Nietzsche came to consider *The Antichrist* as the whole of, and not just first part of, the "Revaluation of All Values."[5]

After this date, the notebooks as well as Nietzsche's correspondence no longer tell of new projects. His only preoccupation during this period is in extracting all of the theoretical and political consequences of the theses contained in *The Antichrist* – a book which he repeatedly refers to as "The Revaluation."[6] And on one of the last pages before delirium set in, we read: "A last word. From now on I will have to have steady hands, a great number of them – immortal hands! – the *Revaluation* should appear in two languages. It would be well to found associations everywhere in order to make available to me, for when the time is right, thousands of partisans."[7]

We can thus conclude that, as much in its original intention as in its formulation, the programme for the revaluation of all values – in which Nietzsche's final philosophy came to be polarized and which constitutes the context in which his fundamental works are elaborated, books such as *The Genealogy of Morals, Twilight of the Idols, The Antichrist*, and *Ecce Homo* – should only be identified with the last three years of Nietzsche's production. What's more: emerging out of the soon-to-be-abandoned *Will to Power*, the programme for the revaluation of all values would seem to be a substitute for this work in progress. As such, it is clear that the *Will to Power*, as a book in and of itself, was abandoned, not merely interrupted, as Nietzsche's sister would have us believe. The "Revaluation" will therefore find its footing, its whole speculative measure, in that which we will call an anthropology of the will and its typologies. As can be seen by reading the notes for the book which Nietzsche abandoned, in this phase the "Revaluation" provided Nietzsche with the structural underpinning he needed and guided him in his attempt to create an all-inclusive system: the will to power. We should also underline the fact that, though it defined Nietzsche's work throughout 1888 and 1889, the programme for the revaluation of values is most clearly explained in *The Antichrist*. This brings us to two further conclusions: first, the revaluation is an essential critique of Christian Morality and how it had come to determine the axiological views of the Western world;[8] and second, if it is true that this programme was abruptly interrupted by delirium, this interruption has to do, not with its theoretic formulation, but rather with the "political" exploitation of its theses. From Nietzsche's point of view, the critique of all values was concluded at that moment in which his consciousness foundered in silence. During the beginning of January 1889, when Nietzsche stopped writing definitively, it almost seems as though it were the writing itself that had finally spent what there was to write.

This brief biographical and thematic outline of the programme for the revaluation has only been made possible in light of the new critical edition of Nietzsche's texts, in which all of the posthumous writings are rigorously gathered and arranged in chronological order. This has given us a new foothold in our understanding of the genesis and the underlying pattern of Nietzsche's last philosophical concerns. But it also raises new interpretive problems. There is one in particular which touches upon the status that this programme gives to the idea of *Eternal Recurrence*. Studies of Nietzsche unanimously take the idea of the repetition of all happenings to be the culmination of Nietzsche's critique of the axiological foundations of Western culture.[9] Heidegger, for example – to refer only to the figure who most marked the interpretation of Nietzsche's last philosophy – superimposes the doctrine of Eternal Recurrence formulated in *Thus Spoke Zarathustra* onto the programme for the revaluation of all values. This led him to establish a connection, which has since then become obvious, between the doctrine of the will to power, as a critique of the axiological paradigms of Western culture, and the theme of the "death of man."[10] Contemporary reflection on humanism has been considerably nourished by this artificial fusion between the theme of the death of man as it occurs in *Thus Spoke Zarathustra* and Nietzsche's theory of nihilism.[11]

Furthermore, the effect of Nietzsche's refutation of values in *Thus Spoke Zarathustra* on that which would orient the plans for the *Revaluation* is much deeper than Nietzschean exegesis would have it. One glaring result of this is in the way that many of the commentators on Nietzschean nihilism have settled upon the Eternal Recurrence as the fulcrum in their analysis of the postmodern condition.[12] Yet, as long as the programme of *revaluation* is identified with the idea of the Eternal Recurrence, the meaning of the fundamental project of Nietzsche's last works will remain compromised by the obscurity of this idea of the eternal recurrence of all things – at once a cosmological representation, an ethical imperative, an apocalyptic fiction, and a Dionysian symbol. The consequences of this misapprehension are obvious. Instead of truly understanding the *revaluation* as one of the most lucid diagnoses of the process of the self-dissolution of contemporary culture's models of legitimacy, Nietzsche's struggle against the moral paradigms of modernity is reduced to just another "new mythology."[13]

One wonders how this reading could possibly have come to be so persuasive among students of Nietzsche? How can we affirm that the Eternal Recurrence is the central pillar of the programme for the revaluation of values, when this idea is absent from all of the works published after 1886 and, in particular, is to be found nowhere in *The Antichrist*, the very work in which Nietzsche's programme on values is actually formulated? Our new understanding of the evolution of the programme for the revaluation of all values casts a new light on the destiny of the Eternal Recurrence and its importance to Nietzsche's work as a whole.

II. Genesis and Destiny of the Idea of the Eternal Recurrence

Just because it might be his only entirely original notion does not mean that the idea of the Eternal Recurrence can be classified as a foundational intuition whose cosmological significance and ethical importance Nietzsche would then explore throughout his work. On the contrary, the evidence now points to the fact that the idea of recurrence is a belated doctrine. Nietzsche's philosophy is, from the beginning, and because of the marked influence of Schopenhauer, a metaphysics of the will. It is the will, in all its manifestations and in its many anthropological avatars, that constitutes the central object of Nietzsche's oeuvre. And yet, at that moment when his work is reaching maturity, that is, nine years after the publication of *The Birth of Tragedy*, and only seven years before it would be abruptly interrupted by delirium, there is the sudden eruption of an idea whose connection to this same philosophy of the will would be so contradictory.

It is not until the summer of 1881, in Sils-Maria, that Nietzsche registers for the first time in his notebooks the idea of an eternal cycle of all events. In spite of the profoundly paradoxical nature of this idea, Nietzsche, carried along by the sudden inspiration, accepts it point blank, as though it were something that, from outside him, had taken hold of his thoughts and demanded that he respond to the truth of everything which it implied.[14]

If the *genesis* of this "inspiration" is one of the great enigmas in the interpretation of Nietzsche, it is crucial, above all, to underline the ambiguity that surrounds its consequences – an ambiguity which will lead to complications in our understanding of the role played by the idea of Eternal Recurrence in the programme for the revaluation of values.

The idea of an exact and infinite repetition of each and every possible event, which had already served to organize *The Gay Science* (1883), is the thematic centrepiece of *Thus Spoke Zarathustra*. However, we know that Nietzsche never actually formulated his doctrine of the Eternal Recurrence in Zarathustra's message. In a letter written on 10 March, 1984 to Franz Overbeck, for example, Nietzsche considered *Thus Spoke Zarathustra* to be a simple preamble to the announcement of the Sils-Maria idea, which in this letter he refers to as "the idea which divides the history of humanity in two parts," and which he admits he is still a long way from being able to represent and communicate.[15] One would have hoped then that in his later works he would have undertaken a rigorous elaboration of the idea of a repetition of all things. Yet, on the contrary, in a piece which Nietzsche concluded at the beginning of 1885 – initially conceived as an autonomous work entitled "Midday and Eternity" and which would eventually be published as the fourth part of *Thus Spoke Zarathustra* – the idea of the Eternal Recurrence is utterly absent. In this same period, Nietzsche begins to commit various projects to the page, all of which were supposed to be part of a major work, and whose titles centred on the idea of the Eternal Recurrence.[16] But, from August 1885 onwards, this idea crops up in just one section of what would become "The Will to Power: Attempt at the Revaluation of all Values."[17]

After this, the doctrine of the Eternal Recurrence almost disappears. In the works published after 1886, the Eternal Recurrence is completely absent, with the exception of just three cases: aphorism 56 of *Beyond Good and Evil* (where it is merely implied); the final chapter of *Twilight of the Idols* (where it is mentioned only to designate the author himself – "the one who taught the Eternal Recurrence");[18] and the chapter dedicated to *Thus Spoke Zarathustra* in *Ecce Homo* (in which it is referred to as constituting the central idea of this work).[19] Not even in the notebooks written during the same period do we find much mention of the Eternal Recurrence.[20]

This eclipse of the idea of the Eternal Recurrence is nothing short of intriguing. After Nietzsche had confessed, in 1884, that *Thus Spoke Zarathustra* was a mere preamble to what he would eventually write about the idea of the Eternal Recurrence, which at the time he still considered himself far from being able to articulate (mysteriously enough, since his earlier works had so wonderfully demonstrated his powers of elucidation), there is a progressive quelling of this idea. At the same time, themes such as the *revaluation of values*, the *will to power* and *nihilism* gradually become the centrepieces of his work.

In spite of the fact that he has moved away from the Sils-Maria inspiration, Nietzsche still creates the fiction of continuity in his work. When he registers in his notebooks the above mentioned programme for the tetralogy, entitling it with the all-inclusive designation of the "Revaluation of All Values", in which *The Antichrist* will figure as the first title, he assigns the title of "Dionysus: The Philosophy of the Eternal Recurrence"[21] to the never realized fourth and last book of the group. And yet the idea itself, of an Eternal Recurrence, is completely absent from *The Antichrist*, that is, from the only book of the four to be effectively brought into existence. And, in the end, Nietzsche would come to consider *The Antichrist* to be the complete realization of the earlier project. How to construe such an omission?

The fundamental question becomes: what role does the idea of the Eternal Recurrence play in the genesis of the project for the *revaluation of all values*, from which, as we have seen, it ended up being excluded? The present chapter will address these questions.

We begin with the hypothesis that there is a necessary tie between the two processes, to wit: the disappearance of the idea of the Eternal

Recurrence from the body of Nietzsche's work starting in 1885, and the beginning of the elaboration of the doctrines of the *will to power* and of *nihilism* which will serve to structure the programme of *revaluation*. One can argue that these last doctrines are the result of an attempt by Nietzsche to respond to the most important ethical and metaphysical problems before him, both of which emerged out of the idea of repetition.

If our hypothesis can be confirmed, the role attributed to the idea of the Eternal Recurrence in the programme of revaluation will have to be reformulated. Contrary to what is normally supposed by the critics, the Sils-Maria inspiration does not turn out to be the fundamental proposal in the programme of the exhaustion of all values. This does not, of course, imply that it has played no role whatsoever. If the doctrine of the Eternal Recurrence is, in fact, a condition for the possibility of the project of the revaluation of values, it is so on the "biographical" plane. It was the transformation of the idea of the *eternal recurrence* into the doctrine of the *will to power* that, as we will try to show, gave rise to the doctrine of *nihilism*, which would, in turn, constitute the fundamental contents of the programme for the revaluation of all values.

Our inquiry will take two different directions. Firstly, we will trace the genesis of the idea of the Eternal Recurrence and the problems which this idea creates in Nietzsche's work after 1881. Secondly, we will not only underline the novelty of the doctrine of the *will to power* and *nihilism* (both arising in 1885) but, more importantly, show to what extent these doctrines should be read as solutions to those problems inscribed in the cosmological and ethical idea of the recurrence of all events.

To ponder the appearance of the idea of the Eternal Recurrence in the writings of Nietzsche is an immense project. As we have already said, Nietzsche always described this idea as having taken the form of pure "inspiration," something which came suddenly to dominate his thinking and force him to search for cosmological and existential truth. In *Ecce Homo*, when he meditates upon the precursors of this inspiration, he refers only to an alteration in his musical tastes.[22] This is certainly not the place to describe the complete evolution of the idea of Recurrence. That would imply a profound examination of Nietzsche's rupture with Schopenhauer's metaphysics, out of which his mature view of nature, his positions on the human condition and, finally, his theory of the will would develop. These were the tendencies which led to his thinking on the revaluation of morals. In this chapter we will concentrate on a vein in Nietzsche's thinking which seems to underlie these tendencies, that is, his notion of the role of guilt – for this is where the real genesis of the project for the revaluation of all values lies.

III. The Phenomenology of Guilt Before the Programme for the Revaluation of All Values

Beginning with *Human, All-too-Human* (1878) morality is defined as the condemnation of existence. In the name of an ideal of justice and of eternity invested with absolute reality, life and its vital instincts have been cursed and turned into the root of the cruelty and ephemeralness of the human condition. This condemnation expresses, according to Nietzsche, a universal phenomenon: the attempt to correct existence, a revolt against life, a dark will bent on avenging vital instincts, on anathematizing the body and its world.[23] To understand the essence of the idea behind morality implies understanding the genesis of the condition of the possibility of this revolt. It is important to inquire into the nature of the paradox of a will that, in the name of an idea of perfecting life, calls for its own annihilation and which sacrifices itself on the altar of values that it engendered in order to judge existence.

Some of the grandeur of Nietzsche's positions on the different moral experiences of the West rests in the fact that he did not formulate just a single response to the question. From the different configurations of the figure of revolt, we can establish the key moments in the basic positions that run through his work. There are three such moments: from 1878 to 1881 – which takes in *Human, All-too-Human, The Wanderer and His Shadow, Mixed Opinions and Maxims,* and *Daybreak*; from 1881 to 1885 – *The Gay Science* and *Thus Spoke Zarathustra*; and after 1885 – *Beyond Good and Evil* and posterior works.

In the period inaugurated by *Human, All-too-Human*, it is the Schopenhauerean programme for the creation of a metaphysical basis for morality which provides what is needed to understand the essence of the will in revolt. This paradigmatic condition, which, in its moral dimension, is attributed to the phenomenon of the revolt of the will against itself, has its origin in the metaphysics of pessimism. For Schopenhauer, the will's search for its own self-destruction as a road to beatitude is not simply an ethical imperative. It has a primitive character – it is found in the origin itself of moral awareness. In *On the Basis of Morality* the experience of remorse is seen as representative of the revolt of life against itself. It offers not only the right condition for the empirical possibility of moral sentiment but the "ratio cognoscendi" of freedom, the metaphysical basis of that moral sentiment. Schopenhauer believes that it is thus possible to demonstrate, immediately and originally, the fact of freedom and, therefore, the moral nature of all human action. According to him, in the experience of remorse (*die Reue*) – that is, in the consciousness of the fragility of the will, of guilt before an act that, in spite of belonging to the past, is recognized by the practical subject as belonging to him (as a manifestation of his immutable individuality) – we are able to see intuitively the essence of the will and, therefore, its moral destiny. For Schopenhauer all of us, when confronted with the sense of the imperfection of action, will return to the *done* in an attempt to *redo* it. Such a sentiment has a metaphysical dimension. "Now as responsibility presupposes a possibility of having acted otherwise and thus freedom in some way, there is to be found indirectly in the consciousness of responsibility the consciousness also of freedom."[24]

This surprising thesis, which affirms the intuitive condition of freedom, as though it could be obtained immediately in the experience of guilt, does not have a descriptive status. In spite of the phenomenological tone that Schopenhauer adopts whenever he speaks of the consciousness of guilt, a reading of his demonstration reveals to what extent the immediate equivalence which he posits between the experience of guilt and the intuition of freedom originates in his attempt to avoid the paradoxes of the Kantian concept of freedom, or, rather, in his attempt to break out of the freedom/morality circle which had organized the *Critique of Practical Reason*. It will be recalled that freedom – an idea of the reason – only acquired objective reality for Kant when it was rigorously deduced from moral law. For its turn, moral law, even though it is a fact of reason, only has an objective basis, its "ratio essendi," in the fact of freedom. As Kant himself affirmed: "One must freely admit it that a kind of circle shows itself here, from which it seems, there is no way out. In the order of efficient causes we assume ourselves to be free in order to think ourselves as under moral laws in the order of ends, and then afterward we think of ourselves subject to these laws because we have attributed freedom of the will to ourselves."[25]

Schopenhauer wanted to break out of this vicious circle, this reciprocal dependency between freedom and morality. At the same time, he intended to strip the sphere of the will of its monopoly on moral experience. How would this be done? On the one hand, he denies moral law the status of a "fact of reason" as was proposed by Kantian formalism. On the other, because he wants to break out of the Kantian circle, he construes freedom not as postulate of reason, but as an intelligible metaphysical property of the ethical subject's own will. Schopenhauer thus displaces one of the terms of the freedom/morality relation. It is no longer the moral fact, as an idea of the reason, but the fact of remorse, that reveals the essence of human morality. And for man, this fact of remorse has a simple and absolute condition. It does not depend on any moral postulate. Guilt is the discovery of the fundamental freedom inscribed in the *intelligible character* of the subject that acts and that leads to the revolt of will against itself.

This metaphysical justification of remorse – and the consequent amplification of its significance as the basis of morality – would inevitably influence Nietzsche's pursuit of the origin of morality's condemnation of existence. Schopenhauer shows Nietzsche the way towards the refutation of the ethic of pessimism. And Nietzsche does nothing more than follow it. The consequences will be enormous. As we will see, Nietzsche never frees himself from Schopenhauer's formulation of morality. In *Human, All-too-Human* he goes no further than to explore the Kantian and Schopenhauerean circularity of the definition of morality and freedom. He merely cuts the Gordian knot of this definition's implied reciprocality, rejecting the thesis which states that the experience of remorse is an original and metaphysical condition. He believes that it is enough to show that this experience is far from being pure and immediate. It presupposes a determined interpretation of the will and its mechanisms, that is, it presupposes the hypothesis of freedom. Thus, in aphorism 39 of *Human, All-too-Human* Nietzsche says the following:

> Schopenhauer concluded otherwise, thus: because certain actions bring after them a feeling of *displeasure* ('consciousness of guilt'), there must exist a sense of accountability; ... From the fact of that feeling of displeasure Schopenhauer believes he can demonstrate a freedom which man must have acquired somehow, not in respect of his actions but in respect of his nature. ... Here the erroneous conclusion is drawn that from the fact of a feeling of displeasure there can be inferred the justification, the rational *admissibility* of this feeling of displeasure; and from this erroneous conclusion Schopenhauer arrives at the fantastic concept of so-called intelligible freedom.[26]

For Nietzsche the reciprocal implication between freedom and morality is exclusively derivative. It is coincidental result of a belief and a false experience: the *belief* in freedom is postulated out of the *experience* of remorse, but the experience of remorse arises only as a result of the fact that the individual supposed himself free. "It is because man *regards* himself as free, not because he is free, that he feels remorse and pangs of conscience."[27]

To liberate man from the yoke of moral values presumes, therefore, a double combat, at once anthropological and metaphysical. What is at stake is the annulment of the condition for the psychological possibility of remorse, and the repudiation of those small mechanisms which lead each one of us to the narrow-minded sense of the finitude of the will, to the false experiences of guilt and the revolt against the self. On the other hand, there is an urgent need to expose the illusions of freedom that underlie the experience of remorse, uncovering the non-contingency of everything that happens and everything that is, as much in us as in the world. Here Nietzsche will have to appeal to a metaphysics of the necessity.

Just by demonstrating the non-contingency of each one of our decisions, each one of our gestures and our renunciations, it is possible to assert their total innocence, their total amorality. "No one is accountable for his deeds, no one for his nature."[28] Or as he states in another aphorism: "Everything is necessity – thus says the new knowledge; and this knowledge itself is necessity. Everything is innocence: and knowledge is the path to insight into this innocence."[29] The critique of values is thus transformed in the period of *Human, All-too-Human* and *Daybreak* into a naturalist metaphysics – demonstrating the fundamental innocence of all actions based on the determined character of their mechanisms – and into a critical anthropology of debilitated wills, "all-too-human" wills, that have been overly exposed to experiences of impotence and self-blame.

In 1881, Nietzsche would receive the "inspiration" for the idea of the Eternal Recurrence. This idea will bring with it a radical reconfiguration of the metaphysics of the necessary and of the innocence of everything that happens. It will also provide a new anthropological explanation for the experience of guilt, forcing Nietzsche to interpret anew the morality of existence.

IV. Time and Morality

In effect, what above all characterizes the period which begins in 1881 with the appearance of the idea of Eternal Recurrence is that Nietzsche's analysis of remorse is pushed back to a period of thinking that predates his works written out of his rupture with Schopenhauer; guilt and revolt of the will are relocated to a moment anterior to the formation of metaphysical presuppositions about freedom and the sentiment of the finitude of the will. Works that post-date 1881 are oriented by the thesis that it is in the universal experience of temporality itself that the origin of the revolt of the will is to be found and, therefore, where the condition for the possibility of morality resides. Nietzsche takes the duplicity itself of the experience of the past – as something which is irrevocable and irreversible – as that primitive experience out of which the revolt of the will erupts against temporal experience. The annulment of the condition of the possibility of morality no longer occurs in the combat with the fiction of freedom (and the way in which it leads to the false experience of remorse), but in a reconversion of the "all-too-human" experience of time into its form of time passed.

In the chapter "On Redemption" in *Thus Spoke Zarathustra* we find the most perfect exposition of this strategy. Nietzsche deduces the will in revolt from the temporal condition of human existence. Many of Nietzsche's readers – and in particular Heidegger – have emphasized the singularity of this nearly "existential analysis" of temporality.[30] Instead of starting from a thesis of the nature of time and exploring merely different forms of its apprehension by the will, Nietzsche seeks to show that the genesis of time is in the subject of the will. Before it is an element in the experience of the world, time is the mode by which the subject which acts only becomes aware of itself through a specific experience of itself.

This experience, which gives rise to itself as time, derives from the individual's discovery of the uniqueness of his own acts. The will has the power to do, even to redo *what it did*, but never to redo the *fact* of having done it. It is the uniqueness of the act, that is its unrepeatability, that introduces will's distance from itself in time. Each one of us can go back to again do what was done, or to redo it, and even destroy it. But we can never return to experience the event itself of doing something. It is this impossibility which creates a disassociation between *that which is done* and the *fact of having done it.* Such a disassociation, according to Nietzsche, means that time is experienced as an immaterial passage, as a film which adheres to the fact of doing and which makes that fact immutable, no matter how mutable that which was done ends up being. "The will cannot will backwards; and that he cannot break time and time's covetousness, that is the will's loneliest melancholy ... That time does not run backwards, that is his wrath ... 'that which was' [*Das, was war*] is the name of the stone he cannot move. ... This, indeed this alone, is what *revenge* is: the will's ill will against time and its 'it was'."[31] It is the will's distance from itself in time, the impossibility of returning to that which was willed that engenders time and, in the same moment, the spirit of revolt, "revenge" (*die Rache*) and the "resentment of the will" (*des Willens Widerwille*).

The will discovers that it is impotent. It then feels time as a feeling of rage, or revolt. From this moment on resentment inevitably contaminates time's mode of being. As such, time constitutes itself as an object of experience of the impure conscience. This conscience is a will in revolt, a will which revolts precisely against time and against everything that occurs in time. The moral condemnation of existence consists thus in the projection onto time of limits inherent to the uniqueness of the will, in its continual dividing of itself, and its deferral of itself in each act.

There is, therefore, already a mechanism of illusion in the most primordial stratum of experience of the self as temporality. Instead of understanding this distancing in time as the result of the uniqueness of the act, that is, its singularity (from whence the impossibility of making the fact of something that has already happened real once again), the irrevocability of the past is felt by the will as an obstacle imposed upon it. The impossibility of annulling the fact of something having happened is thus blamed on time itself. With *time* and *will* in opposition, time can only appear as something which limits *will,* as an interdiction, like "the stone he cannot move" – the false exteriority of time before the one who would convert it into a moral phenomenon. It is as though, putting pressure on each moment of existence, time were a form of "justice," and life, which it moulds, a kind of "punishment." "Everything passes away; therefore everything deserves to pass away. And this too is justice, this law of time that it must devour its children. Thus preached madness."[32] The illusion of a link between *time* and *will* transforms itself into "madness." It is this that gives moral meaning to a conception of time that has been made artificially autonomous, reified. From the illusion of seeing time as something which *happens* comes the madness of affirming that "therefore everything deserved to happen!" (*darum ist alles wert zu vergehen!*) – in which the *happening* suddenly takes on a moral meaning, a "deserving to" (*werten*), a value (*Wert*). Representing time in the figure of "justice" are all the things that exist in time and arise infected by this moral valorization, this guilt. " 'Things are ordered morally according to justice and punishment. Alas, where is redemption from the flux of things and from the punishment called existence?' Thus preached madness."[33] Existence is transformed into a moral phenomenon in that moment in which the uniqueness of doing is pondered from the point of view of time and not from the perspective of the fact of itself alone. For this reason, when a man reflects on himself as existence in time, his only possibility is to discover that he has been infected by the experience of punishment and by the desire for vengeance, by the will to revenge against time. Nietzsche himself would say "*The Spirit of Revenge*, my friends, has so far been the subject of man's best reflection; ... For 'punishment' is what revenge calls itself... ."[34]

V. Nostalgia and Remorse

Let us summarize the four phases in Nietzsche's reconstruction of the genesis of the moral condemnation of existence: (a) experience of the uniqueness of the act and the consequent revolt against its irrevocability; (b) the substantialist interpretation of irrevocability, as though it expressed the dynamism of the "passing" of time; (c) the interpretation of this substantialness as "justice" and "punishment" which is directed at the irrevocable act; and (d) the moral condemnation of existence in general, by its temporality.

The problem with deducing morality from the experience of temporality lies in a process of conversion between two phenomena: that of the experience of time as irrevocability and that of the feeling of revolt against time. For Nietzsche, this conversion is necessary. The "spirit of revenge" is inherent in the temporal condition of human existence. As such, the final basis of morality no longer has its roots in illusion, it is no longer a consequence of the presupposition of freedom (as Nietzsche had argued in *Human, All-too-Human*). Now, morality takes on a universal value; it is seen as an anthropological given, as if the *pathos* of the revolt against life had been inscribed in the experience itself of time.

But Nietzsche is deluding himself here. We can verify that what is tacitly at stake is the *typological* understanding of this same experience of time. It is as though Nietzsche had already formulated the thesis that would organize the theory of the will to power: experiences of time are not universal, rather they are derived from different *types* of will. Indeed, irrevocability of the past in itself cannot be experienced univocally. As Nietzsche will recognize once he begins to explore the inbuilt selectivity of the idea of Eternal Recurrence, it already inevitably contains an unavoidable ambivalence. The irrevocability of the *already done* can be distinguished in two distinct ways: as *nostalgia*, or as *remorse*. In *nostalgia* the will discovers the obstacle of temporal distance because it wants to recuperate the past in order to relive it in its uniqueness, because it recognizes in it the plenitude of a unique conjugation, of a perfect intensity which wants to be repeated. In *remorse*, it is the impossibility of destroying the past, or erasing an act that is seen to be imperfect and which, in its irrevocability, lingers on as a wounded memory which refuses to heal. While in nostalgia temporal deferral is manifest in the property of irreversibility, it is irrevocability which obsesses the guilty conscience. In remorse, as Jankélévitch says, "this is not about reliving an event already lived through, but definitively putting aside the memory of an event, or of a decision; this is not about bringing charming ghosts back to life, but driving away the sinister specters who frighten a guilty conscience."[35] Remorse is the despair which comes of never being able to revoke the irrevocable. For this reason, remorse leads the will into rage against time. The originating "no" which Nietzsche discovers in all of the commandments of value can only be the result of the experience of time as remorse. Nostalgia would never be able to induce "revolt," or the will to revenge. It is precisely the experience of a nothingness beyond repair which follows an absolute – the knowledge of the disappearance of the already lived – that makes the nostalgic consciousness suffer. Remorse, to the contrary, desires the nothingness, or at least the nothingness of a certain past. It is a principle of nihilization. It wants to erase the traces of imperfection from memory. The revolt of remorse against time is, in its essence, the will's revolt against itself, against its finite condition and against the infinitude of its memory.

Thus it is understood that in the description of the human experience of time, the experience which gives birth to the concept of the "spirit of revenge," the experience of the past, "of that which was" (*das, was war*), is not an experience of *nostalgia*. It is not the *irreversible*, but the *irrevocable* that is primordially manifest in our experience of the past. This difference, as we will see below, is decisive to our understanding of the doctrine of the Eternal Recurrence. It is not the mere continual "passing" (*vergehen*) of time, as temporal distance between the present of the will that acts and the series of its acts already carried out; it is not the mere non-repeatability that fills the will with sadness. The impotence of the "spirit of revenge" before time is the despair of never being able to revoke the irrevocable, of never being able to redo an act which is known to be imperfect. It is in this sense that, on this same page, when Nietzsche specifies the meaning of "it was" (*es war*), he is already revealing his understanding of the *typology* of rage against time. " 'It was' – that is the name of the will's gnashing of teeth [*onmachtig gegen das, was getan ist*] and most secret melancholy. Powerless against what has been done, he is an angry spectator of all that is past."[36] It is not "what was lived" but "what was done" (*das, was getan ist*) that inscribes the breach of finitude within the will, the discovery of "impotence" and, consequently, the difference between the irrevocable and the irreversible in the experience of time. Only a will that would like not to have done what it did, only a will that experiences itself as irremissible guilt, unredeemable since it is incapable of undoing the done, in a word, only a will marked by this "remorse" (*Reue*) that Schopenhauer had identified as the originating basis of morality, only it constitutes time according to the figure of the irrevocable, the figure of the incurable petrification of the past.

This already *typological* interpretation of the human constitution of time (of the implicit privilege conferred upon an experience particular to the will – the experience of remorse in the apprehension of time as a sphere of the irremediable) is also apparent in the fact that Nietzsche considers that what causes the will to revolt against time is the impossibility that neither "punishment" nor repentance allows for the retroactive cancellation of the act. It remains unalterable, crystallized in irrevocability, eternally accusing us. "No deed can be annihilated: how could it be undone by punishment."[37] If the will wants the past, it is not to once again set it in motion; the experience of the "it was" is already and always awakened by the desire to annul it, to "erase" the fact of its having been done.

Thus, in this *typological* understanding of the possibility of morality we still find the influence of Schopenhauerean morality, or rather the influence of the way in which Nietzsche had tried to subvert this morality in *Human, All-too-Human*. It is the figure of *remorse* (in which Schopenhauer had invested considerable metaphysical value) which continues to be revealed at the root of the revolt against life and against temporality. We can say that, in *Thus Spoke Zaruthustra*, Nietzsche sought above all to remove from *remorse* this primitive character attributed to it by Schopenhauer. Derived from a precise experience of time, remorse could be seen as arising as an illusion, as the effect of a false interpretation of the structure of irrevocability. Yet, with this gesture, Nietzsche contaminated his own phenomenology of temporality. To strip remorse of its metaphysical status, to reduce it to a simple, impoverished sentiment of time, to an "all-too-human" sentiment, resulted in turning *remorse* into a "human" experience, an experience which concerned Man in all his universality and that would be inscribed in his condition of existing in time.

The diagnosis of morality in *Thus Spoke Zarathustra* is, as such, built upon an ambiguity. Nietzsche wants to start from a pure description of the experience of temporality in order to trace the *pathos* of revenge against life back to it and, therefore, deduce the condition of the possibility for the whole moral valorization of existence. Yet, if the experience of time produces in the will the consciousness of its own finitude, resulting in a *pathos* for revenge against the past, it is because the experience itself of time already finds its genesis in another experience closer to the origin of revolt: that of remorse. And this latter experience no longer has a universal character; it has merely to do with certain kinds of wills – those that, because they do not carry each act to its possible limit, live obsessed with redoing the done.

We can say that there is not one, but two perspectives from which we can understand the condition for the possibility of morality: one *anthropological* and the other *typological*. In the first it is the uniqueness of the act that, in itself, sets off a revolt against time in the will; in the second, the revolt against existence is a predetermined interpretation of this uniqueness. In the anthropological perspective, the spirit of revenge acquires universal status – it is a constituent of man's consciousness as a being that exists in time. Time thus acquires a metaphysical condition. It is its reality, its very passing, in itself irrevocable and unrepeatable, that produces the human condition in man. It is because time is this impassible mass, this monstrous material that in its immateriality reduces everything that exists to nothingness, that man is a being whose most fundamental nature is the revolt against time, against existence, against life, in a word, that man is a "moral" being. Because time exists, man is man. In the typological perspective, the reality of time is dissolved. Not because the human condition is previous to the constitution of temporality as experience. The idea of man as a stable entity also dissolves. What exists are types.[38] And they constitute different modes of temporality. The revolt against time and, therefore, the invention of the figure of time as an irrevocable elapsing, only pertains to the reactive type of will, that will which does not employ the full potential of its power in each moment because it reduces its act to remnants, to the excess of circumstances.[39]

We have already seen to what extent the concept of "the spirit of revenge" is tacitly elaborated on the typological plane. We also saw how this concept is nothing more than a new figure of the concept of "remorse" as it had been constituted in *Human, All-too-Human*. Just as in that book (the first to break with the Schopenhauerean attempt to find a metaphysical basis for Kant's morality), the guilty conscience does not have the status of an intuitive given, nor is it an original source of experience. Repeating the theses of *Human, All-too-Human*, the typological perspective shows that only wills predisposed to thinking themselves impotent curse their actions and rejoice in guilt. Yet, in texts earlier than 1881, the anthropological perspective confers a universal value upon the figure of the "spirit of revenge." We will see that the impasses to which the doctrine of Eternal Recurrence will be driven in *Thus Spoke Zarathustra* derive from this disparity of perspectives.

Indeed, the anthropological and typological perspectives will remain irreducible and will engender distinct strategies for overcoming the "spirit of revenge." In the first, because it is identified with human nature itself, to free man from the "spirit of revenge" is to free man from himself. Overcoming morality implied the death of man and the advent of the over-human. Such a thing would only be possible through the revelation of an alternative temporality, that of the Eternal Recurrence, in which the past is no longer an insurmountable barrier, but is converted into the eternal recurrence of the will to itself. On the contrary, in the typological perspective, since the ultimate condition of the possibility for the moral condemnation of existence is not in temporality itself, but in the will's experience of guilt as it acts in time, to overcome morality, to redeem the will to the *pathos* of the revolt against time, a conversion becomes necessary, not of time, but of the mode for constructing it in the will's experience of itself. In the typological perspective there is a true poietic of time and of its immaterial modulations.

In either of these perspectives the idea of Eternal Recurrence will be called upon to play the role of criteria, of crucial proof. In the typological perspective Eternal Recurrence occurs to him who conceives of it as ethical imperative and selective idea; in the anthropological it occurs as a new physical representation of time that frees all of humanity from its "all-too-human" nature. It is significant that in the first formulations of the Eternal Recurrence it is the typological perspective that orients the programme for the overcoming of the *pathos* of revenge against life. This perspective will be successively overshadowed by the anthropological notion of the "spirit of revenge," until it finally plays itself out in its own aporias. Because of this, we can speak of an evolution of form according to which Nietzsche views the existential impact of the Sils-Maria inspiration upon those to whom it is revealed. While in his first reflections, in particular in *The Gay Science* (1883), the selective dimension of Eternal Recurrence is emphasized, as a nearly apocalyptic revelation, the exterminator of guilty consciousnesses, in *Thus Spoke Zarathustra* its reach is uniquely salvational – it is the "redemptive" message that leads man toward the over-human. The fact that this displacement has gone unnoticed by the most important interpreters of the idea of Eternal Recurrence, who have been unable, for this reason, to recognize the incompatibility between the two ethical programmes contained in the idea, has led Nietzschean exegesis into certain absurdities.[40] By systematically following this evolution we will be able to understand the mechanism by which Nietzsche moved from the idea of the Eternal Recurrence to the programme for the revaluation of all values.

VI. Typologies of Temporality in *The Gay Science*

Nietzsche's first reflections on the impact of the idea of infinite repetition on those to whom it is revealed is founded upon a typological phenomenology of temporality. As a consequence, this impact always manifests itself in the figure of an idea of selectivity. In the notebook from the summer of 1881 that contains the first mention of the Sils-Maria inspiration, Nietzsche says: "Only those who consider their existence to be capable of eternal repetition will remain."[41] Such selective efficacy derives from the inherent ambivalence in any cosmological representation of infinite repetition. It is capable of producing two different antinomian responses in the one who is subjugated by it: either the one who ponders it is annihilated by the very idea, since he is eternally condemned to the pain which the irrevocability of a past that would best be forgotten provokes in him as it obsessively returns to be re-experienced in all its imperfection – a true return of the repressed, as it were; or the promise of repetition would arise as a cosmic confirmation of a past that is actually desired for its own sake, in an access of unconditional nostalgia. That duality of postures that is, it would seem, inbred in the revelation of Eternal Recurrence, is dramatized in aphorism 341 of *The Gay Science*, the first of Nietzsche's works to reveal the Sils-Maria inspiration. There the idea of an infinite repetition is presented in the figure of a demon that suddenly appears in the midst of our solitude to confront us with a new and terrible image of time. His message is that "This life as you live it and have lived it, you will have to live once more and innumerable times more; and there will be nothing new in it, but every pain and every joy and every thought and sigh and everything immeasurably small or great in your life must return to you – all in the same succession and sequence. . . ."[42] In light of this fantastical deliverance Nietzsche asks: "Would you not throw yourself down and gnash your teeth and curse the demon who spoke thus? Or did you once experience a tremendous moment [*oder hast du eimal einen ungeheuren Augenblick erlebt*] when you would have answered him, 'You are a god, and never have I heard anything more godly.' "[43] Since the will to the return of the past can render radically heterogeneous experiences – nostalgia or remorse – the idea of Eternal Recurrence must be comprised of unavoidable existential ambivalence. It induces existential postures that are as distinct from each other as are the ways of seeing the past. For the one in whom memory of the past is always refracted through the knowledge of impotence and a guilty conscience and who, as a consequence, only wants to turn it off, annul it, for this person the idea of infinite recurrence of this past exactly as it was, the idea of the repetition of each and every one of these acts that they want to forget, is a curse, a terrible punishment: this idea annihilates him.

On the other hand, the idea of Eternal Recurrence will confer plenitude to each and every one of the instants of our existence only if this plenitude has already been realized. It is only in one for whom the experience of the past is already contained in this feeling of nostalgia that the idea of the return of this same past can possibly represent "divine thinking." Eternal Recurrence affirms the promise of the repetition of "a tremendous moment" already experienced and which one wants to be lived anew. As Nietzsche asks us, "or did you once experience a tremendous moment"; then, at the conclusion of this same aphorism (341) of *The Gay Science* when we read: "Or how well disposed would you have to become to yourself and to life to *crave nothing more fervently* than this ultimate eternal confirmation and seal?" The "selectivity" that Nietzsche attributes to the idea of recurrence therefore presupposes a typological understanding of temporality. What is expressed in the duality of responses to the revelation of Eternal Recurrence is the duality of postures when confronting the past – remorse or nostalgia.

But this undermines the idea of Eternal Return. As soon as Nietzsche adopts the typological perspective to ponder the inescapable ambivalence of the doctrine of Eternal Return, he annuls, at one stroke, its existential value. The revelation of the Eternal Recurrence of all things ends up by being existentially derivative. It is not the idea of repetition that refigures the experience of temporality. Instead, this idea simply confirms, in cosmological terms, an experience of temporality previously prefigured. It empowers the experience of each past event as a site of the instantaneous plenitude of each act. Nietzsche seems to have been aware of this derivative efficacy when, in 1882, he writes in one of his notebooks: "We want to experience a work of art over and over again! We should fashion our life in this way, so that we have the same wish with each of its parts! This is the main idea! [*Dis der Hauptgedanke*]. Only at the end will the *doctrine* be presented of the repetition of everything that has been, once the tendency has been implanted to create something which can *flourish* a hundred times more strongly in the sunshine of this doctrine!"[44]

It is obvious that "the main idea" (*der Hauptgedanke*) is not the idea of Eternal Recurrence. This particular imperative does not presuppose the idea of repetition. On the contrary. Firstly, we must model each event in our life so that it evokes a nostalgia in us similar to that which we would feel in the contemplation of a work of art. Only in this way can the experience of remorse, of finitude in confrontation with "the already done," be annulled and the moral representation of temporality be overcome. It is over this "aesthetic of nostalgia" already realized that the doctrine of Eternal Recurrence will manifest itself as an ethical maxim. The cosmological representation of each instant as repetition will in the end "create something which can *flourish* a hundred times more strongly in the sunshine of this doctrine!" This presupposed an already incarnate desire for the return to the plenitude of each of the parts of the past. As Nietzsche had declared, the idea of temporal return is merely an "indicator" of this nostalgia and not the condition of its possibility. The imperative upon which it is based is not cosmological but aesthetic. Life must be modelled like a work of art, not for the sake of its infinite repetition, but as a way to eradicate the experience of guilt from our conscience and thus overcome the anthropological conditions of the moral interpretation of existence. But if this is the case, what use is the idea of Recurrence?

Here as well Nietzsche confounds his own explanation of the concept of time. In the greater part of his jottings from the notebooks dedicated to the doctrine of the Eternal Recurrence, this notion is conceived of as though it and the imperative to eradicate guilt were one in the same. As if the formula "My doctrine says: the task is to live your life in such a way that you have to *want* to live again – you will *in any* case!"[45] provided the maxim that would free consciousness from the experience of guilt.[46] In these texts it is the cosmological conception of an infinite and necessary repetition which is converted into an ethical imperative. Nietzsche has caught his doctrine up in a vicious circle. On the one hand the idea of recurrence is simply interpreted as a "divine thought," the absolute affirmation of the plenitude of each moment of existence for the one who had already had the experience, who had already experienced "a tremendous moment" and who has thus seen that this moment can *flourish* a hundred times more strongly in the sunshine of this doctrine. But on the other hand it seems that the same individual would only be induced to perform such an aesthetic modelling of each moment of his existence through the revelation of the idea of Eternal Return. As such, it would appear that when Nietzsche wants to exploit the existential ambivalence of the Sils-Maria inspiration, the criterion of its internal differentiation is displaced by an earlier experience of temporality and a *typological* understanding of the origin of morality is adopted. But, in this case, the idea of repetition is drained of its ethical efficacy: it becomes simply a doctrine that permits empowerment at the level of cosmological representation of an already configured existential posture. On the other hand when Nietzsche wants to see his doctrine as an imperative in whose name each one of us is induced to artistically model each moment of our existence, it becomes a bit forced to presuppose the uniqueness of the representation of Return, as though this doctrine was nothing but affirmative, that is, as though the past were always experienced through the sense of nostalgia.

This circularity between the phenomenology of temporality and the cosmological basis of time's ethic of redemption brings Nietzsche to an impasse. Either the idea of Eternal Return, because it is ambivalent, is an empty imperative, unable to reformulate the experience of time, since existential differentiation is anterior to it, or it arises as a univocal imperative (disguising its ambivalence) and, as such, annulling its ethical impact – since in the end it is an abstract imperative.

VII. The Typological Perspective in *Thus Spoke Zarathustra*

In *Thus Spoke Zarathustra* the "selectivity" of the idea of Eternal Recurrence is completely absent, even if the same is not the case with the typological perspective of temporality that supports this selective interpretation. As an ethical programme, Zarathustra's doctrine is exclusively based on the anthropological perspective of temporality. Because the *pathos* of revenge against time is seen to be inscribed in the very essence of man, the idea of an infinite reversibility, instead of annihilating those wills that cannot tolerate a return to the past, redeems them from revolt. In this way it frees man from his essence and converts him into the "overhuman." Nevertheless, the irreducibility of the phenomenologies of temporality that form a basis for both programmes will again drain the doctrine of Recurrence of its ethicality. And what is most significant is that in *Thus Spoke Zarathustra* the typological understanding of temporality (which presupposes a real difference between remorse and nostalgia as distinctive modes of distinguishing time) already contains an ethical programme, one which will legitimize the formulation of maxims of the will. It is just that this programme does not come through the idea of the Eternal Recurrence. It is nothing more than the reanimation of the natural positivist programme that had oriented *Human, All-too-Human*. The "redemptive" message, rather than being transmitted through the idea of Eternal Recurrence – which, as we will see, merely annuls irreversibility – is directed against remorse, against that sentiment of ambivalence when finally it must confront "the done" (out of repulsion for and, simultaneously, a desire to recuperate it in order to cancel it). "To redeem what is past [*die Vergangnen zu erlosen*] in man and to re-create all 'it was' until the will says, 'Thus I willed it! Thus I shall will it!' [*alles 'Es War' umzuschaffen in ein 'So wolte ich es!'*] – this I called redemption."[47] To overcome the revolt against the past implies understanding it as an absolute expression of the subject that acts. What Nietzsche denounced in the "too human" understanding of the past is the illusion of involuntariness. As long as the will is no longer to be found in one's biography, as long as one does not affirm in each one of one's acts: "Thus I willed it," the past is condemned to remain a "riddle," a "dreadful chance," and it will appear as a series of acts in which the will recognizes itself in its ambivalence, as irremediably part of the will, even though they are acts in which the will is unable to realize itself completely. Every "it was" is a fragment, an enigma, a horrible bit of luck – unless the creative will can declare "Thus I willed it!" Before cosmologically redeeming the past and annulling its irreversibility with the desire for its return such as it was and by affirming it in its necessity in light of the idea of Eternal Recurrence, Nietzsche tries to lead the will toward redeeming the past existentially, to liberating it from the "spirit of revenge." The will declares retrospectively: "Thus I willed it!" and, in this way, confirms each act to be the complete realization of the will it expresses. It redeems itself, firstly, in its revolt against the past, that is, from the experience of remorse, and by doing so cancels the need to express itself morally.

But Nietzsche hardly sees the realization of his programme to surpass all values in this transfiguration, which involves our becoming conscious of our guilt vis-à-vis time. Instead of limiting himself to a typological ethic, as the metamorphosis of the guilty posture, of remorse, into that other – affirming – posture of nostalgia, he conceives of this radical transfiguration of time in terms of the idea of Eternal Recurrence.

Let us look at the way this idea is introduced in the paragraph "On Redemption." There Nietzsche writes: "All 'it was' is a fragment, a riddle, a dreadful accident – until the creative will says to it, 'But thus I willed it.' Until the creative will says to it, 'But thus I willed it; thus I shall will it.' "[48] Some lines below we come across the following: "Who could teach him also to will backwards?" While the declaration "But thus I will it!" merely expresses a change in the representation that I create of my own past, this is the recognition of the univocality of my act and of my whole being – already that other "thus I willed it; thus I shall will it!" contains a declaration of the will. It expresses the nostalgia that this past, complete as such, awakens: a wanting once again to relive the lived. Nietzsche exploits this dislocation to be able to extract from it the anticipated configuration of the idea of Eternal Recurrence when he writes "Who could teach him also to will backwards?"

There is another surprising element in the way Nietzsche reveals the idea of Eternal Return. It is presented as the symbol, the emblem, of an experience of fundamental nostalgia. The will to relive the act of having wanted absolutely in the past induces the will to want the recurrence of all that was wanted. The "redeeming" idea therefore is a response to nostalgia, and not to remorse in confrontation with the past. This link between the experience of nostalgia and the idea of Eternal Recurrence is laid out in the chapter entitled "On the Great Longing" (*Von der grossen Sehnsucht*). Zarathustra, convalescing from the interior metamorphosis suffered after his revelation of the idea of Eternal Recurrence, intones a canticle of nostalgia, a canticle to the dissolution of the temporal differences between "today" and "formerly." "O my soul, I taught you to say 'today' and 'one day' and 'formerly' and to dance away over all Here and There and Yonder."[49]

VIII. Epistemological Solution of the Circle Between the Phenomenology of Temporality and the Ethic of Repetition

In *Thus Spoke Zarathustra* we also discover another strategic dislocation in the exploration of the existential range of the idea of Eternal Recurrence. Nietzsche seems to be looking for a criterion for the differentiation of the antinomian meanings concentrated in this idea, a criterion which would not be given through a prior existential posture, but rather singly via some representation of the essence of time. What is in play here is a perspective which is no longer typological, nor even anthropological, but rather epistemological. Instead of being an experience determined by a past that configures the representation of time in its totality, time is now represented in a way that the relation between the temporal whole and each of its parts can be apprehended, inducing, as a result, distinct postures before time and its passing.

Look, for example, at the chapter entitled "On the Vision and the Riddle": there we find two movements both geared toward a consideration of time, movements in which Nietzsche creates dual perspectives – Zarathustra's and the Dwarf's. The first begins in an experience of the plenitude and autonomy of the instant, raising itself to the contemplation of the Whole, seen as the result of the sum of all discrete temporal singularities until, finally, discovering the finite nature of this totality, it adopts as a reaffirming perspective the plenitude of the instant, seen now as repetition of itself. The second movement, the Dwarf's, starts immediately with the Whole as a circularity of past and future (apparently divergent paths do not contradict each other) from whence he traces the reality of the instant, which, in itself, lacks content of its own, but is seen rather as the simple limit of time which is no longer time.

Zarathustra quizzes the Dwarf about the nature of these paths that diverge outwards from the portico of the instant. The past as well as the future are declared, dogmatically, to be eternities. Then the following question is put to the Dwarf: "But if one were to follow them further and ever further and further: do you think, dwarf, that these paths would be in eternal opposition?" And the Dwarf responds: "Everything straight lies. . . . All truth is crooked, time itself is a circle [*Die Zeit selber ist ein Kreis*]."[50] The Dwarf seems to extract the only conclusion possible when faced with the eternal opposability of the past and the future. If both are eternal, they lead to a circle of temporality. And though Zarathustra becomes exasperated with this response, he considers it superficial. He appeals to the Dwarf to make the instant the centrepiece of his consideration over time. Zarathustra's question is then reformulated in new terms:

> 'Behold this moment! ... From this gateway Moment a long, eternal lane runs *back*: an eternity lies behind us. Must not all things that *can* run have already run along this lane? Must not all things that *can* happen *have* already happened, been done, run past? And if all things have been here before: what do you think of this moment, dwarf? Must not this gateway, too, have been here – before? ... And this slow spider that creeps along the moonlight, and this moonlight itself, and I and you at this gateway whispering together, whispering of eternal things – must we not all have been here before?'[51]

To reveal each instant as a repetition is to reveal to what extent the instant stops being a pure ideal limit of uninterrupted time to be converted into a dense event. The relationship that is established between the elements that fill it (between the spider, the moonlight, the Dwarf and Zarathustra, and, finally, between the universe and each one of its elements co-present in the instant) is hardly fortuitous. The instant acquires the consistency of a discrete and autonomous temporal totality. What is now in play in the notion of the Eternal Recurrence is not the circularity of time, derived from the non-opposability of the paths to the future and to the past, nor even repetition. The circular image of the totality of time expresses a new metaphysical status for the Instant. It is endowed with its own texture, with its own unique reality, at the same time that it is a repetition of itself.

The difference between the Dwarf's answer and that which Zarathustra wants to hear is rooted precisely in the fact of the former not seeing the

Instant as a way of viewing time in its different aspects, but rather wanting to conceive of time in general, in terms of its circular totality, thus weakening the atomicity of each of the moments of this totality.

The existential consequences of this difference of perspectives for the totality-temporal/each-instant-singular relationship are dramatized in this same chapter in the third book of *Thus Spoke Zarathustra*, in the vision of a shepherd into whose mouth a serpent crawls as he sleeps. Zarathustra moves abruptly from the conversation with the Dwarf to the memory of this horrible vision. In this narrative it seems to us that the serpent which slides inside the shepherd symbolizes the linear time of past-present-future that, in its passing, sets up residence inside of man without him being aware of it. In a slow and continual movement, like that of the serpent, time gradually enters us until finally it has completely consumed us. Once awake, the man is already in time, just as the serpent is in his entrails. Zarathustra says that he had tried to save the shepherd by pulling at the serpent's tale. But this, as he said, was in vain. The movement of the serpent, like that of time, goes in a determined direction, it is irreversible. How to evade this being-in-time, how to interrupt this anguish of time's incessant passing on the way to death, this horror of feeling as though one were being continually devoured by time? That is when, suddenly, as Zarathustra relates, a voice rose from within him yelling at the shepherd: "Bite it! Bite it!" And that's what the shepherd did, he bit the serpent, cutting his unending body in half, separating the head from the tail, the past from the future and breaking the continuous totality of time, conquering that dimension of plenitude and autonomy which only the instant can confer. Zarathustra then relates how the shepherd laughed like he'd never heard anyone laugh before.

The image of the serpent should be interpreted as a symbol of the idea of a continuous circle. If the idea of Eternal Recurrence was conceived out of the notion of circular totality, the serpent that doubles back on itself, it leads to a worsening of the experience of temporality as exteriority, the sphere of the involuntary. Each present moment is revealed as merely an ineluctable return of the past, of the "was" in all its immutability. Conversely, if it arises as affirmation of the plenitude of each and every discrete instant, as a real segmentation in the continuum of becoming, then it frees man from this experience and reveals to him the plenitude and the absolute actuality of each instant of his existence.

However, this new metaphysical status will be revealed only to those who interrogate the totality of time starting from the Instant. Only he who has already experienced time as a succession of minimal units (because time is an infinite repetition of itself, to wit the Eternal Recurrence) will be able to affirmatively interpret the idea of repetition and thus, mediated by this idea, cosmologically re-affirm that primordial experience of plenitude, which is the true identification between the will and the act. Only the idea itself of Eternal Recurrence can focus the apprehension of time in the dimension of the Instant. The representation of the idea of Return as a cosmological doctrine creates – in circular fashion – the condition for the possibility of its own revelation. This circularity is similar to that which is already present in *The Gay Science*. While there it has to do with the reciprocal presupposition of an already configured existential posture and with a representation of time that would allow for the empowerment of that posture, in *Thus Spoke Zarathustra* such a shared dynamic (between the existential posture and the representation of time) merely affects the representation of the idea of Eternal Recurrence as a pure cosmological doctrine in which the temporal whole has to be conceived of as the result of an infinite series of atomic instants, even as the atomicity of these instants is based solely on the thesis on the infinite character of the series and, therefore, on the thesis of a limited totality.

This symmetrical deviation in the representation of the temporal whole and of each one of the instants of which it is comprised, has been variously described, particularly in those readings of Nietzsche that have been influenced by the tradition of Husserl and Heidegger's phenomenologies of temporality.[52] Nevertheless, these readings are on shaky ground in conceiving such a circle as a conflict between "intramundane" and "extramundane" conceptions of time. For Eugen Fink, for example, this circularity is a consequence of the fact that Nietzsche was only able to conceive of the idea of the Eternal Recurrence out of the experience of linear time, such as it was represented in the "intramundane" view of things, that is, based on all of that which up until now has been part of the temporal world, only to cancel out, in his explanation of the infinitude of the past, this very same experience in the image of infinite repetition, reducing time to a single, ecstatic dimension.[53] The difficulty in ascending to an "over-human" state lies in this very conflict. Nietzsche still needs to resort to categories and concepts that derive from the all-too-human experience of time with its past–future oppositions, thwarting by the way a positive delineation of that which he was striving to explain. What is created, in Fink's view, is a true "negative hermeneutics of temporality," or the self-dissolution of the temporal categories that serve to orient the *pathos* of "the spirit of revenge." In the end, Fink's reading, rather than revealing the necessary character of the hermeneutic circularity that constitutes the idea of the Eternal Recurrence, reduces Nietszsche's notion to a conceptual black hole. He concludes thusly: "what becomes ambiguous and doubtful about the Nietzschean doctrine of Eternal Recurrence in *Thus Spoke Zarathustra* is the opacity of his concepts of eternity, of repetition, of the course of time and that which runs through it. There is, in Nietzsche, no explicit concept of time."[54] Heidegger sees the outer limits of Nietzsche's theoretical project in this same conceptual weakness. "Nietzsche's reflections on space and time are quite indigent as a whole, and the few thoughts on time, which go beyond traditional notions, are sporadic: indisputable proof that the question of time, indispensable to the principal question of metaphysics, remains closed for him."[55]

Both Fink and Heidegger underestimate the aporias of Eternal Recurrence. In their view these are conceptual and metaphysical limits, not of the doctrine itself, but of the whole of Nietzsche's thought – signs, indeed, of theoretical poverty and blindness.

It is difficult to agree with this reading, since it prevents us from understanding the connection between the difficulties Nietzsche experienced in formulating the idea of the Eternal Recurrence – as a phenomenology of temporality, as an ethical doctrine, and as a cosmological representation – not to mention the whole orientation of Nietzsche's work on the transmutation of all values starting in 1886. Understanding Nietzsche's final philosophy, with its progressive abandonment of the doctrine of Eternal Recurrence and the increasing centrality of the programme of the transmutation of values (with its doctrines of the *will to power* and *nihilism*), calls for a recognition of the *immanent* nature of the aporias of the Eternal Recurrence, and especially those aporias resulting from the undecidability in which Nietzsche maintains the reciprocal implication of his phenomenology of temporality and his ethic of repetition. Eternal Recurrence was never quite carried to its final consequences, not because it was conceptually weak (as Heidegger and Fink would have it), but because it was excessive and its significance was overdetermined. This excess was the result of a deep-seated circularity – more methodological than hermeneutical – which had everything to do with the reciprocal presupposition of the *typological* and *anthropological* perspective of temporality. As we have tried to show, the vicious circle at the root of the idea of Eternal Return lies in the fact that Nietzsche attempts to build a typology of wills based on a phenomenology of temporality (apparently neutral), even though this phenomenology already has in place typological categories which should have illustrated the experience of time. This vicious circle would lead to the progressive disappearance of the idea of Eternal Return in Nietzsche's works. Only Nietzsche's anthropological programme would be affected by the exhaustion of Eternal Return. He would finally break with the equivocation at the base of his doctrine, which was the result of the coexistence of both a typological and an anthropological phenomenology, retaining just one of them. From 1885 onwards, he would concentrate exclusively on the typological. This can be seen in the fourth book of *Thus Spoke Zarathustra*. There we will find no reference at all to the idea of Eternal Return. What we do find is Nietzsche setting up an extremely complicated typology of the wills: "the penitent of the spirit," "the ugliest man," "the voluntary beggar," clearly prepare us for the great typology which will be *The Genealogy of Morals*. After 1886, the critique of moral values would be conducted solely on a typological basis. What is more, this typology of the wills is no longer founded on a phenomenology of temporality. This is the perspective employed in the Second Essay of *The Genealogy of Morals*, "'Guilt,' 'Bad Conscience,' and the Like." The revolt against existence and the spirit of resentment are described in the Second Essay as the correct posture for reactive wills, where all action is reaction and revolt. In this context the transmutation of values would come to mean not a reconversion of human experience in general, but an increase in the exhaustion of typologically decadent values, that is, those engendered by reactive wills.

The most decisive shift between *Thus Spoke Zarathustra* and the works which would come after 1886 is in the abandonment of temporal categories as the principal framing device for the moral condemnation of existence.

This will permit Nietzsche to construct:

1. An ethical typology that does not derive from a phenomenology of temporality but from a psychology of the will.
2. A representation of the instantaneity and pure present of each voluntary act that is not itself based on a representation of temporality.

The fundamental architecture of the future programme for the transmutation of values originates in these theoretical innovations.

IX. The Doctrine of the Will to Power

As we have already mentioned above, the notebooks of 1884 and 1885 demonstrate the extent to which Nietszche had begun to back away from the various formulations of the idea of the Eternal Recurrence.

The doctrine of the will to power, which first makes itself felt in these same notebooks, will respond directly to this need for a new theory. It will maintain the previous conception of the purity of the act. In each instant acting is not a transition from potential to the act itself, from the desire to do something to its realization, but rather the act itself in a definitive sense. However, this is also where the principal shift occurs, this pure presence of each act is no longer based on a doctrine of time, but on a physics of the will. Schematically, this doctrine can be represented by its principal postulates:[56]

1. The functional nature of the will. The will in its entirety only acts against other wills. It is always a gathering of dynamic relations: "every force can only expend itself on what resists."[57]
2. The thesis of the instantaneity of the will. The will exists solely as a manifestation against another will. Wills confront each other in a single instant. Their identity is changed by time since in the following instant another will is already acting. As Nietzsche says: "Supposing that the world had a certain quantum of force at its disposal, then it is obvious that every displacement of power at any point would affect the whole system."[58] This is why there is no causal conditioning in uninterrupted time, but always an absolute and instantaneous reformulation of all relations of force. "Two successive states, the one 'cause,' the other 'effect': this is false. The first has nothing to effect, the second has been effected by nothing. It is a question of a struggle between two elements of unequal power: a new arrangement of forces is achieved according to the measure of power of each of them. The second condition is something fundamentally different from the first (not its effect): the essential thing is that the factions in struggle emerge with different quanta of power."[59]
3. The relation between forces in each moment of their conflict is governed by a "principle of the better," in which is grounded the deterministic conclusion of each event in nature. The resultant of this dynamic conflict is only aleatory from the perspective of each of the forces present. Taken together, as the copossibility of a multiple, this perspective is absolutely necessary as each force, in its essential instantaneity, extracts its final consequence from each instant and so reaches its maximum power. As such, the necessity of the physical event does not result in any conformity to universal laws (which would mean that its essence would have to depend on a transcendent instance), nor the inclusion of each event on the wheel of Eternal Return. This necessity is now a process of internal generation. "I take good care not to talk of chemical 'laws': that has a moral aftertaste. It is rather a matter of the absolute establishment of power relations: the stronger becomes master of the weaker to the extent that the weaker cannot assert its degree of autonomy – here there is no mercy, no forbearance, even less a respect for 'laws'!"[60] Nietzsche adopts a localizing and instantaneous conception of determinism "There is no law: every power at every moment draws its ultimate conclusion. It is precisely on the lack of a mezzo termine that calculability rests."[61]

It is important to underline that these three dynamic principles upon which Nietzsche would construct his doctrine of the will to power presuppose a fundamental duality between the perspective of each individual will and that of the regulated relation of the multiplicity of wills in conflict in each local morphology. From the perspective of singularity, each will is radically unconditioned, spontaneous, and represents the pure impulse, endowed by a free determination, of an immanent finality and the struggle for the infinite increase of power. From the general perspective of morphology the resultant is always determined. Nietzsche's problem is in conciliating this duality of perspectives while maintaining the instantaneity of the will as a principle. They cannot be considered two distinct moments, one in which the individual will begins to act in unconditioned fashion and the other in which it achieves a regulated resultant in the context of copossibility. It was precisely to solve this problem that Nietzsche established the difference between the concepts of *will* and *power*.[62] The first represents the interior and unconditioned face of force while the second is the resultant in the context of local copossibility.

With the doctrine of the will to power, Nietzsche constructs a representation of action as pure present and complete in each instant without requiring the instant to be derived from a temporal conception or from any representation of a cosmological totality. Significantly, this doctrine appears for the first time in 1886 in *Beyond Good and Evil*. There, in aphorism 22 Nietzsche writes:

> 'nature's conformity to law,' of which you physicists talk so proudly, as though – why, it exists only owing to your interpretation and bad 'philology' ... and somebody might come along who, with opposite intentions and modes of interpretation, could read out of the same 'nature,' and with regard to the same phenomenon, rather the tyrannically inconsiderate and relentless enforcement of claims of power ... but he might, nevertheless, end by asserting the same about this world as you do, namely, that it has a 'necessary' and 'calculable' course, *not* because laws obtain in it, but because they are absolutely *lacking*, and every power draws its ultimate consequences at every moment.[63]

It is hardly strange, therefore, that in this same work, in the very next aphorism, Nietzsche announces the creation of a new discipline: the "morphology and *the doctrine of the development of the will to power.*"[64] This is also the first book in which the idea of Eternal Return is entirely absent.

X. The Will to Power and Nihilism

It is important to ask to what extent the abandonment of the idea of Eternal Recurrence, as a basis for the representation of the instantaneity and the immanent plenitude of acting, made the doctrine of nihilism possible. There are two important reasons for this fact.

Firstly, Nietzsche – now that he is in possession (1885) of the doctrine of the will to power – reduces the cosmology of the Eternal Recurrence to a mere reactive interpretation. Secondly, and precisely in its new manifestation as the "morphology and *the doctrine of the will to power*," it will come to form the basis of the new understanding of the condition for the possibility of morality, providing structure for a new typology of wills. This is the import of the famous fragment of 10 June, 1887, written in Lenzer Heide, which provides us with a germ for the most important work of Nietzsche's late period – *The Genealogy of Morals*.[65] Indeed, Nietzsche began work on this book that very same day and it was concluded a month later. There, for the first time, Nietzsche presents us with the devaluation of all values; this he considers to be the essence of contemporary culture, the logical endgame of this same system of values, or even, more pointedly, the consequence of a very specific axiology – Christian morality. Here, for the first time, Eternal Return is also presented as the terminal point in the thinking through of this process, as "the most extreme form of nihilism," and it is emphasized in exactly the same terms in which it was dramatized in *The Gay Science* and *Thus Spoke Zarathustra*.[66]

It is also in this fragment that Nietzsche conceives a strategy for overcoming nihilism. Significantly, it is not through the affirmative sense of the idea of the Eternal Recurrence that this is realized. There is no redeeming imperative of the idea of repetition. Contrary to what occurs in those works in which the "nothing eternal" of repetition gets converted into the divine blessing of each moment of existence in the eyes of those who have already moulded each act as though it were a work of art, into "tremendous instants," now the idea of infinite repetition no longer frees man from his revolt against existence; instead, it exacerbates his condition, irremediably closing him in upon himself.

The overcoming of nihilism and, therefore, of the idea itself of Eternal Recurrence, now seen as the culmination of nihilism, is not taken as a reconfiguration of the experience of time. The conversion by the reactive wills of the "no" to existence into a "yes" to this same existence is not here mediated by the idea of Eternal Return. It is only in paragraph 7 that we read: "If we remove finality from the process, can we *nevertheless* still affirm the process? – This would be the case if something within that process were being *achieved* at its every moment – and always the same."

Inevitably, the critics see in this passage a reference to the idea of eternal repetition of this "same."[67] But is this really plausible? It is possible to see this "same" in the context of the doctrine of the will to power. To the extent that, in each instant, all forces realize the full extent of their power as pure presence, since the previous moment is of no consequence, but merely a radically different configuration of forces determined by a new, local, and instantaneous copossibility, each moment always reaches the same point. It is just that this "same" is purely intensive. It is always the same *quantum* of power that is present in the contest of forces in conflict, even if their vectorial appropriation by each single force varies instant to instant and, as such, continues to engender new forms of power. The "yes" to existence demands recognition, not only of that absolute optimization which brings itself up to date in each moment of the process, but also the identification between the essence of each event and each individual act. And each event is nothing more than the result of the will of each and every individual in conflict in local groupings of intensities. Nietzsche can now say: "*Every fundamental trait* which underlies *everything* that happens, which expresses itself in everything that happens, ought to lead an individual who felt it as *his* fundamental trait to welcome triumphantly every moment of general existence. The point would be precisely to experience this fundamental trait in oneself as good, as valuable, with pleasure."[68] The cancellation of the conditions for the possibility of a moral interpretation of existence and its temporality are transformed into a recognition of the equivalence between the most characteristic features (*der Grundcharakterzug*) of each event and the essence of each individual. This would mean feeling this essence as good and valuable. The individual who reaches this understanding is led to "welcome triumphantly every moment of general existence," just as he had prospered from existence under other paradigms in *The Gay Science* and *Thus Spoke Zarathustra*. But now, saying "yes" to existence is no longer mediated by this idea. Nor could it be, since it belongs uniquely to the history of nihilism.

The older circularity has been broken. In the breach between the two perspectives – the reactive and the affirmative – the doctrine of the will to power had, in the meantime, flourished.

XI. The New Understanding of the Condition of the Possibility for the Moral Interpretation of Existence

Nietzsche has now arrived at an understanding of the process of moral devaluation as it has played out in the life of his times – and his new view of the problem is very much different from that which is found in *Thus Spoke Zarathustra*. The revolt against existence is no longer a consequence of human nature itself, determined, as it was, by time. His new understanding first unfolds in the Lenzer Heide fragment in the ninth paragraph; it is a notion that will come to structure the whole of *The Genealogy of Morals*:

Now, *morality* protected life from despair and from the plunge into nothingness for those men and classes who were violated and oppressed by *men*: for powerlessness against men, *not* powerlessness against nature, is what engenders the most desperate bitterness against existence. Morality treated the despots, the men of violence, the "masters" in general, as the enemies against whom the common man must be protected, i.e., *first of all encouraged, strengthened.* Consequently, morality taught the deepest *hatred* and *contempt* for what is the rulers' fundamental trait: *their will to power.*[69]

It is no longer powerlessness against nature and its essential temporality – as Zarathustra had claimed – but *powerlessness against men* that provokes the more desperate revolt against existence and which excites the moral response. As Nietzsche tirelessly affirms in the Second and Third Essays of *The Genealogy of Morals*, the result is a highly determined interpretation of the relations of power that constitute every event. It is the weaker wills, those who are violated and oppressed in relations of power, who give rise to morality as a way of warding off their own despair.

Nietzsche's morphology of the will to power will eventually come to reconfigure the typology of wills underlying the phenomenology of time that was delineated in *Thus Spoke Zarathustra*. While in the earlier book this typology was founded, as we have seen, on temporal categories and on the opposition between remorse and nostalgia, now it is exclusively "physiological." However, here too it is essentially dualistic. Nietzsche considers just two types: the "unfortunate" (*die schlechtweggekommen*) and the "stronger ones" (*die Stärksten*). The first are characterized by "the *will to destruction* as the will of a still deeper instinct, the instinct for self-destruction, the *will into nothingness* [*des Willens ins Nichts*]."[70] The interpretation of the morality of existence is pursued only by the "unfortunate"; it is a form of self-justification, a way for them to transcend their "nihilizing" will. Opposed to them are the "stronger ones." They are defined by Nietzsche in the following terms, as "The most moderate, those who have no *need* of extreme articles of faith, who not only concede but even love a good deal of contingency and nonsense, who can think of a man with a considerable moderation of his value and not therefore become small and weak: the richest in health, who are equal to the most misfortunes and therefore less afraid of misfortune...."[71] The overcoming of morality does not demand that man be transfigured. It effects the self-perishing of those who engender morality and who find only there a justification for their inferiority, for their "no" to existence. While in *Thus Spoke Zarathustra* the overcoming of morality and the transformation towards the over-human implies the adherence to an article of extreme faith – the idea of the eternal repetition of the same – now the contrary is the case. From an anthropological point of view, superior men, the "stronger ones," are not simply an ideal in Zarathustra's message, but are already realized. They are men "who *are sure of their power* and who represent with conscious pride the strength man has achieved."[72] And that which defines their power is precisely the fact that it is not dependent on any manner of cosmological representation, or doctrine of temporality. They "have no *need* of extreme articles of faith." They have already found the fullness of man independent from the idea of Eternal Return, or rather, in spite of it. For this reason, the last paragraph comprises a single question: "What would such a man think of eternal recurrence?"

How to send weak wills, the "unfortunate," to their annihilation? How to manage a selection between affirmative wills and reactive wills? How to describe the idea which now, by its ambivalence, has created a true split between those who think it? In a word, what is the "selective idea" now? Significantly, Nietzsche writes: "If sufferer, the oppressed man, *lost his belief* in having a *right* to his contempt for the will to power, he would enter the stage of hopeless desperation. This would be the case if this trait were essential to life, if it turned out that even that 'will to morality' was just concealing this 'will to power,' that even that hatred and contempt is still a power-will."[73] This is a radical change in Nietzsche's programme. The revelation which is now capable of leading reactive wills to despair, that most terrible of revelations, is not the idea of Eternal Return; it is the idea that even the experience of guilt, even in the "will to morality" the will to power, as essence of the world, is part of the equation. The "unfortunate one" suddenly figures out that he has lost the legitimacy to revolt against those who oppress him, as if, in them, there were only the struggle to increase power. Even in their oppressed being and in their revolt against those who oppress them, the "unfortunate ones" express the very same struggle for power. Only in them it appears as a reactive action, as revolt and the spirit of revenge. By discovering the truth of the theory of the will to power, the "unfortunate one," as Nietzsche says, descends into "the phase of hopeless desperation" and collapse.

Morality no longer belongs to the temporal finitude of human existence – which was the case in *Thus Spoke Zarathustra*. From 1885 onward, it is inherent in the specific *type* of will. Consequently, the destruction of morality does not involve a reconversion of human nature, freeing it from the yoke of the past through the idea of infinite recurrence. Morality's condition as possibility does not have to be cancelled, only its self-destructive logic need be disturbed. This is why Eternal Return is now considered for only its reactive value. "The *unhealthiest* kind of man in Europe (of all classes) is the ground of this nihilism: they will feel that belief in the eternal recurrence is a *curse* which, once you are struck by it, makes you no longer baulk at any action; not being passively extinguished, but *making* everything that is so senseless and aimless be extinguished: although it is only a spasm, a blind rage on realizing that everything has existed for eternities – including this moment of nihilism and lust for destruction. – The *value of such a crisis* is that it *cleanses*..."[74]

In Nietzsche's eyes, the decadence of Western culture represents the end of a cycle – of decadent morality, of resenting wills, of all those who fail to feel each event as the expression of their own essence. The programme for the transmutation of all values will receive privileged treatment in *The Antichrist*. The process of the exhaustion of the models of ethical and epistemological legitimacy that characterize the nihilist condition in modern times is seen by Nietzsche to be the direct consequence of a specific systemic collapse and a breakdown in values: in short, the failure of Christianity's moral hypothesis. And it was precisely with the description of this process of self-destruction of Christian morality that Nietzsche began the Lenzer Heide fragment.

The doctrine of nihilism, as a negative logic of morality, emerges out of the profound alteration of Nietzsche's view of the role of the idea of the Eternal Recurrence. The idea of infinite repetition cannot free human existence from its temporal condition, because the origin of the revolt against universal existence does not reside in time. On the contrary, it rises out of this final idea in the process of moral exhaustion. The self-annihilation of the Eternal Recurrence is brought to term by the revelation of the doctrine of the will to power. We can say that nihilism occurred to Nietzsche as the essence of the history of Western rationality – a symptom of the fate of the West's values. And this happened at that moment when he realized that, as a prophet, he was just another moment in the revelation of that same destiny.

The disappearance of the idea of the Eternal Recurrence from all of Nietzsche's post-1886 writings was a sign of the fact that Nietzsche had abandoned his supreme idea to the fate of nihilism itself, that same nihilism which the idea was meant to eradicate and beyond which Nietzsche will now move.

6

Nihilism According to Nietzsche

The genius – but, perhaps for this reason, the great equivocation – of Nietzsche's reading of the European cultural condition at the end of the nineteenth century, consists in the fact that he condenses a multiplicity of symptoms of the crisis of the models of rationality inherited from modernity in the figure of a single and decisive event: the advent of nihilism. For Nietzsche, phenomena such as aesthetic romanticism, the success of the mechanistic paradigm of the life sciences, philosophical pessimism or the emergence of European socialist movements are hardly seen as timely attempts by the West at internal reformulations of models of aesthetic, epistemological, moral or political legitimization, but moments in a process of an absolute exhaustion of the possibility itself of legitimization in general. This devaluation of all values and the radical loss of foundation is, according to Nietzsche, not only a necessary process, but an irreversible one. Nietzsche views this as an extreme consequence of the bankruptcy of the very models of legitimization themselves.

Nihilism would encompass European consciousness in an inescapable paradox: that of living in a moment ulterior to the dissolution of the models of the legitimization of values, upon which it itself had been constructed, without, however, the means to consider such an epochal position as an expression of a privilege, as this would presuppose that the final basis of such models still existed: notions of conscience, progress, and overcoming.

Nietzsche presents the doctrine of nihilism as a description and, at the same time, as a practical accomplishment of the exhaustion of this process of delegitimization of Western values. Nihilism thus becomes the title of a general interpretation of Western culture and a political and aesthetical manifesto for the subsequent centuries.

As historical narrative, the doctrine of nihilism is built upon the model of negative dialectics. According to Nietzsche the decadence of values originated with the earliest taking of positions in the West. It was with Socratic ethics (and Christianity's reclamation of them) that, in the name of equating happiness with knowledge, the foundations of civilization in Art had shifted to foundations based on Knowledge. Ever since, life had become the victim of reason with its self-destructive logic. Ironically,

Nietzsche fails to free himself from the fascination for historicism that he so lucidly denounces in the second *Untimely Meditation*. To the extent that he tries to describe nihilism as a unique event, it was impossible for his reading of the West to avoid maintaining as well some of the logical awkwardness to which the great nineteenth-century philosophies of history had succumbed. Nietzsche was the victim of an excessive appreciation for Hegelianism. He believes he can break with historicism simply by rejecting the categories of *progress* and *overcoming*.

It was with this inverted Hegelianism that Nietzsche most clearly manifested himself, not only in his role as the son of his century, but as a representative of the central categories of a culture against which he would position himself. Indeed, more than a particular concept, the notion of *decadence* is the historical and moral category par excellence by which the West read the origin of its destiny. It was always as "a fall," or a "period of degeneracy," that each epoch or people described their particular epochal place. Hesiod's myth of the five ages, upon which the Greek tradition was built, is, in this respect, as eloquent as it is decisive in the construction of the West's historical consciousness.

Nevertheless, it would be an error to reduce the doctrine of nihilism to a negative teleology. Nietzsche's attachment to the category of *decadence* is not exhausted simply in the inversion of the illuminist idea of "progress." On the contrary, the very genesis of this doctrine derives from a fundamental reformulation of the notion of "decadence" as a historical category. From 1886 onwards (the year that marks the beginning of Nietzsche's systematic reflection on the logic of self-dissolution of Western values) the concept of "decadence" takes on a primordially anthropological meaning. Decadence designates, not the result of an historical process, but the characterization of a determined psychological line. As Nietzsche declares in *The Twilight of the Idols*: "To choose what is harmful to oneself, to be *attracted* by 'disinterested' motives, almost constitutes the formula for *decadence*."[1] This mutation of meaning, the shift from an historical category to an anthropological one, with its adoption of expressions such as *décadence* and *décadent*, which are inherited from the more conceptual tradition of the French "psychologists" Taine and Bourget, led Nietzsche to a different appreciation of the fundamental evolution of the culture of his period. Decadence had nothing to do with a logic of the development of humanity, or with a situation of minority when faced with its origin. It should be seen more in the sense invoked by the title of Freud's famous work, *Civilization and its Discontents*, and the fact that humanity had adopted values that were contrary to its self-affirmation, which is to say, typologically "decadent" values. As such, the situation of crisis in which humanity has put itself, by the bankruptcy of these same values, seems, paradoxically, to be an expression of some new vigour, of some vital growth. "The concept of decadence. – Waste, decay, elimination need not be condemned: they are necessary consequences of life, of the growth of life. The phenomenon of decadence is as necessary as any increase and advance of life: one is in no position to abolish it. Reason demands, on the contrary, that we do justice to it."[2] It is precisely to designate the fundamental ambivalence in the process of the dissolution of decadent values, for which the concept of decadence as an historical category is no longer useful, that Nietzsche adopts, starting in 1886, the concept of nihilism.

Nietzsche's reading of the genealogy of nihilism is constructed upon the model of a negative dialectic. This is no longer the case in terms of the way Nietzsche considers the possibility of overcoming nihilism. The devaluation of all values does not correspond to a single moment of determined negativity that would permit, in and of itself, the dialectical construction of a new basis, a new ground for new values. What it does do is to put humanity in a situation of insecurity and essential danger. The West had already experienced a similar internal dissolution of its axiological models. But this undoing, instead of being translated into new modes of existence, led to a worsening of decadence. According to Nietzsche, that was the most decisive lesson of the Renaissance. In its excess, the culture of Dante and Machiavelli had finally reached the point of a total reversal of Christian morals. As Nietzsche says in *The Antichrist*, "*Cesare Borgia as Pope* ... Do you understand me? ... with this, Christianity was *abolished*! – What happened? A German monk, Luther, came to Rome. This monk whose body had all the vindictive instincts of a wounded priest, flew into a rage in Rome *against* the Renaissance ... Instead of feeling the most profound gratitude at the scale of what had taken place, the fact that Christianity had been overcome at its source."[3] The nihilist condition that, according to Nietzsche, characterizes the culture of the end of the nineteenth century, corresponds, in its fundamental ambiguity, to a second "chance" for decadence. Its essential feature is the result of the fact that European consciousness is, for the first time, confronted with not only the self-dissolution of Christian morals, but with the bankruptcy of all ethical categories which had found their paradigm in Christian morality.

This is why it was so important to prevent the repetition of that process of a mere axiological overcoming of decadence which asphyxiated the world of possibilities opened by the Italian Renaissance. The paradox which constitutes the nihilistic condition of our modernity cannot be simply dissolved or got around by the recuperation of values whose bankruptcy is at the very root of its origin. It has to be experienced in its essence. "Why is the advent of nihilism now so necessary? It is because that is where our very own values have found their final moment, because nihilism is the logic of our highest values and ideas pushed to the extreme, because we first have to experience nihilism in order to discover what was, finally, the *value* of these 'values' ... We are waiting for the arrival, at any moment, of new values."[4]

As an interpretation of the history of the moral mechanisms of the West, the doctrine of nihilism contains a strong duality of perspectives. It conciliates an *historicist* vision of phenomena of civilization, presuming them to be linked by a narrow internal logic (the result of a process of the dissolution of self-founding models of the West), with a *vitalist* reading, in light of which each historical configuration presents a single "chance" for producing the superior forms of civilization.

This duality of perspectives finds rigorous expression in what is probably the most significant of Nietzsche's texts on the phenomenon of nihilism. We refer to the fragment from the late notebooks, written on 10 June, 1887, which Nietzsche himself entitled *The European Nihilism*.[5] In just sixteen paragraphs Nietzsche (a) reconstructs the fundamental moments of what he considers to be the process of self-dissolution of Christian morality; (b) situates the idea of Eternal Return in this context as its culmination; (c) plots the metaphysical basis of a new "yes to all things" beyond "the death of God"; (d) reveals the central theses of his anthropology of the will to power, and establishes, based on them, the genealogy of Christian morals; and, finally, (e) underlines the selective reach of the crisis produced by nihilism, tracing the contours of the figure of "stronger men" which the crisis will allow us to see. Thus, in a single and indeed fragmentary text, from his late notebooks, Nietzsche elaborates not only those themes that, since Heidegger, are central to his late philosophy (nihilism, the will to power, the Eternal Recurrence, the revaluation of values and the over-human) but he shows them for the first time as moments in a logic that is immanent in the condition of European culture itself.

The importance of this text also resides in the fact that it contains that which can be considered to be Nietzsche's "political programme," his struggle for a new "hierarchy of forces" (*die Rangordnung der Kräfte*). With exquisite clarity, Nietzsche traces the figure of "those who turned out badly" (*schlechtweggekommen*), not only from a "physiological" perspective, as the "*unhealthiest* kind of man," but, fundamentally, from an ethical perspective, as the one who revolts against existence, whose action is oriented by a principle of destruction, by a "will to nothingness." This is why Nietzsche rejects the sociological interpretation of the concept of "hierarchy." As he said, this interpretation would have to be constituted out of "all existing social orders" since "those who turned out badly" can be found "in all classes" (*in allen Ständen*). The "strongest ones" (*die Stärksten*), which the crisis in moral values will allow to emerge, are equally defined by purely ethical criteria. They are "The most moderate, those who have no *need* of extreme dogmas, those who not only concede but love a good measure of chance and nonsense, those who can conceive of man with a significant reduction in his value without thereby becoming small and weak: the richest in health who can cope with the most misfortunes and so have no great fear of misfortunes – men who *are sure of their power* and represent with conscious pride the *achievement* of human strength" (§15). This text allows us to understand to what extent the Nazi recuperation of the ideal of the superior man was only made possible by sacrificing one of the profoundest ethical and anthropological theses of the doctrine of the will to power. *The European Nihilism* confronts us, then, with the theoretical nucleus of Nietzsche's final philosophy.

In spite of having been written exactly one century ago and of having been the object of many editions, the text of *The European Nihilism* is presented in the Colli and Montinari edition of 1980 in novel fashion. The fact is that the history of the publication of Nietzsche's notebooks is anything but happy. The complete version of this fragment was only published once in the *princeps* edition (1901) of Nietzsche's posthumous work, a work which, with its miscast title *The Will to Power* (*Der Wille zur Macht*), contained only 483 texts extracted from the notebooks. All later editions, including the octavo edition of 1911, since then considered to be the canonical version, derived from the "pocket edition" of 1906 (which compiles, under the same title, 1067 fragments, and which, just as the first one, was under the direction of Peter Gast and Elisabeth Forester-Nietzsche), present *The European Nihilism* in four distinct fragments. The first paragraph of the original version there corresponds to the 4th fragment, the second to the 5th, and the third to the 114th. Finally, the 4th through the 16th correspond to the 55th. This adulteration cannot but gravely compromise the intelligibility of this text. Not only because it divides it into four false fragments, but it also inserts them into different chapters of book I of this artificial work, known as *The Will to Power*. In this particular editorial arrangement *The European Nihilism* loses the central line of its argument and thus all that gives it its unique character, which is the fact that it is the most systematic text ever written by Nietzsche about the genealogy of nihilism.

It is only the recent critical edition, directed by the Italians Giorgio Colli and Mazzino Montinari (1967), which has restored, with all due rigour, *The European Nihilism* to its original format, just as Nietzsche had written it on 10 June, 1887. We can therefore say that it has only been for a dozen years that we have had access to this important document on the Nietzschean conception of Western civilizational decadence.

It is also important to underline that, as well as a philological reconstitution, the Colli and Montinari edition, by adopting a strictly chronological criterion for the organization of Nietzsche's works and, therefore, giving us the chance to understand the place this text occupies in the evolution of Nietzsche's thought, brings a new intelligibility to *The European Nihilism*. In fact, in light of this new edition, the Lenzer Heide text can now be seen as a decisive moment in the formulation of Nietzsche's final philosophy. It is an authentic turning point: it closes a cycle in his work (which has at its centre the idea of Eternal Return) and initiates another (that which is oriented by the doctrine of the will to power). Thus, we understand today that this text, in which the idea of an infinite repetition is presented for the first time as the consequence of the logic itself of the devaluation of the values produced by Christian morality, chronologically marks the definitive disappearance of the idea of Eternal Return from Nietzsche's published works. While *The Gay Science, Thus Spoke Zarathustra*, and *Beyond Good and Evil*, that is, all works after 1881, display the idea of a cyclical repetition of all events, *The Genealogy of Morals*, written immediately following the stay in Lenzer Heide, as well as all the works which are posterior to it, never again refer to this circular representation of time, or, if they do, as in the case of *Twilight of the Idols* or *Ecce Homo*, it is in a purely autobiographical context (when he refers to himself, he does so with the designation *he that taught Eternal Recurrence*). Looked at chronologically, *The European Nihilism* displays therefore a surprising isomorphism between its content and the place that it occupies in the evolution of Nietzsche's philosophy, that is, between, on one hand, the theoretical gesture by which Nietzsche disengages himself from the idea of the Eternal Recurrence and, on the other, the effective disappearance of this same idea from the body of his texts.

Its "typological" interpretation of the origin of value judgments also marks the Lenzer Heide text as a turning point. This interpretation is to be found in §§9–15, which anticipate (though schematically) the principal theses of *The Genealogy of Morals*. Here, for the first time, Nietzsche abandons that which we could call the "existential perspective" that oriented his earlier works. The interpretation of action as a moral phenomenon no longer results in a revolt against the essential temporality of human existence, as it did in *Thus Spoke Zarathustra*, nor in an illusion about the true dimension of the will, as happened in *Beyond Good and Evil*. Now it is merely an expression of a determined type of will. As Nietzsche affirms in §9 of the Lenzer Heide text, it is "the abused and oppressed classes of men" who need morals, not only as a way to protect themselves "from despair and the leap into nothingness" but as well as a weapon against the "the powerful, the violent, the 'master' in general." We know the importance that this typological conception of morality attains in *The Genealogy of Morals*: it forms a basis there for the thesis on the reactive origin of moral judgments as expression of the inversion of values on the part of those who are "oppressed." In addition to this thematic concurrence between the Lenzer Heide fragment and *The Genealogy of Morals*, it is also true that it was written in a flow of creative and inspired intensity in less than a month and that directly following his sojourn at Lenzer Heide (the manuscript was sent to his publisher on 30 July that same year, in 1887). The fact that this text on *The European Nihilism* is the most systematic of Nietzsche's entire output adds force to the hypothesis that it corresponds to a decisive moment in the formulation of the arguments that orient the works of the final period (*Twilight of the Idols, The Antichrist, The Wagner Case, Nietzsche Contra Wagner,* and *Ecce Homo*) and which achieve their first fullness in *The Genealogy of Morals*.

It is perhaps in its status as a turning point in Nietzsche's philosophy, one which marks the closure of that period of works written around the notion of the Eternal Recurrence – *The Gay Science, Thus Spoke Zarathustra,* and *Beyond Good and Evil* – and the beginning of the great formulations of the doctrine of the will to power, that we can find the source of the fundamental ambiguity that, as we shall see, the text of *The European Nihilism* manifests.

Hidden under the auspices of an apparent univocality, which emerges out of the central line of thought enabled by Nietzsche's negative teleology of Christian morals, are a set of essentially distinctive narratives that adopt different postulates about morals and their genesis and that, as a consequence, come to different conclusions about their bankruptcy.

One of the first of these narratives, which we can refer to as *epistemological*, is constructed around the opposition between life and truth. This corresponds to §§1–4. In these paragraphs morality has the nature of a necessary illusion used to justify life and conceal the fundamental fragility of the human condition, thereby redeeming life's temporal finitude. As Nietzsche writes, "It conferred on man an absolute *value*, in contrast to his smallness and contingency in the flux of becoming and passing away" (§1). In the epistemological narrative Nietzsche conceives of morality as an affirmative strategy of life itself. Understanding man as a moral being, as a will determined by absolute values that elevate his status, whether metaphysical or epistemological, redeems his ephemerality, his fragility, his insignificance in the flow from birth to death. Evil and contingency are given meaning. Morals presume in man the ability to know absolute values and the final meaning of things. This thesis expresses a revolution in Nietzsche's thinking. Contrary to what we were given to believe in *Human, All-too-Human*, and which became his final formulation in *Thus Spoke Zarathustra*, morality, in the Lenzer Heide text, is no longer a condemnation of temporal existence in favour of some distant eternity. In its most primordial sense, morality had to have been, according to the 1887 text, the first "yes" to existence. It represented the first response of civilization to the non-meaning of pain and death. As Nietzsche says, "it prevented man from despising himself as man, from taking against life, from despairing of knowing [*Erkennen*]: it was a *means of preservation*" (§1). He concludes this first paragraph with the seemingly strange thesis "in sum: morality was the great *antidote* against practical and theoretical *nihilism.*" Nihilism is for the first time conceived, not as an event of culture, not as the effect of the irreversible dissolution of values, of practices and of interpretations, but as a pure and primordial fact of existence as such. What Nietzsche calls "practical and theoretical nihilism" would be inherent in the contingency of life and of death; it would be the purest non-meaning of individual and collective existence taken as whole. And morality, with its fictions and values, its categories of truth and necessity, would be the principal "antidote" against this absolute nothingness, against this primordial nihilism.

The question confronting Nietzsche in the interior of this narrative is that which has to do with the origin of a consciousness in revolt, and also with the beginning of an understanding of a world and of man who says "no" to life. If morals are, in their essence, an affirmation, an antidote against despair and nothingness, from whence the negation, whence the "no" to life and life's joys? Here Nietzsche also reformulates his diagnosis put forth in *Thus Spoke Zarathustra*. The "no" to life is not evidence of a moral interpretation of existence but, paradoxically, the effect of the dissolution of this moral interpretation. The revolt is the consequence of the dialectic of knowledge itself, or better, of the dimension of the truth that all of fiction is based on.

In these first four paragraphs – which condense the epistemological narrative – Nietzsche locates the inversion of the "yes" directly in the sphere of values and their mechanisms of voluntary falsification. This inversion is seen as a corollary to morality itself (to the principle of truth) that, in questioning the basis for value judgments, had led to the discovery of their origin in illusion. "But among the forces nurtured by morality was *truthfulness: this* ultimately turns on morality, discovers its *teleology*, the *partiality* of its viewpoint – and now the *insight* into this long-ingrained mendacity, which one despairs of throwing off, acts precisely as a stimulus. To nihilism"(§2). The bankruptcy of this morality would thus be inscribed in its own originating logic, in the antagonism between life and truth. "This antagonism – *not* valuing what we know [*erkennen*], and no longer being *permitted* to value what we would like to hoodwink ourselves with – results in a disintegration process" (§2).

Nietzsche therefore distinguishes two types of nihilism. That which he calls the "first nihilism," is inherent to the very condition of existence and its lack of meaning. The "second nihilism" is simply the consequence of the self-dissolution of the strategies of resistance, of the sabotaging of that antidote to the first nihilism, to wit morals. Its main characteristic is the experience of disappointment, of seeing through illusion, of no longer being able to take seriously the tools of belief in life and the world. It is the result of a generalized melancholy. The logic of nihilism is identified with knowledge itself: uncritical dogmatism vis-à-vis the value of morals gives rise to a critique of fundamentals which, in turn, leads to radical scepticism against the pretensions of life itself.

In this perspective, therefore, nihilism, that is, the lack of confidence in any absolute basis whatsoever of human finitude, cannot be the result of the logic itself of life. To the extent that life is an essential quest for self-affirmation, nihilism can only come from something that is not life. This is where morality condenses the whole of the weight of the phenomenon of nihilism. As a fragile response to the necessity to affirm life – fragile because it is built upon illusion and the pretensions of truth – morality itself is solely responsible for the world's current disenchantment. If the response to the first nihilism had not been given in the figure of the illusion of values, the discovery of its illusion would never have led to the despair that defines the second nihilism.

But this is not the only characterization of nihilism which we find in the Lenzer Heide text. The second narrative can be found in §§9–15. The principal rupture with the earlier one lies in the *typological* perspective which is adopted. Morality is no longer the consequence of a demand made by life in general, but that of a determined *type* of existence. It is no longer life as a whole which calls for an antidote to despair. Morality in these paragraphs is present as simply the expression of a certain mode of life, that of "the kind of people and classes who were violated and oppressed by *people*." As Nietzsche says: "*morality* has protected life from despair and the leap into nothingness in the kind of people and classes who were violated and oppressed by *people*: for it is powerlessness in the face of people, *not* powerlessness in the face of nature, that generates the most desperate embitterment against existence" (§9). It is glaringly apparent that Nietzsche's thinking here runs counter to his own system of morals. What disappears is the whole universe of *Thus Spoke Zarathustra*. Morality in Zarathustra is presented as though it had arisen out of a certain impotency before nature. The invention of a world of eternal values, in the name of which life and its ephemerality is condemned, is the consequence of the will which suffers over the irrevocability of all beings and all events. Morality in this sense is the "spirit of vengeance," of the revolt against time and the permanent "was" of everything that exists. This "spirit of vengeance" has two principal features: it is universal, that is, it affects each and every will, each and every individual, and, on the other hand, it expresses impotency vis-à-vis nature, it is burdened by the mere fact of having to exist in a world that is essentially temporal and utterly determined by its irrevocability. Freeing humanity of morality is one and the same with freeing the will from this "spirit of vengeance." But within the framework of *Thus Spoke Zarathustra*, this was only made possible by the idea of the Eternal Recurrence. Via the infinite recurrence of each element of universal existence, nature revealed itself as the redeemer of nature, redeemer of this "impotency" before the "this was," before time. This is because morality was conceived as a consequence of the essential feature of nature and time; the overcoming of morality imposed new metaphors of the world and of time. And freeing the world of time itself, freeing nature from its irrevocable temporality, was to free man from himself, from his too-human nature, that is, from being condemned by time – creating the over-man. And this new poetics, this vision of a new experience of time, could only be declared in the context of prophecy, by a gospel brought to men by someone beyond men and the gods, someone like Zarathustra.

This is precisely the interpretation that the Lenzer Heide text abandons. In 1887 Nietzsche comes to see that morality, in its sense of a revolt against life, originates not in some impotency before nature, but in an impotency before men. This change in perspective brings two fundamental consequences in its wake. The first is that morality is no longer an expression of the human condition, it is no longer inscribed in the nature of the will as a whole, but rather merely characterizes certain wills, infecting only those men, those "people and classes who were violated and oppressed by *people*." Morality therefore is the expression of a *type* of will. The second consequence has to do with the object of revolt. Because it is only the people who are violated and oppressed by other people who are driven to revolt, their "spirit of vengeance" does not target life as a whole, or nature as a temporal condition. The revolt, in the first instance, is against those who oppress them. Morality is that interpretation which makes out of affirmative people contemptible beings, which transforms those who are the holders of power into enemies of humanity. It is only in this sense that morality is converted into a general condemnation of nature, as a condemnation of the most intimate essence of everything that exists. In condemning those who hold power, the violated and oppressed condemn that which runs deepest in all of life: the tendency toward domination, the will to power. As Nietzsche says: "Morality has treated the powerful, the violent, the 'masters' in general as the enemies against whom the common man must be protected, i.e., *first of all encouraged, strengthened.* Consequently morality has taught to *hate* and *despise* most profoundly what is the fundamental characteristic of the rulers: *their will to power*" (§9).

This new characterization of the origin of the morality is the same which will come to organize *The Genealogy of Morals*, which Nietzsche begins shortly after 10 June, 1887 and which would be sent to his publisher a mere six weeks later. There we will find two absolutely new strategies. On the one hand, Nietzsche seeks to explain the appearance of morality via a description of a certain type of will: that of the weak, of the slaves, of the oppressed. Morality is thus explained not by the "spirit of vengeance" – which would target time and its "was" – but by "resentment" – which aims to infect strong wills, the holders of power, with guilt. On the other hand, the overcoming of morality no longer presumes a new cosmology, or a new poetics of time and its eternal recurrence. This is why the idea of Eternal Recurrence is completely absent from *The Genealogy of Morals* – as it will be absent from all of the other books which Nietzsche will publish after 1887. The destruction of the conditions for the possibility of morality now turns to the presentation of the features that define the holders of power as representative of those of the whole of will, of all living beings, in a word, it now turns to the demonstration of the fact that everything is "Will to Power."

The whole of this programme is announced in §9 of the Lenzer Heide text:

> To abolish, deny, break down this morality: that would mean providing the most hated drive with an *opposite* sensation and evaluation. If the sufferer, the oppressed man *lost his belief* in having a *right* to his contempt for the will to power, he would enter the stage of hopeless desperation. This would be the case if this trait were essential to life, if it turned out that even that 'will to morality' was just concealing this 'will to power,' that even that hatred and contempt is still a power-will [*Machwille*]. The oppressed man would realize that he is *in the same boat* as the oppressor and that he has no *prerogative* over him, no *higher status* than him.

The programme for the erosion of morality is essentially theoretical. The battle against oppressed wills is worked out on a plane of representations of the world, on a plane of beliefs. As Nietzsche says: "If the sufferer, the oppressed man *lost his belief* in having a *right* to his contempt for the will to power, he would enter the stage of hopeless desperation." And this dimension of belief is underlined in §10: "*Provided that the belief in this morality collapses*, those who turned out badly would no longer have their consolation – and they would *perish*." This would be possible by demonstrating to the victim and to the oppressed that even their revolt against the holders of power testifies to the hidden presence of the will to power, which constitutes their own fundamental motivation. If, in *Thus Spoke Zarathustra*, the new gospel brought with it the revelation of the Eternal Return, in *The Genealogy of Morals* what is displayed – not revealed – is the decisive argument against all moral belief: the world as will to power.

Yet, also within the typological narrative, the Lenzer Heide text maintains a dialectical understanding of this process of moral erosion. It is as though Nietzsche understood that the new message, the demonstration that everything is will to power, belonged as well to the internal logic of morality. No prophet of the will to power is required. Weak wills and the oppressed, in their own movement toward revolt and resentment, lead to the destruction of that very morality which they had invented in order to legitimize their contempt for the holders of power. In the typological narrative nihilism also appears, therefore, as a consequence of this process of self-dissolution of morality. In the narrative that we have called "epistemological" (§§1–4), self-dissolution is an effect of voluntary delusion. Value judgments are victims of their own corollaries, they are the cause of their own perishing.

It is this same dialectic, though applied to the logic of the revolt of the oppressed, that organized the typological narrative in §§11–12. It is the will to destruction, the same which had created morality as a way to justify the revolt against the holders of power, that now takes on morality itself as the object of its revolt and it is against morality that it exercises itself. As in the first narrative, the bankruptcy of morality leads as well to a phenomenon of inversion within the process of continuous intensification. The will to destruction, driven to the extreme of its logical conclusion, ultimately destroys its own basis, that is, the morality that legitimizes it.

> This *perishing* presents itself as a – *self-ruination*, as an instinctive selection of that which *must destroy*. *Symptoms* of this self-destruction by those who turned out badly: self-vivisection, poisoning, intoxication, romanticism, above all the instinctive need for actions which make *deadly enemies* of the powerful (– as if one were breeding one's own executioners); the *will to destruction* as the will of an even deeper instinct, the instinct of self-destruction, of the *will into nothingness* (§11).

Emphasis is given to the fact that the "nothingness" towards which the bankruptcy of morality leads is no longer an expression of generalized scepticism about the possibility for any meaning whatsoever in existence, which the first narrative points to, but is rather the consequence of a will, or better, of a determined *type* of will. If in the *epistemological* narrative nihilism arose as a final event of the process of the development of knowledge, in the *typological* narrative nihilism is the extreme result of "the *will to destruction* as the will of an even deeper instinct, the instinct of self-destruction, of the *will into nothingness* [*des Willens ins Nichts*]" (§11). The first narrative pursues a logic of knowledge and its self-destructive dialectic, the second a logic of negative will and of its metamorphosis into nothingness.

Clearly distinct as to the genealogy they establish for the nihilist condition of European culture, the narratives which we have called *epistemological* and *typological* are different as well in the way in which they evaluate the constitutive ambivalence of the crisis produced by the bankruptcy of previous value judgments. The first aligns itself with a historicist perspective. By identifying the logic of nihilism with the logic of knowledge, the dissolution of morals ends up by emerging as an expression of progress, as a consequence of the development of a specific rationality, not only critical but technical as well. The power with which critical reason targets morality, with the sole aim of denouncing the falsity of its foundations, would be thus merely a corollary of the domination achieved by technical reason over nature. According to Nietzsche it was this domination – which brought man greater confidence in his own power and destiny – that precluded the necessity for the foundation of the morals of human existence. "In fact we no longer need an antidote against *first* nihilism so much: life is no longer so uncertain, contingent, senseless in our Europe. Such an immense *multiplication* of the *value* of man, of the value of evil etc. is not so necessary now; we can stand a significant *reduction* in this value and concede a good deal of nonsense and chance: the *power* that man has achieved now permits a *reduction* in the disciplinary measures, of which the moral interpretation was the strongest. 'God' is much too extreme a hypothesis" (§3). Even if life is deprived of morality – with the consequent loss of its metaphysical basis – the fact itself of being able to dispense with morality is a sign of new vigour. Herein resides (in accordance with the *epistemological* perspective) the ambiguity of the nihilism of modernity. This is why a bankruptcy of values is not simply a "collapse," or "degeneration," but a necessary event in the affirmation of life. It is the specifically negative character, essential to the fundamental recuperation of life, which lends nihilism its status as a negative dialectic that comes very close to being an eschatology.

It is actually this understanding of a "dialectic" of the European cultural malaise that is present in the *typological* paradigm, even if, because of the fact that it is formulated upon different postulates, its historical significance is questionable. Paragraph 14 affirms the "purifying" importance of the moral crisis. It is just that, here, it is not life in its entirety, or Man, who come out strengthened by the crisis. The categories of "life" or "humanity," which structure the *epistemological* narrative, do not play any role here. "Purification" is now conceived as a process which internally fractures life itself, which produces hierarchical effects among men. It comes down to being a selection among powers, leading to the decay of "the kind of people and classes who were violated and oppressed by *people*," and, in counterpoint, elevating the "strongest." The destruction of morality based on a will to nothingness destroys the unfortunate themselves, "*those who turned out badly*," since they are only able to legitimize their existence within the ambit of morality. "Nihilism as a symptom of the fact that those who turned out badly have no consolation left: that they destroy in order to be destroyed, that, relieved of morality, they no longer have any reason to 'surrender themselves'" (§12). Contrary to this, only the ones who have no need of belief, no need of dogmas about the absolute value of man, will be elevated by this crisis. "Who will prove to be the *strongest* in this? The most moderate, those who have no *need* of extreme dogmas, those who not only concede but love a good measure of chance and nonsense, those who can conceive of man with a significant reduction in his value without thereby becoming small and weak: the richest in health who can cope with the most misfortunes and so have no great fear of misfortunes – men who *are sure of their power* and represent with conscious pride the *achievement* of human strength"(§15). Because they "are sure of their power," those who love chance and nonsense will be prepared to resist the decay of morality and to reveal themselves as the strongest. As such, since morality is no longer the expression of one of life's necessities, the moral crisis has nothing to do with life in general, but merely serves to close the cycle of reactive morality and, with it, to condemn the dissolution of the weak wills to which it had given rise.

The *typological* perspective also conceives the process of self-dissolution of values as a moment of necessary negativity within a negative teleology. By representing the destruction, not as the exhaustion of a determined logic, but as the consequence of a "will to nothingness," negativity itself is no longer just an abstract moment of the dialectic of morality, but takes on an empirical dimension. Negativity embodies itself in the "*those who turned out badly.*" That is why only their true disappearance will allow for the overcoming of negation and lead toward the exhaustion of morals. This is where the negative dialectic of nihilism acquires a strangely selective meaning, a strangely *apocalyptic* dimension.

Faced with this huge disparity in the views of nihilism we can perhaps better understand what it was that actually led the editors of the fictitious work, *The Will to Power*, to break up the text of *The European Nihilism*, which we have discussed above. It was all about trying to erase its fundamental contradiction. By separating the four first paragraphs from each other, Nietzsche's sister and Peter Gast caused the epistemological narrative to disappear; on the other hand, by beginning the rest of the text with §4, they created the illusion of homogeneity between the culminating moment in the *epistemological* narrative – the idea of the Eternal Recurrence – and the whole of the *typological* narrative. We do not know if this was done deliberately, or simply in order to maintain consistency; we only know that the result was, on one hand, the dissolution of the contradiction between the epistemological perspective and the typology of nihilism through the cancellation of the textual duality via which it was revealed, and, on other hand, the promotion of the idea of the Eternal Recurrence as the culminating topic of Nietzsche's reading of nihilism.

But the contradictions in Nietzsche must be understood and not artificially dissolved. It is an undeniable fact that, given the way in which these contradictions are included in the June 1887 text, he conceived of the two perspectives on nihilism, if not as univocals, at least as convergences. Understanding this text implies understanding how those narratives could occur to Nietzsche as unified.

It is our view that producing this unity would have been the function of that which we can consider the third of these narratives of nihilism present in the Lenzer Heide text. This can be found in §§ 5–8, and has at its centre the idea of the Eternal Recurrence. In these paragraphs Nietzsche seems to set out his "metaphysics," that is, his thesis on the condition of the possibility for a non-moral meaning of existence. As such, this metaphysical narrative appears to be the *positive opposite* of the other two. Both the *epistemological* perspective and the *typological* face the question of the meaning of existence solely from the logic of its exhaustion. They try to describe the process of the conversion of the theological thesis (according to which everything has a basis, that is, is part of a creator's plan, including evil) into the thesis of nihilism, or of the absolute absence of basis, of a total "in vain." They are therefore framed negatively according to their dialectic. Yet the function of the idea of the Eternal Recurrence seems, on the contrary, to permit the revelation of existence as positive, as an absolute fact, beyond the absence of all interpretations, all moral beliefs. Nevertheless, it is important to underline the fact that the revelation of the positive fact of a senseless existence is not the result of a simple negation of moral sense. Nietzsche does not limit himself to opposing a new interpretation of the world to the bankruptcy of all previous interpretations – which would be to ignore the truth and the historical breadth of the phenomenon of nihilism. The overcoming of nihilism, the overcoming of the belief that everything is "in vain," will have to be achieved on the basis of maximization, of an absolute furthering of the process itself of the bankruptcy of all interpretations. The decisive importance that Nietzsche attributes to the idea of the Eternal Recurrence is precisely the result of this cosmological idea being a representation of a radically silent, unspoken world, that is, of its being the most "paralyzing" *negation* of the meaning of existence because of the denial of all finality. Paragraphs 5 and 6, which deliberate over the terminal moments of the mockery of knowledge, present the idea of the Eternal Recurrence as the terminal point in this process. "Let us think this thought in its most terrible form: existence as it is, without sense or aim, but inevitably returning, without a finale in nothingness: 'the eternal return.' This is the most extreme form of nihilism: nothingness (the 'senseless') eternally! [*das Nichts* (*das 'Sinnlose'*) *ewig*]. European form of

Buddhism: energy of knowledge [*Wissen*] and strength *forces* one into such a belief. It is the *most scientific* of all possible hypotheses. We deny final goals: if existence had one, it would have to have been reached" (§6). The idea of the Eternal Recurrence thus terminates, according to the *epistemological* perspective, Christian morality in and of itself: if Christianity depends upon an eschatological representation of the world, the thesis of the infinite cycle undermines its roots at their profoundest.

The Eternal Recurrence plays an identical role in creating the effect of mockery in the *typological narrative*. The representation of an Eternal Recurrence of all things is also seen as the final moment in the bankruptcy of morality, although here, as one would expect, the impact is selective. It is the unfortunate, the oppressed man, Nietzsche tells us in §14, who will face the Eternal Recurrence as the ultimate form of self-destruction. "The *unhealthiest* kind of man in Europe (of all classes) is the ground of this nihilism: they will feel that belief in the eternal recurrence is a *curse* which, once you are struck by it, makes you no longer baulk at any action; not being passively extinguished, but *making* everything that is so senseless and aimless be extinguished: although it is only a spasm, a blind rage on realizing that everything has existed for eternities – including this moment of nihilism and lust for destruction." The oppressed man will then try to destroy everything that is revealed in this idea to be meaningless and endless, including his own existence.

It is now necessary to raise the important question. Beyond its appalling and despair-inspiring significance, does the idea of the Eternal Recurrence contain within it some redemptive importance? Is there some dimension – cosmological, ethical, or aesthetic – in the idea of infinite recurrence that might lead to a will beyond the will to destruction? Where is the affirmative face of this idea in which Nietzsche now discovers the final chapter in the story of the will in revolt?

Such ambivalence, such a fusion between an abyssal, negative interpretation and an affirmation of the infinite was, as we have seen, the nucleus of the ethical impact of the idea of the Eternal Recurrence, as much in *The Gay Science* as in *Thus Spoke Zarathustra*. The idea was always presented there as the condition of something that imposed a decision, that obliged a radical cut between significations. In 1883, in *The Gay Science*, it took the form of a demon that had invaded our midnight dreams. In 1884, in Zarathustra's words, it appeared as an enigma, as an image that needed to be deciphered, not because it was obscure, vague or indeterminate, but because it demanded a decision be made, a choice between the Dwarf's perspective, for whom time was circular and everything was equal, and the shepherd's perspective, who had cut off the head of the serpent of time and laughed before the eternity of each instant. In all of his writings on the Eternal Recurrence Nietzsche explores this constructive stridency, this unsupportable oscillation between two experiences, two radically opposed conceptions of the world, of man and of time.

Is that perhaps what is occurring in the Lenzer Heide text? We could be led to think that it is precisely in the moment that nihilism closes in around itself, that the idea of the Eternal Recurrence creates a possibility for revealing the basis itself of existence, both in cosmic as well as human terms. Indeed, even if this cosmological explanation expresses the lack of a theological or a teleological basis for human existence, cancelling both the hypothesis of a creator God and that of a final cause of becoming, it does not invalidate the figure of a basis, or reject the possibility of a meaning of existence.

On the contrary, with the idea of the Eternal Return the only thing that is exhausted is a specific model for a basis, the moral and conceptual model of the meaning of existence as transcendence, whether in the figure of an archaeology, or in that of an eschatology. Nihilism's inversion of morality, by denying any form of transcendence, becomes the victim of its own logic, since it believes that denying everything that exceeds the facticity of existence is, at the same time, to deny the possibility of any meaning for that which exists. As Nietzsche writes: "*One* interpretation has collapsed, but because it was considered *the* interpretation, it appears as though there is no sense in existence whatsoever, as though everything is *in vain*" (§4). The idea of the Eternal Recurrence breaks this connection between meaning and transcendence.

Does this mean that now, that is, in the 1887 text, this signifies that the idea of the Eternal Recurrence is at once the most extreme cancellation of any form of transcendence and, at the same time, the most radical revelation of a meaning of existence in the brutal fact of one's simply existing? Can we say that by inscribing the idea of the Eternal Recurrence in the history of nihilism, Nietzsche is also providing nihilism itself with an affirmative dimension? Would there also be a similar ambivalence at the heart of the Eternal Recurrence as a nihilist idea?

This seems to be the perspective of the Lenzer Heide text. In effect, Nietzsche begins by showing to what extent the representation of the totality of time as an infinite circle is the most nihilistic of all ideas. The representation of "existence as it is, without sense or aim, but inevitably returning, without a finale in nothingness: 'the eternal return'" (§6), is still, not only the consequence of a foundational moral model, but its most extreme form by virtue of the fact that it is inverted. The question now is whether the idea itself of the Eternal Recurrence is producing a final inversion of perspectives and, through an exhaustion of all values, will come to reveal the meaning of existence without meaning. Does "existence as it is, without sense or aim, but inevitably returning, without a finale in nothingness" lead not to nothingness, but rather to the liberation of an absolute "yes"?

A first reading of the text leaves us with the impression that it is the idea of the Eternal Recurrence that, by itself alone, can force a second inversion: the negation of a model of meaning in favour of affirming a new paradigm which it alone, through its formulation, can reveal – the concept of a meaning as absolute immanence, that is, with the immediate coincidence of each event with its own essence as pure act. The idea of the Eternal Recurrence would thus absorb all of transcendence, even in its most insignificant immanencies – each instant – thereby revealing the source of the meaning of existence.

Apparently, this is the meaning that comes out of paragraph 7. Nietzsche asks: "If we remove finality from the process, can we *nevertheless* still affirm the process? This would be the case if something within that process were being *achieved* at its every moment – and always the same" (§7). The impression is given here that Nietzsche is describing the affirmative face of the idea of the Eternal Return. The nihilist version could be reduced to the despair felt when facing the lack of any end whatsoever of the whole of the cosmological process. The affirmative version will consist in, *in spite of this,* accepting this process. The "yes" to this process would only require that we presuppose "something within that process were being *achieved* at its every moment – and always the same." There seems to be no doubt that this "something" within the process goes back to the idea of the Eternal Return. It seems that only in the context of the idea of the eternal repetition of all things can there exist something that is always attained in each moment, and is "always the same." Indeed, conceiving existence as infinite duration without an object or finality, the idea of Eternal Return causes each instant to arise as an absolute immanence, as the centre of time in its totality. Each moment in the process returns, not to an origin or finality, but simply to a series of identical instants of which it is the repetition. Each event is a pure act, an absolute coincidence between itself and its essence. The instant is no longer a mark of the ephemeralness of human existence "in the flux of becoming and passing away" (§1), but has been converted into a basis for itself and for the totality of becoming.

However, a more attentive reading of the Lenzer Heide text will completely subvert this interpretation. Nowhere does Nietzsche ever say that it is the idea of the Eternal Recurrence that contains the "yes" to each moment of the process. On the contrary, he shows that such a "yes" had already been enunciated at a certain moment in the history of ideas – and quite independently of the idea of the Eternal Recurrence. Let us look once again at the previously cited passage: "If we remove finality from the process, can we *nevertheless* still affirm the process? – This would be the case if something within that process were being *achieved* at its every moment – and always the same. Spinoza reached such an affirmative position, to the extent that every moment has a *logical* necessity: and with the logicality of his fundamental instinct he was triumphant that the world was constituted in *such* a manner" (§7). The "yes" to each moment in the process, in spite of there being no finality for the whole, had already been formulated by Spinoza. Spinoza inverted the concept of meaning by absorbing it within existence itself. In affirming a metaphysical likeness between the essence of each of the existents in the univocality of God and his modes, Spinoza would discover the immanent necessity of each event, the reason for its being such as it is and not any other way. Spinoza was able to arrive at the supreme position of saying "yes" to all things. However, Nietzsche considered the kind of affirmation arrived at by Spinoza too particular. "But his case is just an individual case" (§8). Nietzsche never recognized the pantheism that supports this way of conceiving the immanent character of the meaning of each event. The likeness between essence and existence, according to Nietzsche, should be conceived, not as the singularity of the whole and each of its modes, but as the univocality of each event in and of itself, in the fullness of instants. The likeness between the thing and its basis, beyond any teleology, is the likeness between that which each instant wants to reach and the act of reaching it. Yet, is this notion that the idea of the Eternal Recurrence is a representation of each instant still not too pantheistic? To absolutely affirm the "something" that is reached within the process and in each of its moments, which "is always the same," simply because this "something" is integrated into the whole, because this something belongs to an immense cycle of things and happenings, is this not to say that it is one more experience of the divine, now cast in the figure of an eternal whole? And yet, could we still say "yes" to each instant of existence without adopting either Spinoza's model of pantheist univocality, or the idea of the Eternal Recurrence?

What is most revealing in the Lenzer Heide text is that this is precisely what Nietzsche does do. Let us go back to that moment in which Spinoza's "yes" is invoked:

> Spinoza reached such an affirmative position, to the extent that every moment has a *logical* necessity: and with the logicality of his fundamental instinct he was triumphant that the world was constituted in *such* a manner. But his case is just an individual case. *Every fundamental characteristic* at the basis of *every* event, as expressed in every event, would need to impel any individual who felt it was his fundamental characteristic to welcome triumphantly every moment of existence in general. It would need this fundamental characteristic in oneself to be felt precisely as good, valuable, with pleasure (§7,8).

Spinoza's response is too particular. And, as such, too artificial. It presupposes an immense conceptual machinery, a terribly complex ontological and teleological system. For Nietzsche this is completely unnecessary. The "yes" that he now wants to express is much simpler. There are just two necessary conditions: (a) the knowledge of what is fundamental in each event, the knowledge of the essential structure of each moment in progress; and (b) the feeling of pleasure provoked by this essential "something" which underlies each event.

This is what comes across in paragraph 8. It is enough, in the first instance, that each individual feels that *his* fundamental characteristic is exactly that which underlies each event so that, if he feels this fundamental characteristic in himself as pleasure, as something good and valuable, he will "welcome triumphantly every moment of existence in general."

Where is the idea of the Eternal Recurrence in this "yes"? The individual triumphantly approves each instant of universal existence only if he feels with pleasure, as good and valuable, the "fundamental characteristic" that underlies each moment. The great question of the Lenzer Heide text therefore shifts from the idea of the Eternal Recurrence – which is always presented as the final chapter of the history of nihilism – to an understanding of what this "fundamental characteristic" might be.

And, directly in the second paragraph, where the narrative on the origin of morality we have referred to as *typological* begins, Nietzsche explains what the significance of this *Grundcharakterzug* is. Let us cite the passage once again. "Consequently morality has taught to *hate* and *despise* most profoundly what is the fundamental characteristic of the rulers [*der Grundcharakterzug der Herrschenden*]: *their will to power*" (§9). This is where the theory of the will to power begins to constitute the basis for the new "yes" to each moment of universal existence. The one who recognizes in himself this manifestation of the will to power will be able to triumphantly sanction each instant, affirm that "something," always the same, which is produced in each moment of the process.

We will find as well that the theory of the will to power is not merely a substitute for the idea of the Eternal Recurrence in its role as the idea that forms a basis of the new "yes" to all things. It also takes on the status of a truly decisive idea in terms of wills. The concept of the will to power, as the fundamental characteristic that underlies each action and each event, allows us to understand, in one and the same moment: (a) the origin of morality, (b) the erosion of morality, and (c) the new "yes" to universal existence. This simultaneity is the sense in which the will to power itself contains, in its essence, the fundamental ambivalence of existence. It leads as much to the invention of morality (as the revolt of the oppressed against the holders of power), as it elevates affirmative wills to the overcoming of the nihilistic self-eroding of morality, via the sanctioning of each moment of the process. But this essential ambivalence in the idea of the will to power already presupposes a typological understanding of will. It is only those who feel oppressed that have the necessity for morality, the need to hate and condemn the will of the dominators. It is on this level that the theory of the will to power explains the origin of morality. This is why this origin is always genealogical, that is, it presupposes a diagnosis of the *type* of will in play, an analysis of the lineage of wills that express themselves through value judgments. It is only the oppressed wills that secrete morality as a strategy of revolt against the dominators. And they are the same wills that lead to nihilism. Instigated by the spirit of destruction, they revert to morality itself and carry it to the point of erosion, destroying, thus, their own basis. By losing belief in the validity of judgments that legitimize their revolt against the affirmative wills, they end up disconsolate. And they end up in exactly the same place as the principle they oppose, the place of the powerful, and they force the powerful to become their hangmen, perpetuating the final nothingness. "Nihilism as a symptom of the fact that those who turned out badly have no consolation left: that they destroy in order to be destroyed, that, relieved of morality, they no longer have any reason to 'surrender themselves' – that they position themselves on the territory of the opposing principle and *want power* for themselves, too, by *forcing* the powerful to be their executioners. This is the European form of Buddhism: *doing no*, after all existence has lost its 'sense'" (§ 12).

As with the *epistemological* narrative, the *typological* narrative of the idea of the Eternal Return also becomes a condition of the last moment in the process of the self-erosion of morality. This is what we find in paragraphs 13 and 14. Nietzsche tells us that nihilism implies a diminution of those collective energies which power European civilization. This is the point in which a general scepticism begins to arise as the fallout of that infinite struggle among interpretations of man and of the world. This endemic fatigue explains the similarity between the appearance of Buddhism in the East, with its suspension of all beliefs, with its godless teleology, and the way in which European Science has led to the idea of the Eternal Return, to the idea of a cosmic totality, with no built-in finality. As Nietzsche says: "A certain spiritual fatigue – reaching the point of hopeless skepticism directed *against* philosophers as a result of the long struggle between philosophical opinions – likewise characterizes the by no means *lowly* standing of these nihilists. Think of the situation in which Buddha appeared. The doctrine of the eternal recurrence would have *erudite* presuppositions (such as the teacher Buddha had, e.g. concept of causality etc.)" (§13). In the typological narrative, the idea of the Eternal Recurrence is also seen to parallel the doctrine of Buddhism because it requires "erudite presuppositions," it requires a minimal cosmology, even if it is just the simple concept of "causality." Yet, in the typological narrative, the idea of the Eternal Recurrence does not only express the culminating point, the final effect of a self-dissolution of moral interpretations of existence. It is also seen as a strategy of oppressed wills. We recall that in the epistemological narrative the Eternal Recurrence is an idea to which morality is led once all of its illusions about the final meaning of existence have dissolved. "Let us think this thought in its most terrible form: existence as it is, without sense or aim, but inevitably returning, without a finale in nothingness: 'the eternal return.' This is the most extreme form of nihilism: nothingness (the 'senseless') eternally! European form of Buddhism: energy of knowledge and strength *forces* one into such a belief. It is the *most scientific* of all possible hypotheses. We deny final goals: if existence had one, it would have to have been reached" (§ 6). The idea of the Eternal Recurrence, within the dialectic of knowledge, is the consequence of a science that, based on the principle of truth at all costs, denies the idea of "finality" because therein it discovers the mechanism of illusion, of self-enchantment. It is the need to know that necessitates this disenchantment before the world. The Eternal Recurrence is what is left after all illusions have dissolved. It is, for this very reason, the most extreme form of nihilism.

The role played by Eternal Recurrence inside the typological narrative expresses a reactive will. It is the moment in which resentment and revenge turn against themselves, only to be led towards the most terrible despair. The Eternal Recurrence, which is presented here as a "curse" engendered by oppressed wills, embodies another form of nihilism: that of the pleasure of destruction. It is no longer simply a state of disenchantment that is at stake, the discovery that everything that exists is nothingness, but the actual desire to transform everything that exists into nothingness. "The *unhealthiest* kind of man in Europe (of all classes) is the ground of this nihilism: they will feel that belief in the eternal recurrence is a *curse* which, once you are struck by it, makes you no longer baulk at any action; not being passively extinguished, but *making* everything that is so senseless and aimless be extinguished: although it is only a spasm, a blind rage on realizing that everything has existed for eternities – including this moment of nihilism and lust for destruction" (§14).

This is why the Eternal Recurrence no longer needs to be presented to humanity as a way of inducing, through its ethical ambiguity, different responses to the meaning of each instant of existence. The idea of Eternal Recurrence (because it is basically a chapter in the story of nihilism and its movement toward despair and destruction) immediately has the effect of a decision. And this effect now occurs on the anthropological rather than the ethical plane. The lust for destruction, which the idea that everything has already existed for an eternity legitimizes, forces a natural selection among wills, separating them along typological lines, and clarifies the hierarchy of forces. "The *value of such a crisis* is that it *cleanses*, that it forces together related elements and makes them ruin each other, that it allocates common tasks to people of opposing mentalities – also bringing to light the weaker, more insecure among them and thus initiating a *hierarchy of forces* from the point of view of health: acknowledging commanders as commanders, obeyers as obeyers. At one remove from all existing social orders, of course" (§14). The idea of the Eternal Return, the last chapter in a story of multiple metamorphoses of wills oppressed in their spirit of revolt against the holders of power, does not only exhaust a certain model of meaning, as in the case of the epistemological narrative, but it produces a crisis, it produces a decision that effects the totality of wills. And this crisis not only fulfills an internal logic, it not only allows for the bankruptcy of all illusions, it "cleanses," as it selects certain wills who, themselves, had invented morality for the purposes of self-justification. The dialectic of knowledge leads to disenchantment; the dialectic of wills in revolt terminates – following the revolt against the self – in exhaustion and finally in a nearly apocalyptic cleansing.

How can affirmative wills survive this crisis? What criterion is needed to intensify them, to clarify them in a new hierarchy of forces? Could it be that an affirmative interpretation of the idea of the Eternal Recurrence would raise them to a condition of will which would allow them to say "yes" to all things? Once more, the idea of the Eternal Recurrence plays no positive role in the affirmative conclusion of nihilism, in the strategy for exiting nihilism. Contrary to what occurs in *The Gay Science* and *Thus Spoke Zarathustra*, affirmation, the interior intensification of forces in each will, fails to take meaning from the idea of infinite repetition. It is not due to a sudden understanding through affirmation of the eternity that repeats itself in every instant that wills will overcome their "spirit of revenge" and liberate themselves from morality. Nietzsche is very clear about this. Affirmative wills, sovereign wills, are characterized by not needing any representation of the world, of men, of eternity, or of repetition. They are those that, as Nietzsche says, "have no need of extreme dogmas" in order to affirm their absolute approval of each instant. "Who will prove to be the *strongest* in this? The most moderate, those who have no *need* of extreme dogmas, those who not only concede but love a good measure of chance and nonsense, those who can conceive of man with a significant reduction in his value without thereby becoming small and weak: the richest in health who can cope with the most misfortunes and so have no great fear of misfortunes – men who *are sure of their power* and represent with conscious pride the *achievement* of human strength" (§15). The strongest are not those who subscribe to some kind of understanding of the idea of the Eternal Recurrence. They are those who are "sure of their power," that is, who recognize in each of their actions, and underlying each moment of their existence, this fundamental characteristic which is their will to power. It is the doctrine of the will to power, and not the idea of the Eternal Recurrence, which will come to explain the affirmative conclusions that are possible in the crisis of nihilism, that nihilism which finds its end with the idea of the Eternal Recurrence. It is the doctrine of the will to power that not only explains how morality arose in the first place, but how the idea of the Eternal Return arose as a paradoxical consequence of morality, and, finally, that explains how the crisis created from the appearance of nihilism – and, with it, the idea of the Eternal Recurrence – creates another crisis internally, a process of the cleansing of wills, freeing those stronger wills from the spirit of resentment and directing them towards the affirmation of each event in universal existence. It is only because these strong wills, these superior men – who not only "concede but love a good measure of chance and nonsense" – are raised to the level of conscious pride in their strength, that they are able to affirm the whole of existence.

It should be clear how the doctrine of the Eternal Recurrence came to subtly link various narratives of the genesis of non-sense. The analogous status, which the idea of the Eternal Recurrence has in the *epistemological* and the *typological* narrative, produces, between them, the appearance of univocality. The *epistemological* narrative actually seems to serve as the historical introduction to the *typological*, as though the logic of science were nothing more than the development of a "will to nothingness." Nietzsche leaves open the hypothesis that the dialectic of knowledge might be the trap used by the will to destruction to orchestrate its own demise via the curse that it itself produced.

In the ambivalence that structures *The European Nihilism*, it is the fundamental duality that runs through the doctrine of nihilism (the parallel adoption of historicist and vitalist postulates) that, through the idea of the Eternal Recurrence, finds a precarious overcoming. The final paragraph reinforces this mechanism: "How would such a man think of the eternal recurrence?" (§16) asks Nietzsche.

For those men who will revel in the crisis of nihilism, like "the strongest," for those who "have no need of extreme dogmas" (§15), what would be the meaning of this idea of the exact repetition of all events and, therefore, the repetition of the process of the crisis itself and its effects of "cleansing?" Nietzsche does not respond. Nor does he have to respond. The destiny of these stronger men no longer depends on the way in which they conceive of the idea of the Eternal Recurrence, but solely on how they feel, with pleasure and lust after, as though it were something of value, this most "fundamental characteristic" which is their will to power. This is why the idea of the Eternal Recurrence is left out of *The Genealogy of Morals*, and of all other books after this text of 10 June, 1887. If Nietzsche refers to it again, it is only as a biographical reference, as happens in *Ecce Homo*, when he explains the genesis of *Thus Spoke Zarathustra*.

Shall we then continue to consider the idea of the Eternal Recurrence as the culminating idea of Nietzsche's final philosophy, as the main subject of Nietzsche's late works?

Notes

Translator's Preface

[1] George Steiner, *Errata: An Examined Life*, Phoenix: London, 1997, p. 83.
[2] *The Basic Writings of Neitzsche*, edited and translated by Walter Kaufmann, Random House: New York, 2000, p. xxiii.
[3] Ibid., p. ix.

1 Nietzsche's Place in the Aesthetics of Postmodernity

[1] *The Birth of Tragedy: The Basic Writings of Nietzsche*, edited and translated by Walter Kaufmann, New York: Random House, 2000, p. 60. (Translator's note: I wish to thank Filipe Ferreira for bibliographic assistance).

[2] "Kant labored energetically to define the distinctive character of the aesthetic domain. His point of departure here was the analysis of the judgment of taste, which is certainly directed towards something subjective, namely the free play of the imagination, but which manifests more than mere preference, being orientated rather towards intersubjective agreement. Although aesthetic objects belong neither to the sphere of phenomena knowable by means of the categories of the understanding, nor to the sphere of free acts subject to the legislation of practical reason, works of art (and those of natural beauty) are accessible to *objective judgment*." J. Habermas, "Die Moderne – ein unvollendetes Projekt" in *Die Moderne – ein unvollendetes Projekt. Philosophisch-politische Aufsätze*, Reclam Verlag: Leipzig, 1990, p. 44. English translation: "Modernity: An Unfinished Project" in *Habermas and the Unfinished Project of Modernity: Critical Essays on the Philosophical Discourse of Modernity*, ed. Maurizio Passerin d'Entreves and Seyla Benhabib, MIT Press: Cambridge, Massachusetts, 1997. Habermas's references to the Kantian aesthetic occur regularly. For an overview of the connection between Habermas's programme of the communication act and the aesthetic theory see Rainer Rochlitz, "De l'expression au sens. Perspectives Esthétiques chez Habermas" in *Revue Internationale de Philosophie* 4/1995, n. 194, pp. 405–435.

[3] "[T]he aesthetic for him [Habermas] has remained an aesthetic of the beautiful." Lyotard, "Résponse à la question: qu'est-ce que le postmoderne?" in *Critique*, 419, April 1982, p. 365. (My translation.)

[4] "In his *Critique of Judgment* Kant outlines, rapidly and almost without realizing it, another solution to the problem of sublime painting. One cannot, he writes,

represent the power of infinite might or absolute magnitude within space and time because they are pure Ideas. But one can at least allude to them, or 'evoke' them by means of what he baptizes a 'negative presentation.' As an example of this paradox of a representation which represents nothing, Kant cites Mosaic law which forbids the making of graven images." J.F. Lyotard *L'Inhumain*, Galilée: Paris, 1988, p. 96. English translation: *The Inhuman: Reflections on Time*, translated by Geoffrey Bennington and Rachel Bowlby, Polity Press: Cambridge, 1991, p. 85.

⁵ "This is only an indication, but it prefigures the Minimalist and abstractionist solutions painting will use to try to escape the figurative prison." *Ibid.*

⁶ "Avant-garde art abandons the role of identification that the work previously played in relation to the community of addressees. Even when conceived, as it was by Kant, as a *de jure* horizon or presumption rather than a *de facto* reality, a *sensus communis* (which, moreover, Kant refers to only when writing about beauty, not the sublime) does not manage to achieve stability when it comes to interrogative works of art." Lyotard, *L'Inhumain*, p. 115. English translation: p.104. For a well-founded discussion on the lack of a "sensus communis" in Kant associated with the sublime, see Paul Crowther, "The Kantian Sublime, the Avant Garde and the Postmodern: A Critique of Lyotard." *New Formations*, Spring 1989, 7: 67–75.

⁷ J. F. Lyotard and Jacob Rogozinski, *L'Autre Journal*, December 1985, p. 34. [My translation.]

⁸ Lyotard, *L'Inhumain*, p. 149. English translation: p. 137.

⁹ Those interested in a more in-depth analysis of the debate between Lyotard and Habermas can turn to a large body of literature. I would draw your attention to the most important presentation of this theme, a work by Albrecht Wellmer, *Zur Dialektik von Moderne und Postmoderne nach Adorno*, Suhrkamp Frankfurt am Main, 1988, as well as to the small book by Manfred Frank, *Die Grenzen der Verständigung. Ein Geistergespräch zwischen Lyotard und Habermas*, Suhrkamp, Frankfurt am Main, 1988, and to an article by Richard Rorty, "Habermas, Lyotard et la Postmodernité" in *Critique* no. 442, March 1984, pp. 181–197. Wellmer is available in English in: "The Dialectic of Modernism and Postmodernism: The Critique of Reason since Adorno" in *The Persistence of Modernity: Essays on Aesthetics, Ethics and Postmodernism*, translated by David Midgley, Polity Press: Cambridge, 1991.

¹⁰ *Critique of Judgment*, translated by Werner S. Pluhar, Hackett Publishing Company: Indianapolis, 1987, p. 159.

¹¹ *Ibid.*, p. 79.

¹² Schiller, English translation: *On the Aesthetic Education of Man: In a Series of Letters*, translated by Elizabeth M. Wilkinson and L.A. Willoughby, Clarendon Press: Oxford, 1983, p. 215.

¹³ "It is, therefore, one of the most important tasks of education to subject man to form even in his purely physical life, and to make him aesthetic in every domain over which beauty is capable of extending her sway; since it is only out of the aesthetic, not out of the physical state that the moral can develop. If man is, in every single case, to possess the power of enlarging his judgment and his will into the judgment of the species as a whole ... if he is to be fit and ready to raise himself out of the restricted cycle of natural ends towards rational purposes, then he must already have prepared himself for the latter within the limits of the former, and

have realized his physical destiny with a certain freedom of the spirit, that is, in accordance with the laws of beauty." Schiller, *ibid.*, p. 215. In another passage Schiller goes on to affirm: "Though it may be his needs which drive man into society, and reason which instils within him the principles of social behavior, beauty alone can confer upon him a social character. Taste alone brings harmony into society, because it fosters harmony in the individual. ... All other forms of communication divide society, because they relate exclusively either to the private receptivity or to the private proficiency of its individual members, hence to that which distinguishes man from man; only the aesthetic mode of communication unites society, because it relates to that which is common to all." *Ibid.*

[14] J. Habermas, *The Philosophical Discourse of Modernity*, MIT Press: Cambridge, Massachusetts, 1987, p. 45.

[15] "Die Moderne – ein unvollendetes Projekt," p. 52. English translation: p. 53.

[16] *The Philosophical Discourse of Modernity*, p. 49.

[17] "With Nietzsche's entrance into the discourse of modernity, the argument shifts, from the ground up. To begin with, reason was conceived as a reconciling self-knowledge, then as a liberating appropriation, and finally as a compensatory remembrance, so that it could emerge as the equivalent for the unifying power of religion and overcome the bipartitions of modernity by means of its own driving forces. Three times this attempt to tailor the concept of reason to the programme of an intrinsic dialectic of enlightenment miscarried. In the context of this constellation, Nietzsche had no choice but to submit subject-centred reason yet again to an immanent critique – or to give up the programme entirely. Nietzsche opts for the second alternative." *The Philosophical Discourse of Modernity*, pp. 85–6.

[18] The emblematic work of French Nietzscheanism is *Nietzsche aujourd'hui?*, 2 vols, Col. 10/18, UGE: Paris, 1973, which contains the talks and debates from the Cerisy-la-Salle International Colloquium on Nietzsche, held in June 1972. There is now a significant grouping of studies of this philosophical movement. See especially: David B. Allison, ed., *The New Nietzsche: Contemporary Styles of Interpretation*, MIT Press: Cambridge, Massachusetts and London, 1985; Keith Ansell-Pearson and Howard Caygill, eds, *The Fate of the New Nietzsche*, Avebury: Aldershot, 1993; Ernst Behler, "Nietzsche and Deconstruction," in Volker Dürr, Reinhold Grimm and Kathy Harms, eds, *Nietzsche: Literature and Values*, University of Wisconsin Press: Madison, 1988 (pp. 180–98); Michael Allen Gillespie and Tracy B. Strong, eds, *Nietzsche's New Seas: Explorations in Philosophy, Aesthetics, and Politics*, University of Chicago Press: Chicago and London, 1988; David Farrell Krell and David Wood, eds, *Exceedingly Nietzsche: Aspects of Contemporary Nietzsche-Interpretation*, Routledge: London and New York, 1988.

[19] Cf. *Du Sublime* by Jean-Luc Nancy and Michel Deguy, Belim: Paris, 1988 and also J. Derrida, Ph. Lacoue-Labarthe, J.L. Nancy, J.F. Lyotard *et al.*, *La Faculté de juger*, Minuit: Paris, 1985. But the most important study continues to be *Leçons sur l'Analytique du sublime*, by J.F. Lyotard, Galilée: Paris, 1991. Here, over more than three hundred pages, Lyotard gives us an exhaustive commentary on §23–29 of the *Critique of Judgment*, precisely those sections which make up the "Analytic of the Sublime." English translations: Jean-Francois Courtine *et al.*, *Of the Sublime: Presence in Question*, translated by Jeffrey S. Librett, SUNY Press: New York, J.F. Lyotard,

1993, *Lessons on the Analytic of the Sublime: Kant's Critique of Judgment* [sections 23–29], translated from the French by Elizabeth Rottenberg, Stanford University Press: California, 1994.

[20] Alain Boyer, André Comte-Sponville, Vincent Descombes, Luc Ferry, Robert Legros, Philippe Raynaud, Alain Renaut, Pierre André Taguieff, *Pourquoi nous ne, sommes pas nietzschéens*, Grasset: Paris, 1991. English translation: *Why We Are Not Nietzscheans*, translated by Robert de Loaiza, University of Chicago Press: Chicago, 1997.

[21] The most significant cases of this absence is represented by two collections of recent studies dedicated to the *sublime*: *Du Sublime*, already referred to and *Das Erhabene. Zwischen Grenzerfahrung und Grössenwahn*, by Christine Pries, Weinheim, 1989. Jean-Luc Nancy, in his study "L'offrande sublime" in which, along with a commentary on the "Analytic of the Sublime" in the *Critique of Judgment*, he traces one story of the meditation on the sublime in contemporary thought, which includes references to Benjamin, Heidegger, Adorno, and Bataille, makes the following comment in a footnote: "I must not omit to mention at least once the name of Nietzsche, who thought, in one sense or several, something of the sublime, even if he hardly thematized it as such." *Du Sublime*, p. 39, n.3. But nowhere is this "sublime in a certain sense" which Nietzsche would have pondered mentioned, nor is it ever shown that he worked systematically at this theme. Nietzsche's aesthetic is a permanent fixture in both of these volumes, albeit only at an implicit level. And when it appears more explicitly, as in *Erhabene*, in "Die Verwindung der Erhabenen – Nietzsche" by Norbert Bolz, the sublime is only referred to – and always in the vaguest of ways – in reference to *The Gay Science* and *Thus Spoke Zarathustra*, especially in the commentary on the chapter "Von den Erhabenen" (cf. pp. 165–17). Likewise, in a recent work, Marc Richir reconstructs the place of the aesthetic of the sublime in political thought from Kant onwards – including considerations of Fichte, Hegel, Schelling, Michelet, and Heidegger. In his introduction he says "the largest gap in our considerations of the philosophers is Nietzsche. But ... to consider him thoroughly we would need a whole book." English translations of two of these works can be found in: Jean-Luc Nancy, "The Sublime Offering" in *Of the Sublime: Presence in Question*, pp. 25–53.

[22] Among the studies of Nietzsche's aesthetic, the only ones that refer to the category of the sublime in *The Birth of Tragedy* are *Aesthetische Lebensformen bei Nietzsche* by Rudolf Reuber, Willhelm Fink Verlag: Munich, 1989, and Bertram Schmidt, *Der ethische Aspekt der Musik. Nietzsches «Geburt der Tragoedie» und die Weiner Klassische Musik*, Königshausen & Neumann: Würzburg, 1991. However, in both cases, there is a failure to understand the link between the Nietzschean theory and the Kantian tradition of the sublime. While Reuber locates the tradition of the sublime, in its opposition to the *beautiful*, in the tradition of the aesthetic of the *ugly* – inaugurated by Karl Rosenkranz in his *Ästhetick des Hässlichen* (1853) (cf. Reuber, pp. 76–96), Schmidt simply suspends an analysis of the consequences of his discovery that the Dionysian originates in Schiller's Sublime. After affirming that "his [Nietzsche's] concept of Dionysian is similar to the concept of Schiller's *Sublime*: the pleasure in suffering, the 'marvelous mixture and duplicity of affections' is analogous to the 'mixed feeling' of the *Sublime* in the Schillerean sense"

(p. 50), Schmidt adds that "an analysis of this analogy would outstrip the reach of the present work" (*ibid.*). Only after 1991 did systematic interpretations of *The Birth of Tragedy* based on the aesthetic of the sublime appear. One example is John Sallis's *Crossings, Nietzsche and the Space of Tragedy*, University of Chicago Press: Chicago and London, 1991, and another is Michael Harr's *Nietzsche et la Métaphysique*, Gallimard, Paris, 1993. Though neither book makes any references to Lyotard's recent readings of the "Analytic of the Sublime," they do, however, bespeak a consciousness of the theme's, let's say, "postmodern" plots. Nevertheless, in both cases, the reading is based exclusively on maintaining a parallelism between Kant and Nietzsche. This creates two important limitations: (a) the task of determining the history of the reception of the *Critique of Judgment* within Nietzsche's work is neglected; that is, the transformation of the Kantian sublime into Schopenhauer's metaphysic and thus into Wagner's expressionist aesthetic is not reconstructed; (b) there is a total absence of hermeneutical reservations in the establishment of the Kant/Nietzsche parallel. Neither Sallis nor Harr ever suspected the possibility that their interpretation of the Kantian theory of the sublime is already contaminated by the Nietzschean tonalities which underlie the renaissance in interest in the "Analytic of the Sublime." English Translation: Michael Harr, *Nietzsche and Metaphysics*, translated from the French by Michael Gendre, SUNY Press: New York, 1996.

[23] This process of transferring the effects of an aesthetic mockery of the real, which had originated in *The Birth of Tragedy*, to the Kantian theory of the sublime, without any examination of Nietzsche's own return to Kant via this same theory of the sublime, truly began in 1978 with Jacques Derrida's *La Vérité en Peinture*, Flammarion: Paris, 1978. Through a rigorous reading of the theory of the sublime in the *Critique of Judgment* in the chapter entitled "Le Colossal," Derrida showed how Kant had first described the experience of the representation of the irrepresentable, the impossible presence of presence. Yet, his discovery is informed solely by the theories of art put forth by Benjamin and Heidegger. Nietzsche is there, always present, but only in the epochal plots of the theory of the sublime and never as a moment in the history of the metaphysic of the irrepresentable constructed around the polarity beautiful/sublime. As such, those hesitations that, in the tradition of the aesthetic of the sublime, run through the entirety of this experience of a presentification of the irrepresentable – for example, as Derrida shows in the Hegelian interpretation of Kant, the hesitation between "*knowing*, or rather of thinking, whether one must *think* (as Hegel thinks) sublimity, set out from the thought of sublimity, or on the contrary (as Kant figures) from presentation, inadequate to this thought, of the sublime, etc." – never affect Nietzsche's text. (English translation: Derrida, J., *The Truth in Painting*, translated from the French by Geoff Bennington and Ian MacLeod, University of Chicago Press: Chicago, 1987, p. 134.) He does not belong to this history; he merely furnishes it with its untouchable horizon. To read *The Birth of Tragedy* through the theory of the sublime would be to upset the veracity of the absolute eccentricity of Nietzsche's aesthetic in a tradition that, in the final analysis, finds its line of escape in the sublime.

[24] Arthur Schopenhauer, *The World as Will and Representation I*, translation by E.F. Payne, Dover Publications, Inc: New York, 1969, pp. 201–2.

[25] "The beautiful and the sublime are similar in some respects. We like both for their own sake, and both presuppose that we make judgment of reflection rather either a judgment of sense or a logically determinative one. Hence in neither of them does our liking depend on a sensation, such as that of the agreeable, nor on a determinate concept, as does our liking of the good; yet we do refer the liking to concepts, though it is indeterminate which concepts these are ... That is also why both kinds of judgment are *singular* ones that nonetheless proclaim themselves universally valid for all subjects." Kant, *Critique of Judgment*, p. 97.

[26] "The beautiful in nature concerns the form of the object, which consists in [the object's] being bounded. But the sublime can also be found in a formless object, insofar as we present *unboundedness*, either [as] in the object or because the object prompts us to present it, while we add to this unboundedness the thought of its totality." *Ibid.*, p. 8.

[27] "For the one liking ([that for]) the beautiful) carries with it directly a feeling of life's being furthered, and hence is compatible with charms and with an imagination at play. But the other liking (the feeling of the sublime) is a pleasure that arises only indirectly: it is produced by the feeling of a momentary inhibition of the vital forces followed immediately by an outpouring of them that is all the stronger. Hence it is an emotion, and so it seems to be seriousness, rather than play, in the imagination's activity." *Ibid.*

[28] *Ibid.*, pp. 97–8.

[29] "Alexander Baumgarten produced with this intention a general aesthetic of all that is beautiful, in which he started from the concept of perfection of knowledge of the senses, and hence of knowledge of perception. But in this case also, the subjective part is at once done with as soon as this concept is established, and he proceeds to the objective part, and to that which is practical and is related thereto. But even here, the merit was reserved for Kant of investigating seriously and profoundly the *stimulation itself*, in consequence of which we call the object giving rise to it *beautiful*, in order, if possible, to discover its constituent elements and conditions in our nature." *The World as Will and Representation*, I, p. 530.

[30] *Ibid.*, pp. 530–1.

[31] *Ibid.*, p. 206.

[32] "The subjective correlative of time and space in themselves, as empty forms, was called by Kant pure sensibility, and this expression may be retained, as Kant was the pioneer here, although it is not quite suitable; for sensibility presupposes matter. The subjective correlative of matter or of causality, for the two are one and the same, is the understanding, and it is nothing more than this. ... The first, simplest, everpresent manifestation of understanding is perception of the actual world. This is in every way knowledge of the cause from effect, and therefore all perception is intellectual." *Ibid.*, p. 11.

[33] "In the first book the world was shown to be mere *representation*, object for a subject. In the second book, we considered it from its other side, and found that this is *will*, which proved to be simply what this world is besides being representation. In accordance with this knowledge, we called the world as

representation, both as a whole and in its parts, *the objectivity of the will,* which accordingly means the will become object, i.e., representation." *Ibid.,* p. 169.

[34] *Ibid.,* p. 170.

[35] "[I]n so far as the subject knows as an *individual,* the Ideas will also lie quite outside the sphere of its knowledge as such. Therefore, if the Ideas are to become object of knowledge, this can happen only by abolishing individuality in the knowing subject." *Ibid.,* p. 169.

[36] "[T]he transition that is possible, but to be regarded only as an exception, from the common knowledge of particular things to knowledge of the Idea takes place suddenly, since knowledge tears itself free from the service of the will precisely by the subject's ceasing to be merely individual, and being now a pure will-less subject of knowledge. Such a subject of knowledge no longer follows relations in accordance with the principle of sufficient reason; on the contrary, it rests in fixed contemplation of the object presented to it out of its connexion with any other, and rises into this." *Ibid.,* p. 178.

[37] *Ibid.,* p. 202.

[38] *Ibid.,* p. 205.

[39] *Ibid.*

[40] This moral destiny of the aesthetic of the sublime is well presented by Leonel Ribeiro dos Santos in his study "Sentiment of the Sublime and Moral Experience." As he writes: "If ... we go on to examine that which Kant considers to be sublime and the conditions to which this sentiment is submitted, the more the aesthetic nature of this sentiment will seem to be implicated. What is even more patent is its intimate connection with ideas of reason and with moral feeling or disposition." *A razão sensível,* Colibri: Lisbon, 1994, p. 94. [My translation.]

[41] *The World as will and Representation,* I, p. 205.

[42] *Ibid.*

[43] *Ibid.,* p. 207.

[44] *Ibid.,* p. 252.

[45] *Ibid.,* pp. 252–3.

[46] *Ibid.,* p. 207.

[47] *Ibid.,* p. 253.

[48] *The World as Will and Representation* II, SW II, p. 433.

[49] Perhaps it is in this link between the aesthetic of the sublime and the theory of the tragedy that the metaphysics of pessimism most closely approaches the inheritance of Schiller, Lessing, and Schelling. For an analysis of the place of tragedy as figure of the sublime within Romantic dramaturgy, see "Tragédie et sublimité. L'interprétation speculative de *l'Oedipe Roi* au seule de l'idéalisme allemand" by Jean-François Courtine, in his *Exstase de la Raison. Essais sur Schelling,* Galilée: Paris, 1990, pp. 75–111.

[50] *The World as Will and Representation,* II, p. 433.

[51] As George Steiner has shown, in this use of tragedy as metaphor for the absolute of existence, Schopenhauer repeats the basis of the aesthetics of the tragic of German Idealism. See *Antigones,* Clarendon Press: New York, 1986.

[52] Early in paragraph 16 Schopenhauer resorts to the metaphor of the stage to illustrate the ambivalent condition of human existence, which is simultaneously

concrete and abstract. "In the former he is abandoned to all the storms of reality and to the influence of the present; he must struggle, suffer, and die like the animal. But his life in the abstract, as it stands before his rational consciousness, is the calm reflection of his life in the concrete, and of the world in which he lives; ... In respect of this withdrawal into reflection, he is like an actor who has played his part in one scene, and takes his place in the audience until he must appear again. In the audience he quietly looks on at whatever may happen, even though it be the preparation of his own death (in the play); but then he again goes on the stage, and acts and suffers as he must." *The World as Will and Representation*, I, p. 85.

[53] *The World as Will and Representation*, II, p. 433.

[54] It is this complete annulment of the gift that truly marks the transcendental category of tragedy. Even though he does not consider the link between the theory of tragedy and the aesthetic of the sublime, Philonenko gives us an excellent description of this ontological, as well as moral, cancellation in the metaphysics of pessimism and in the constitution of tragedy as a transcendental figure. "Schopenhauer wants ideality of time and space to have some effect on the real and moral nullity of all phenomena manifested therein. First the real nullity: all phenomena is nothing more than a simulacrum of being, and Schopenhauer reduces the *Erscheinung* to the Kantian sense of *Schein*. Secondly, moral nullity: the simple *Schein* which develops on the last level of reality as it is defined by Plato cannot even attempt to have an ethical meaning, as its consistency is null. The ontological and moral nullity of the experience of the world is the founding moment of the transcendental category of tragedy: there is no meaning to birth, there is no meaning in living and death is simply what it is, a nothing. But this moment, in and of itself, reveals its consequence: conceived in this way, the transcendental category of tragedy justifies and insures pessimism." [My translation.] "Brève méditation sur la philosophie de la tragédie de Schopenhauer" in *Le transcendental et la pensée moderne*, PUF: Paris, 1990, p. 296.

[55] *The World as Will and Representation*, I, pp. 255–6.

[56] *Ibid.*, p. 257.

[57] We know that the characterization of music as a condition of objectless representation, in spite of being paradoxical in its dependence upon Western art's mimetic tradition, would be fulfilled in the musical aesthetic of the nineteenth- and the early twentieth-century works of Mahler, Strauss, Schoenberg and Berg. See Michelle Biget, "Compositeurs allemands lecteurs de Schopenhauer, 1850–1920" in Roger-Pol Droit, ed., *Présences de Schopenhauer*, Grasset: Paris, 1989, pp. 174–86.

[58] For example, Wagner always said that *Der Ring des Nibelungen* was finished before he had discovered Schopenhauer in 1854. Nevertheless, as Richard Hollindrake shows us, even though in the 1853 edition the last scene makes an apology for Woltan's power, the edition of *Gesammelte Schriften und Dichtung* of 1873 substitutes the concept of "power" for "love," and Woltan embodies the experience of negation of the world. See *Nietzsche, Wagner and the Philosophy of Pessimism*, George Allen & Unwin: London, 1982, especially pp. 57–8.

[59] For a historico-philological reconstitution of the relationship of reciprocal

influence between Nietzsche and Wagner see Mazzino Montinari, "Nietzsche und Wagner vor hundert Jahren" in *Nietzsche – Studien*, 7 (1978), pp. 288–307.

[60] Wagner, *Beethoven*, in Jubilaeumsausgabe, Band 9, Insel Verlag: Frankfurt am Main, 1983, pp. 56–7. English translation: *Beethoven*, by Richard Wagner, trans. Edward Dannreuthe, ed. William Reeves, London, 1903 (3rd edn) pp. 23–30.

[61] For an understanding of the place of Eduard Hanslick and his formalist model in the history of the aesthetics of music, see Dahlhaus, C. *Aesthetics of Music*, translated from the German by William W. Austin, Cambridge University Press: Cambridge (1982).

[62] "To the question – what is to be expressed with all this material? The answer will be: *musical ideas*. Now, a musical idea, reproduced in its entirety, is not only an object of intrinsic beauty, but also an end in itself, and not a means for representing feelings and thoughts. The essence of music is *sound and motion*." *Vom Musicalisch-Schönen. Ein Beitrag zur Revision der Ästhetik der Tonkunst*, Breitkopf & Härtel: Wiesbaden, 1989, p. 59. (1st edn, Leipzig, 1854). English translation: Eduard Hanslick, *Beautiful in Music. A contribution to the revisal of Musical Aesthetics*, trans. Gustav Cohen, Novello, Ewer & Co: London and New York, 1891.

[63] Jean-Jacques Nattiez summarizes the theses of this work in the following fashion: (a) music awakens the senses; (a) therefore the senses are not contained in the music; and (c) the beautiful in music does not reside in the feelings of the composer, or the listener, but in the pure contemplation of the form: the composer should not try to excite feeling. Nattiez comes to the following conclusion: "With this essay, Western aesthetics seesaws. It is no longer concerned with the study of sensations produced by a form – and Hanslick reminds us of the meaning of the word *aesthesis* – but of the form itself." Jean-Jacques Nattiez, "Hanslick ou les apories de l'immanence" in *Le Combat de Chronos et d'Orphée*, Christian Bourgois Editeur: Paris, 1993, p. 59. [My translation above.]

[64] *Vom Musikalisch-Schönen*, p. 7. [My translation.]

[65] In the 1854 edition Hanslick only discusses Wagner's *Work of the Art of the Future* (1850) and the theses presented therein about the heart as the organ of sound. In later editions Hanslick takes to task the definition of music as the "art of expression" [*Kunst des Ausdrucks*], as well as the thesis that would see music as a means for the immediate apprehension of the world's essence. Here he is looking precisely at Wagner's essay *Beethoven* (1870). It is surprising that in criticizing Wagner's text, he fails to understand that it represents a response to his own formalist notions. In fact, Hanslick does not consider the distinction made here for the first time by Wagner between an aesthetic of the beautiful, as an aesthetic of forms, and an aesthetic of the sublime, as an aesthetic of the senses. Nor does he see that via this distinction Wagner is able to save his expressionist definition of music.

[66] *Beethoven*, p. 83. English translation: pp. 71–71.

[67] *Ibid.*, p. 73. English translation: pp. 55–6.

[68] Nietzsche had always been tormented by Wagner's aesthetic correlation between the sublime, the ineffable, and the divine. But only in 1888, in *The Wagner Case*, did he really let it be understood to what extent he was conscious of the fact the it was the beautiful/sublime opposition that functioned in Wagner as the

motor behind this correlation. It is worth citing in its entirety paragraph 6, in which Nietzsche satirizes the Wagnerian aesthetic: "What is beautiful has a fly in its ointment: we know that. Why, then, have beauty? why not rather that which is great, sublime, gigantic – that which moves *masses*? – Once more: it is easier to be gigantic than to be beautiful; we know that" ... "German youths, horned Siegfrieds, and other Wagnerians – require the sublime, the profound, the overwhelming" ... "They all have the same logic 'Whoever throws us is strong; whoever elevates us is divine, whoever leads us to have intimations is profound.' Let us make up our minds, honored musicians: we want to throw then, we want to elevate them, we want to lead them to have intimations. That much we are capable of" ... "Regarding the matter of inducing intimations: this is the point of departure of our concept of 'style'. Above all, no thought! Nothing is more compromising than a thought, the throng yet of unborn thoughts, the promise of future thoughts, the world as it was before God created it – a recrudescence of chaos. – Chaos induces intimations. To speak in the language of the master: infinity, but without melody. Secondly, as far as throwing people is concerned, this really belongs partly to physiology" ... "Above all, however, *passion* throws people. Let us reach an understanding about passion. Nothing is cheaper than passion. One can dispense with all virtues of counterpoint, one need not have learned a thing – passion is one ability we always have. Beauty is difficult: beware of beauty! – And *melody*" ... "Nothing is more dangerous than a beautiful melody" ... "A final bit of advice! Perhaps it includes everything else. *Let us be idealists!* This is, if not the cleverest thing we can do at least the wisest. To elevate men one has to be sublime oneself. Let us walk on walk on clouds, let us harangue the infinite, let us surround ourselves with symbols!" *The Wagner Case*, §6, *Friedrich Nietzsche, Werke, Kritische Studienausgabe*, (KSA) *VI*, pp. 24–5. English translation: Walter Kaufmann, ed. and translator, *The Basic Writings of Nietzsche*, Modern Library: New York, 2000, p. 623.

[69] *Beethoven*, p. 87. English translation: pp. 77–8.

[70] *Ibid.*

2 The Individual and Individuality in Nietzsche

[1] *Werke, Kritische Studienausgabe* (hereafter KSA), eds, Georgio Colli and Mazzino Montinari, Verlag de Gruyter: Berlin/New York, 1967, XII, 9 (84); *The Will To Power*, ed. by W. Kaufmann, translated by W. Kaufmann and R.J. Hollingdale, Vintage: New York, 1967, § 379. (Translator's note: All further references for *The Will to Power* are to the Kaufmann ed. and will be indicated by WP. "The Individual and Individuality in Nietzsche" was first translated into English by Christopher Rollason, for *Pli*, 12 (2001). For the present translation of this chapter, I have relied heavily on Rollason's superb translation of the Nabais text. Rollason's version has been recently re-published in *A Companion to Nietzsche*, Keith Ansell Pearson (ed), Blackwell: London, 2006. The version published in *Pli* (and later in the Blackwell book) underwent heavy editing by the editor[s] of that magazine and certain crucial passages that were in the original Portuguese version were omitted from the published, English versions, thereby eliminating the central thesis of the

article concerning the disappearance of the idea of the Eternal Recurrence after 1885. The present translation restores these passages and, in doing so, will significantly challenge the canonical sanctification of the doctrine of the Eternal Return in, especially, Anglo-American Nietzsche studies.

[2] KSA, IX (158). (Translator's note: many of the citations in the present chapter are from Nietzsche's posthumous writings. This is the case where only the KSA reference is provided. Where no translator is indicated the passage was translated by the editors of *Pli*).

[3] G.W. Leibniz, letter to Arnauld of 30 April 1687, *Philosophische Schriften*, ed. Gerhardt, vol. II, p. 97.

[4] The lack of a specific description of the concept of the individual in Nietzsche has lead some scholars to see a negation of the individual in his theory of the will to power, and the predominance of an undifferentiated continuum. In the words of Eugen Fink in *Nietzsches Philosophie* (French trans., Hildenberg, Minuit: Paris, 1965): "The world is not composed of things, it is a single flux of life, a 'sea' in which there are waves but nothing is permanent" (p. 207) and, again: "Starting out from a basic conception of being as becoming, Nietzsche denies the individual, finite being. There is no such thing as being because, in the end, there is no such thing as individuation" (p. 210).

[5] *The World as Will and Representation*, I, p. 113.

[6] cf. Immanuel Kant, *Critique of Pure Reason* (*Kritik der reinen Vernunft*), AK B 473/ A 445 and ff.

[7] "The solution to the third antinomy, whose subject was the idea of freedom, merits special consideration insofar as for us it is very remarkable that Kant is obliged precisely here, in connection with the Idea of Freedom, to speak in greater detail about the thing in itself." *The World as Will and Representation*, p. 501.

[8] Schopenhauer, *Parerga und Paralipomena I*, S.W., V. p. 270.

[9] Schopenhauer, *The World as Will and Representation*, IV, §63, S.W., I, p. 674. [My translation.]

[10] KSA, I, pp. 26–7. English translation: *The Birth of Tragedy and Other Writings*, translated by Ronald Speirs, Cambridge University Press: Cambridge, 1999, p. 15.

[11] "We, however, who consist of and are completely trapped in semblance, are compelled to feel this semblance to be that which truly is not [*Wahrhaft-Nichtseiende*], i.e. a continual Becoming in time, space, and causality – in other words, empirical reality." *Ibid.*, KSA, I, pp. 38–9. English translation: Speirs, 1999, p. 26.

[12] "If we add to this horror the blissful ecstasy which arises from the innermost ground of man, indeed of nature itself, whenever this breakdown of the *principium individuationis* occurs, we catch a glimpse of the essence of the *Dionysiac*, which is best conveyed by the analogy of *intoxication*. ... Now, hearing this gospel of universal harmony, each person feels himself to be not simply united, reconciled or merged with his neighbor, but quite literally one with him, as if the veil of maya had been torn apart, so that mere shreds of it flutter before the mysterious primordial unity [*das Ur-ein*]." *Ibid.*, KSA, I, p. 30. English translation: Speirs, 1999, p. 17–18.

[13] "One might even describe Apollo as the magnificent divine image of the

principium individuationis, whose gestures and gaze speak to us of all the intense pleasure, wisdom and beauty of 'semblance'." *Ibid.*, KSA, I, p. 28. English translation: p. 17.

[14] "As an ethical divinity Apollo demands measure from all who belong to him and, so that they may respect that meaure, knowledge of themselves." *Ibid.*, KSA, I, p. 40. English translation: Speirs, 1999, p. 27.

[15] "But how do we regain ourselves? How can man know himself? He is a dark and concealed thing. ... The young soul looks back upon life with the question: what have you until now truly loved? What does your soul have to do with the series of these venerated objects in front of you? Perhaps through their essence and their sequence they give you a law, the fundamental law of your proper self." *Schopenhauer as Educator*, KSA, I, p. 340.

[16] *Ibid.*, KSA, I, p. 338.

[17] It is significant that it should be through the figure of Apollo that Nietzsche distinguishes himself from Schopenhauer. Dionysus will only return after 1885, with the theory of the Will to Power, in which the universal Whole no longer opposes the *principium individuationis*, but rather becomes its expression.

[18] "Here, at this moment of supreme danger for the will, *art* approaches as a saving sorceress with the power to heal. Art alone can re-direct those repulsive thoughts about the terrible and the absurd nature of existence into representations with which man can live." KSA, I, p. 57. English translation: Speirs, 1999, p. 40.

[19] *Schopenhauer as Educator*, KSA, I, pp. 374–5.

[20] KSA, II, p. 29. English translation: *Human, All-too-Human*, translated by R.J. Hollingdale, Cambridge University Press: Cambridge, 1995, p. 15.

[21] *Ibid.*, KSA, II, p. 30. English translation: Hollingdale, 1995, p. 16.

[22] KSA, IX, 6 (158).

[23] Nietzsche was inspired by Jacob Burckhardt's *The Civilization of the Renaissance in Italy* (1860), especially the second part with its description of the development of the individual as a self-sufficient individuality. See the second part, entitled "The Development of the Individual."

[24] *Human, All-too-Human*, KSA, II, p. 103. English translation: Hollingdale, 1995, p. 57.

[25] KSA, IX, 6 (80).

[26] KSA, IX, 6 (158).

[27] KSA, IX, 6 (293).

[28] KSA, IX, 7 (62); WP 331.

[29] KSA, IX, 7 (62); WP 331.

[30] "[A]ll is eternal, unbecome [*ungeworden*]," KSA, IX, 11 (157).

[31] KSA, IX, II (202).

[32] KSA, IX, 11 (156).

[33] "All becoming moves itself in the repetition of a determinate number of absolutely identical states," KSA, IX, 11 (245).

[34] KSA, IX, 11 (148).

[35] KSA, IX, 18 (3). [My translation.]

[36] KSA, III, p. 570.

[37] KSA, IX, 11 (161).

[38] KSA, IX, 11 (202).

[39] We are taking up Giorgio Colli's thesis from his work *Scritti su Nietzsche*, Adelphi Editore: Milan, 1980, in the chapter dedicated to the posthumous fragments from the autumn of 1884 to autumn of 1885, according to which Nietzsche's theory of the Will to Power only appeared in this period, not only because only then did Nietzsche deliberately adopt the metaphysical perspective as a way of endowing the world with the force of an explicative viewpoint, but also because it is only from this point on that he begins to develop the fundamental philosophical project entitled, precisely, *The Will to Power*.

[40] KSA, XI, 36 (34); WP 618.

[41] KSA, XI, 36 (31); WP 619.

[42] *Beyond Good and Evil*, KSA, V, p. 54. English translation: *Basic Writings of Nietzsche*, ed. and trans. by Walter Kaufmann, Random House: New York, 2000, pp. 237–8.

[43] KSA, IX, II (156).

[44] KSA, IX, II (7).

[45] KSA, XI, 27 (27).

[46] KSA, XIII, II (III); WP 704.

[47] KSA, XIII, II (73); WP 715.

[48] KSA, XIII, 14 (79): WP 634.

[49] KSA, XIII, 14 (79): WP 635.

[50] KSA, XI, 38 (12); WP 1067.

[51] KSA, XII, 2 (148); WP 643.

[52] KSA, XIII, 14 (80).

[53] Nietzsche accepts the existence of a multidimensional space, absolute in that it is unlike a separate substance existing only in itself but as the result of the co-localizations of forces. "I believe in absolute space as the substratum of force: the latter limits and forms. Time eternal. But space and time do not exist in themselves." KSA, XI, 36 (25); WP 545.

[54] KSA, XIII, 14 (98).

[55] KSA, XII, 2 (85); WP 557.

[56] KSA, XII, 2 (142); WP 632.

[57] KSA, XIII, 11 (77); WP 694.

[58] KSA, XIII, 14 (80).

[59] KSA, XII, 5 (12).

[60] KSA, XI, 36 (20); WP 637.

[61] KSA, XI, 34 (247).

[62] KSA, XI, 35 (59).

[63] KSA, XII, 2 (149); WP 556.

[64] *Human, All-too-Human*, KSA, II, p. 20. English translation: p. 9.

[65] KSA, XII, 2 (157); WP 564.

[66] It is in this sense that Nietzsche considers thought as part of the essence of will: "feeling and more precisely various types of feelings much be recognized as ingredients of the will, and secondly also thought: in each act of the will a thought commands – and one should not believe that this thought can separate itself from

volition, as if then [after separation] volition would still be left over." KSA, XI, 38 (8).

⁶⁷ KSA, XII, 5 (64).
⁶⁸ KSA, XI, 11 (32). [My translation.]
⁶⁹ KSA, XIII, 11 (83); WP 674.
⁷⁰ KSA, XII, 2 (143).
⁷¹ KSA, XII, 2 (175). Nietzsche's criticism of Darwinism touches precisely on the inversion of perspectives in its explanation of external/internal relations in the genesis of living forms. "The influence of 'external circumstances' is overestimated to the point of nonsense by Darwin; what is essential about the life-process is just the gigantic creative power which produces forms working from within while using and exploiting 'external circumstances'." KSA, XII, 7 (25).
⁷² Nietzsche is able to deny his own notion of "cause" based on the model of copossibility among individuals. As he says: "'Cause' and 'effect' ... That means: the separation of the event into action and passion." KSA, XII, 7 (1). All individuals are absolutely active. "What is 'passive'? To resist and react. To be hampered in forward-grasping movement: thus an act of resistance and reaction. What is 'active'? Striding towards power." KSA, 5 (64).
⁷³ KSA, XIII, 14 (113). [My translation.]
⁷⁴ KSA, XII, 5 (71).
⁷⁵ It is also the model of copossiblity that allows Nietzsche to conceive the tie between the spontaneous nature of each individual and the regulated character of each and every one of the events that comprise his biography. "Let us here dismiss the two popular concepts 'necessity' and 'law': the former introduces a false constraint into the world, the latter a false freedom. 'Things' do not behave regularly, according to a *rule*... There is no obedience here: for that something is as it is, as strong or as weak, is not the consequence of an obedience to a rule or a compulsion – The degree of resistance and the degree of superior power – this is the question in every event: if, for our day-to-day calculations, we know how to express this in formulas and 'laws', so much the better for us! ... There is no law: every power draws its ultimate consequence at every moment, Calculability exists precisely because things are unable to be other that they are." KSA, XIII, 14 (79); WP 634.
⁷⁶ This fragment (the Lenzer Heide text of 1887) is dealt with extensively in the last chapter of this book.
⁷⁷ KSA, XII, 7 (38); WP 1032.

3 Necessity and Contingency in Nietzsche's Early Writings

¹ *Ecce Homo*, KSA, VI, p. 296. English translation: *The Genealogy of Morals and Ecce Homo*, translated by Walter Kaufmann, Random House: New York, 1989, p. 258.
² *Dithyrambs of Dionysus*, translated by R.J. Hollingdale, Black Swan Books: Redding Ridge, 1984.
³ These essays (like everything that Nietzsche wrote before the autumn of 1869) are not included in the Colli and Montinari critical edition, our principal source of

Nietzsche's works in this study. This edition begins with the published writings from the Basel period. For this reason the works spoken about here are taken from the five-volume edition *Friedrich Nietzsche. Werke und Briefe. Historisch-Kritische Gesamtausabe*, edited by Hans Joachim Mene, Carl Koch, and Karl Schlechta, C.H. Beck'sche Verlagsbuchhandlung: Munich, 1933–40.

[4] English translation: "Fate and History: Thoughts," in Keith Ansell Pearson and Duncan Large, eds, *The Nietzsche Reader*, Blackwell: London, 2006, p. 13. Translated by Duncan Large.

[5] *Ibid.*, p. 13.

[6] *Ibid.*, p. 14.

[7] *Ibid.*, p. 14.

[8] *Ibid.*, p. 15.

[9] *Freedom of Will and Fate*, in *ibid.*, p. 17.

[10] *Ibid.*, p. 17.

[11] *Ibid.*

[12] *Ibid.* p. 14.

[13] *Ibid.*

[14] On this confusion in *Thus Spoke Zarathustra* see Chapter 5 below, especially the sections entitled "Time and Morality" and "The Typological Perspective in *Thus Spoke Zarathustra*."

[15] "The solution of the third antinomy, whose subject was the Idea of freedom, merits special consideration ... In general, this is the point where Kant's philosophy leads to mine, or mine springs from his as its parent stem." (*The World as Will and Representation*, I, p. 501.)

[16] "For us it is very remarkable that Kant is obliged precisely here, in connexion with the *Idea of freedom*, to speak in greater detail about the *thing-in-itself*, hitherto seen only in the background. This is very easy for us to understand after we have recognized the thing-in-itself as the *will*. ... For the rest, it is just this intended solution of the sham third antinomy that gives Kant the opportunity to express very beautifully the profoundest ideas of his whole philosophy ... but above all, the discussion of the contrast between the empirical and intelligible characters which I number among the most admirable things ever said by man." (*Ibid.*, pp. 501–5.)

[17] "Every efficient cause, however, must have a *character*, that is, a rule according to which it manifest its causality, and without which it would not be a cause. According to this we should have in every subject of the world of sense, first, an *empirical character*, through which its acts, as phenomena, stand with other phenomena in an unbroken connection, according to permanent laws of nature, and could be derived from them as their conditions, and in connection with them form the links of one and the same series in the order of nature. Secondly, we should have to allow to it an *intelligible character* also, by which, it is true, it becomes the cause of the same acts as phenomena, but which itself is not subject to any conditions of sensibility, and never phenomenal. We might call the former the character of such a thing as a phenomena, in the latter the character of the thing by itself. According to its intelligible character, this active subject would not depend on conditions of time, for time is only the condition of phenomena, and not of things by themselves. In it no *act* would *arise* or *perish*, neither would it be subject

therefore to the law of determination in time and of all that is changeable, namely, that everything *which happens* must have its cause in the *phenomena* (of the previous state). In one word its causality, so far as it is intelligible, would not have a place in the series of empirical conditions by which the event is rendered necessary in the world of sense." Kant, *Critique of Pure Reason*, translated by F. Max Müller, Anchor Books: New York, 1966, p. 370.

[18] "For we are speaking here of the absolutely first beginning, not according to time, but according to causality. If, for instance, at this moment I rise from my chair with perfect freedom, without the necessary determining influence of natural causes, a new series has its absolute beginning in this event, with all its natural consequences *ad infinitum*, although, with regard to time, this event is only the continuation of a preceding series. For this determination and this act do not belong to the succession of merely natural effects, nor are they a mere continuation of them, but the determining natural causes completely stop before it, so far as this event is concerned, which no doubt follows them, and does not *result* from them, and may therefore be called an absolutely first beginning in a series of phenomena, not with reference to time, but with reference to causality." *Ibid.*, p. 322.

[19] S. W., III, p. 707. English translation: *On the Basis of Morality*, translated by E.F.J. Payne, Berghahm Books: Providence, 1995, p. 112.

[20] KSA I, pp. 374–5. English translation: "Schopenhauer as Educator" in *Untimely Meditations*, translated by R.J. Hollingdale, Cambridge University Press: Cambridge, 1997, p. 155.

[21] *Ibid.*, p. 127.

[22] KSA, I, 56. English translation: in *The Basic Writings of Nietzsche*, edited and translated by Walter Kaufmann, Random House: New York, 2000 (first ed. 1967), p. 60.

[23] KSA, I, p. 257. English translation: "On the Uses and Disadvantages of History for Life," in *Untimely Meditations*, translated by R.J. Hollingdale, p. 67.

[24] *Ibid.*, p. 59.

[25] *Ibid.*

[26] *Ibid.*, p. 67.

[27] "History belongs above all to the man of deeds and power, to him who fights a great fight, who needs models, teachers, comforters and cannot find them among his contemporaries." (*Ibid.* p. 67) ... "He learns from it that the greatness that once existed was in any event once *possible* and may thus be possible again." (*Ibid.* p. 69.)

[28] *Ibid.*, p. 70.

[29] *Ibid.*, p. 74.

[30] *Ibid.*, pp. 75–6.

[31] *Ibid.*, p. 76.

[32] *Ibid.*, p. 66.

[33] *The World As Will and Representation*, I, pp. 182–3.

4 Nietzsche and Stoicism

[1] KSA, VI, p. 274; English translation: in *The Basic Writings of Nietzsche*, edited and translated by Walter Kaufmann, Random House: New York, 2000, p. 688.

[2] *Ibid.*, p. 688.

[3] Because Nietzsche and not the philosophy of the Portico is the object of this chapter, in which we will try to analyse the way in which Nietzsche conceived of Stoicism, we recommend that the reader refer to one of the most important books dedicated to all of the central aspects of Stoicism, especially for an analysis of the ethical programme of the Stoics. See Victor Goldschmidt, *Le système stoïcien et l'idée de temps*, Vrin: Paris, 1977.

[4] See the commentary on this aphorism at the end of this chapter.

[5] On the importance of the influence of Stoicism, it is worth reading Michel Spanneut's classic, *Permanence du stoïcisme, de Zenon à Malraux*, ed., J. Duculot, S. A: Gembloux, 1973. There you will find two pages dedicated to Nietzsche. In addition to the diverse and contradictory ways in which Nietzsche appreciated Stoicism, Spanneut lays out Nietzsche's most important points of affinity, that is, (a) the idea of the Eternal Recurrence, (b) the programme for the assent to destiny as the basis for the autonomous ideal of the will, and (c) the model for the world as Will (*cf.* pp. 352–3).

[6] Charles Andler, *Nietzsche, sa vie et sa pensée*, Gallimard: Paris, 1958, vol. II, pp. 406–8.

[7] Georges Morel, *Nietzsche, Introduction à une première lecture*, Aubier-Montaigne: Paris, 1971, vol. II, pp. 284–5.

[8] *Cf.* Jean Granier, *Le probléme de la Verité dans la philosophie de Nietzsche*, Seuil: Paris, 1966, pp. 414–15.

[9] See Gilles Deleuze, *Logique du Sens*, Minuit: Paris, 1969.

[10] Gilles Deleuze, *Nietzsche et la philosophie*, P.U.F.: Paris, 1962, p. 20. English translation: *Nietzsche and philosophy*, translated by High Tomlinson, Athlone: London, 1983.

[11] Because Nietzsche's essay was not included in the Colli and Montinari edition, we have used the Hans Joachim Mette and Karl Schlechta edition. Both the German and the Latin version of *De Laertii Diogenis fontibus* are published in volume IV, pp. 217–359. An exposition of the theses according to which Diocles of Magnesia had been the source of the whole of book VII on the Portico occupy pp. 223–5.

[12] Nietzsche's argument (*ibid.*, pp. 229–36) is based almost exclusively on a passage at the beginning of the 10th Book of Diogenes Laertius. It can be summed up as follows: Diocles of Magnesia, who, according to what we know via Diogenes, so praised Epicurus in the book III of his lost work, would be the same author, also referred to by Diogenes, indicated in the work *Twenty-Four Proofs to Diocles in Twelve Books* by the Stoic, Sócio, (whom Nietzsche demonstrates as being the one who was known to be Seneca's teacher). Furthermore, according to Diogenes, this work which refutes Diocle also defames Epicurus. This being the case, Nietzsche concludes, Diocles of Magnesia can only be the enemy of the Portico and its detractor.

[13] Pindar, *Pythian Odes* II, v. 73, cited by Nietzsche, *ibid.*, p. 222. On the

importance of this maxim as an appeal to the conquest of radical individuality throughout Nietzsche's philosophy of the Will to Power, see Chapter 2, above.

¹⁴ "How different is the Stoic in the middle of the same misfortune instructed by experience and dominating himself through concepts!" ["Wie anders steht unter dem gleichen Missgeschick der stoische, an der Erfahrung belehrte, durch Begriffe sich beherrschende Mensch da!"] KSA, I, p. 890. [My translation.]

¹⁵ According to Nietzsche, in Dionysian ecstasy the veil of Maya is stripped away and man suddenly accedes to the primordial unity that, as in Schopenhauer, is identified with the world of the thing-in-itself. Cf. *The Birth of Tragedy*, KSA, I, pp. 27–8. English translation: *The Basic Writings of Nietzsche*, p. 37.

¹⁶ *Human, All-too-Human*, KSA II, p. 129. English translation: Hollingdale, R. J., translator. *Human, All-Too-Human*, Cambridge University Press: Cambridge, 1999, p. 73.

¹⁷ "*Socrates* – If all goes well, the time will come when one will take up the memorabilia of Socrates rather than the Bible as a guide to morals and reason, and when Montaigne and Horace will be employed as forerunners and signposts to an understanding of this simplest and most imperishable of intercessors. The pathways of the most various philosophical modes of life lead back to him; at bottom they are the modes of life of the various temperaments confirmed and established by reason and habit and all of them directed towards joy in living and in one's own self; from which one might conclude that Socrates' most personal characteristic was a participation in every temperament. Socrates excels the founder of Christianity in being able to be serious cheerfully and in possessing that *wisdom full of roguishness* that constitutes the finest state of the human soul. And he also possessed the finer intellect." *The Wanderer and His Shadow* KSA, II, pp. 591–2, see also op. cit., 6 and 72, pp. 542 and 584, respectively. English Translation: in *Human, All-too-Human*, p. 332.

¹⁸ "He who desires little more of things than knowledge of them easily finds repose of soul ..." Ibid., p 41. [KSA, II, p. 75.] "All we require, and what can be given us only now the individual sciences have attained their present level, is a *chemistry* of the moral, religious and aesthetic conceptions and sensations." [*Op. cit.* I, KSA, II, p. 24.] *Ibid.*, p. 12.

¹⁹ See the whole of the third chapter of *Human, All-too-Human*, entitled "The Religious Life."

²⁰ KSA, XI, 34 (39). English translation: *Daybreak*, translated by R.J. Hollingdale, Cambridge University Press: Cambridge, 1997, p. 82.

²¹ Posthumous Writings, *Friedrich Nietzsche, Sämtliche Werke, Kritische Studienausgabe*, Band 11, April–June 1885, 34[39]. [My translation].

²² *Daybreak* 139, KSA, XI, p. 34 (39). English translation: *Daybreak* 139, p. 13. (English trans.: *Daybreak* 139, p. 139).

²³ This distinction is evidence of the existential rather than the political nature of Nietzsche's aristocratic ideal. As Deleuze shows, the distinction between the morality of the master and that of the slave must be considered typologically, that is, solely based upon the way in which they organize and enact the will. Cf. *Nietzsche et la Philosophie*, pp. 164–7.

²⁴ KSA, III, pp. 316–17. English translation: *Daybreak*, §546, p. 219.

[25] We don't have enough information to be able to determine with any precision exactly which of the Stoics Nietzsche had read. In reference to a letter to F. Overbeck, of August 1879, Charles Andler purports that Nietzsche had gathered much of his information about the Stoics from Constant Martha's reading of Roman Moralists; cf. *Nietzsche, sa vie et sa pensée*, vol. II, pp. 215–17. This is a likely hypothesis, especially when we consider that in the whole of Nietzsche's works there is only one citation from the Portico: Epictetus's *Manual* (fifth paragraph) is cited in *Vermischte Meinungen und Spruche* 386, S. W., II, 528–9 (see note 27 below). As Colli and Montinari note, even this citation could have been taken from Schopenhauer, either from *The World as Will and Representation*, or from the *Parerga*; cf. KSA, XIV, p. 134.

[26] KSA, IX, 7 (71). [My translation.]

[27] Throughout his work, Nietzsche will renew his call for a knowledge of Nature, loyalty to its law and necessity. For example in *The Gay Science* he has the following to say: "We, however, *want to become those we are* – human beings who are new, unique, incomparable, who give themselves laws, who create themselves. To that end we must become the best learners and discoverers of everything that is lawful and necessary in the world: we must become *physicists* in order to be able to be *creators* in this sense – while hitherto all valuations and ideals have been based on *ignorance* of physics or were constructed so as to *contradict* it. Therefore: long live physics! And even more so that which *compels* us to turn to physics – our honesty! *The Gay Science*, 335, KSA, III, pp. 563–4. English translation: *The Gay Science*, ed. and translated by W. Kaufmann, Random House: New York, 1974, p. 266. See as well Alain Juranville, *Physique de Nietzsche*, Denoel/Gonthier: Paris, 1973.

[28] Nietzsche not only condensed the essence of his "morality" into the *amor fati* equation, but also an expression of that which would be one of the most intimate expressions of his own experience: "For now the necessary ... Love what is necessary! *Amor fati*, that will be my morality." KSA, IX, 15 (20) [My translation]. In *Ecce Homo* he would also tell us: "My formula for greatness in a human being is *amor fati*: that one wants nothing to be different, not forward, not backward, not in all eternity. Not merely bear what is necessary ... but *love* it." (*Ibid.*, (Kaufmann) p. 714. The same subject would be taken up in *Nietzsche Contra Wagner*: "As my innermost nature teaches me, whatever is necessary – as seen from the heights and in the sense of a *great* economy – is also the useful par excellence: one should not only bear it, one should *love* it. *Amor fati*: that is my inmost nature." KSA, VI, p. 436. English translation: *The Portable Nietzsche*, p. 680.

[29] *Human, All-too-Human*, KSA II, p. 105. English translation: p. 58.

[30] *Assorted Opinions and Maxims* 386, KSA, II, pp. 528–9. English translation is included in: *ibid.*, p. 296.

[31] See the last chapter of this book, "Nihilism According to Nietzsche."

[32] In aphorism 341 in *The Gay Science* Nietzsche writes: "The question in each and every thing, 'Do you desire this once more and innumerable times more?' would lie upon your actions as the greatest weight. Or how well disposed would you have to become to yourself and to life *to crave nothing more fervently* than this ultimate eternal confirmation and seal?" KSA, III, p. 570. English translation: p. 274.

[33] See the beautiful hymn to eternity and the wholeness of the Universe, or as Nietzsche calls it «das Ja – und Amen-Lied» in *Thus Spoke Zarathustra*, III. *The Seven Seals*, KSA, IV, pp. 287–91. English translation in *The Portable Nietzsche*, p. 340.

[34] "The doctrine of the 'eternal recurrence,' that is, of the unconditional and infinitely repeated circular course of all things – this doctrine of Zarathustra *might* in the end have been taught already by Heraclitus. At least the Stoa has traces of it, and the Stoics inherited almost all of their principal notions from Heraclitus." *Ecce Homo*, KSA, VI, p. 313. English translation: pp. 729–30.

[35] Cf. Emile Bréhier, *Chrysippe*, Félix Alcan, Paris, 1910, p. 158.

[36] For an exhaustive analysis of the cosmological, logical, and ethical reach of the doctrine of the Eternal Recurrence in the Stoa see Jonathan Barnes "La doctrine du Retour Eternel," in *Les Stoiciens et leur Logique*, Vrin: Paris, 1978, pp. 3–20. The bibliography on this subject is nearly unlimited; see Joan Stambaugh, *Nietzsche's thought of Eternal Return*, the Johns Hopkins University Press: Baltimore and London, 1972. Karl Löwith, *Nietzsches Philosophie der ewigen Wiederkehr des Gleichen*, Kohlhamer: Stuttgart, 1956, and Pierre Klossowski, *Nietzsche et le cercle vicieux*, Mercure de France: Paris, 1969.

[37] KSA, IX, 12 (141). [My translation.]

[38] "... hence I, too, shall say what it is that I wish from myself today, and what was the first thought to run across my heart this year – what thought shall be for me the reason, warranty, and sweetness of my life henceforth. I want to learn more and more to see as beautiful what is necessary in things; then I shall be one of those who make things beautiful. *Amor fati*: let that be my love henceforth!" *The Gay Science*, aphorism 276; KSA, III, p. 521. English translation: p. 223.

[39] Cf. *The Gay Science*, aphorism 341; KSA, III, p. 570. English translation: p. 274.

[40] KSA, III, p. 544. English translation: p. 245.

[41] KSA, III, p. 383. English translation: pp. 85–6. With respect to this, aphorism 326 is also worth citing: "Is our life really painful and burdensome enough to make it advantageous to exchange it for a Stoic way of life and petrification? We are *not so badly off* that we have to be as badly off as Stoics." (English translation: p. 257).

[42] Nietzsche is a victim of that same confusion that Victor Goldschmidt exposed, between the general and permanent imperturbability of primitive scepticism in Stoicism and the active readiness for correct action at opportune moments. Goldschmidt, *Le système stoïcien et l'idée de temps*, p. 135. See chapter 5, "La théorie de l'action," as well as chapter 6, "La morale en acte," pp. 125–210.

[43] *Beyond Good and Evil* 227, KSA, V, p. 162. English translation: in *The Basic Writings of Nietzsche*, p. 345.

[44] This principle, as is well known, underwent various formulations; cf. Hans von Arnim, *Stoicorum Veterum Fragmenta*, III, Teubner: Stuttgart, 1964, p. 4 and following. Nietzsche refers only to its trivial form, as moral naturalism, that is, as though he were expressing the principle of living according to moral laws that had emerged out of nature.

[45] *Beyond Good and Evil*, 9, KSA, V, pp. 21–2. English translation: *Basic Writings of Nietzsche*, p. 205.

[46] Hans von Arnim, *Stoicorum Veterum Fragmenta*, III, 5,14.

[47] *Ibid.*, III, 4,12.

⁴⁸ *De finibus*, IV, 14, in *ibid.*, III, 5, 26.

⁴⁹ *De finibus*, III, 9, 31, in *ibid.*, III, 6, 6.

⁵⁰ Cited by Nicola Festa, *I frammenti degli stoici antichi*, Georg Olms Verlag: Hildesheim, 1971, p. 59.

⁵¹ For an analysis of the various formulations of this maxim and the meaning of each of its terms see Damianos Tsekourakis, *Studies in the terminology of early Stoic ethics*, Franz Steiner Verlag: Wiesbaden, 1974, especially chap. I, pp. 1–61.

⁵² XXX see 36 Cf. *Beyond Good and Evil* 36, KSA, V, pp. 54–5. English translation: *The Basic Writings of Nietzsche*, p. 237.

⁵³ Kaufmann, *Basic Writings*, pp. 205–6.

⁵⁴ There is a flagrant isomorphism between the physics of the Stoics and the physics of the Will to Power. Among many points of affinity, we should draw attention to the radical materialism of both, the affirmation of the world as will, the rejections of atomism in favor of a fundamental continuism, the structural conception of causality, as well as the already referred to idea of the Eternal Recurrence. See Sambursky's classic study, *Physics of the Stoics*, Routledge and Kegan Paul: London, 1959.

5 The Role of the Idea of the Eternal Recurrence in the Genesis of the Project for the Revaluation of All Values

¹ This occurs in fragment number 2 [100] in KSA, XII, pointedly dated by Nietzsche "Sils-Maria, Summer of 1886." Here we can read "The Will to Power. Attempt at a revaluation of all values." The first plans for an important work entitled *The Will to Power* date from the Summer of 1885 (cf. KSA, XI, p. 39 [I]), which at the time carried the subtitle "Attempt at A New Interpretation of all Events."

² Cf. KSA, XIII, 22 [14].

³ In *Ecce Homo* Nietzsche relates the most important moments in the composition of *The Antichrist*: "Immediately upon finishing this work [*Twilight of the Idols*], without losing even one day, I attacked the tremendous task of the *Revaluation*." (KSA, VI, p. 355.) English translation: *The Genealogy of Morals* and *Ecce Homo*, ed. and trans. by Walter Kaufmann, Random House: New York, 1989, p. 315. We know as well from this account that, in spite of the fact that the preface was written on 3 September, *The Antichrist* was only concluded on the 30th of the same month. "On the 30th of September, great victory" ... "On the same day I wrote the preface for the *Twilight of Idols*: correcting the printer's proofs of that book by my recreation in September." (KSA, VI, p. 356. English translation: p. 316.)

In fact, in the belated preface to *Twilight of the Idols* we read: "Turin, September 30, 1888, *on the day when the first book of the Revaluation of All Values was completed.*" (KSA, VI, p. 58. English translation: in *The Portable Nietzsche*, p. 466.)

⁴ Cited by Colli and Montinari in *Chronik zu Nietzsches Leben*, included in KSA, XV, p. 58.

⁵ "This is the first evidence that Nietzsche considers *The Antichrist* as the whole

of the 'Revaluation','' the editors write, commenting on the letter cited above. KSA, XV, p. 186.

⁶ See for example the following passage from a letter to Paul Deussen dated 26 November, 1888: "My 'Revaluation of All Values', whose principal title [*Haupttitel*] is 'The Antichrist', is finished. In the next years, I must occupy myself with the translation of this work into seven languages: the first edition in each of these languages, about a million copies." Cit. in KSA, XV, p. 187. (Translator's version.)

⁷ 2 KSA, XIII, 25 [11]. [My translation.]

⁸ "The uncovering of Christian morality is an event without parallel, a real catastrophe." (KSA, VI, p. 373.) English translation: Kaufmann, 1989, p. 333.) Nietzsche wrote at the end of *Ecce Homo*, referring to *The Antichrist*. "He that is enlightened about that, is a force majeure, a destiny – he breaks the history of mankind in two. One lives before him, or one lives after him." (*Ibid.*) In the same notebook of 1886, where for the first time he mentions "the revaluation of all values," he writes: "Starting point: it is an *error* to point to 'social hardship' or 'physiological degeneration' or even corruption as the *cause* of nihilism. These can still be interpreted in very different ways. Instead, it's in a *very particular interpretation*, the Christian-moral one, that nihilism is found." (KSA, XII, 2 [127]). English translation: *Writings from the Late Notebooks*, trans. Kate Sturge, Cambridge University Press: Cambridge, 2003, p. 83.

⁹ The paradigmantic works are by Klossowski, *Nietzsche et le cercle vicieux*, Deleuze, *Nietzsche et la Philosophie*, Wolfgang Muller-Lauter, *Nietzsche Seine Philosophie der Gegensatze und seiner Philosophie*, Walter de Gruyter: Berlin/New York, 1971, Karl Lowith, *Nietzsches Philosophie der ewigen Wiederkehr des Gleichen*, Kohlhammer: Stutgart, 1956, Joan Stambaugh, *Nietzsche's thought of eternal return*, Bernd Magnus, *Nietzsche's Existential Imperative*, Indiana University Press: Bloomington & London, 1978. And most recently Gunter Abel, *Nietzsche, Die Dynamik der Willen zur Macht und die ewige Wiederkehr*, Walter de Gruyter: Berlin/New York, 1984.

¹⁰ This is the central thesis of Heidegger's *Was Heisst Denken?*, Max Niemeyer Verlag: Tübingen, 1954. For Heidegger, revaluing all values would be to cancel the condition for the possibility of the whole moral devaluation of existence. Not only this, but, according to Heidegger, Nietzsche would have seen such a basis in the existential figure of the "spirit of revenge" (*der Geist der Rache*) – which is defined as a revolt again the irrevocability of the past. To unleash the consciousness of revolt against the past and, thus, the revolt against existence in general, would therefore imply the acceptance of the idea of the Eternal Recurrence, that is to say, the revaluation of man in the over-human.

¹¹ Deleuze's reading of the way Nietzsche prepares Foucault's fundamental theses is significant. "What does Foucault mean when he says there is no point in crying over the death of man?" ... "Foucault, like Nietzsche, can only sketch in something embryonic and not yet functional. Nietzsche said that man imprisoned life, but the superman is what frees life *within man himself*, to the benefit of another form, and so on" ... "And is this unlimited finity or superfold not what Nietzsche had already designated with the name of eternal return?" Gilles Deleuze, *Foucault*, Minuit: Paris, 1986. English translation: *Foucault*, translated by Seán Hand, University of Minnesota Press: Minneapolis, 1988, pp. 130–1. The link between the

reflection on "the death of man" – identified certainly by Heidegger with the end of the metaphysics of the subject – and the basis of the philosophy of Nietzsche can also be found in the programmatic text, "Les fins de l'homme," by Jacques Derrida, in *Marges de la Philosophie*, Minuit: Paris, 1972. English translation: *Margins of Philosophy*, translated by Alan Bass, University of Chicago Press: Chicago, 1982. See, as well, Gianni Vattimo's *Al di la des soggetto. Nietzsche, Heidegger and l'hermeneutica*, Feltrinelli: Milano, 1981, where this link between Nietzsche and Heidegger is taken up precisely around this theme of the "death of man."

[12] Gianni Vattimo comes to the same conclusion: "Indeed, the scattered and often incoherent theories of post-modernity acquire rigor and philosophical credibility when seen in relation to the Nietzschean problematic of the overcoming of metaphysics." *La fine della modernità*, Garzanti: Milan, 1985, p. 9. Translated into English as: *The End of Modernity: Nihilism and hermeneutics in post-modern culture*, translated by Jon R. Snyder, Polity: Cambridge, 1988, p.1.

[13] This is Habermas's interpretation in the chapter dedicated to Nietzsche in *Der philosophische Diskurs der Moderne*, Suhrkamp: Frankfurt am Main, 1985.

[14] "Now I shall relate the history of *Zarathustra*. The fundamental conception of this work, the idea of the eternal recurrence, this highest formula of affirmation that is at all attainable, belongs in August 1881: it was penned on a sheet with the notation underneath, "6000 feet beyond man and time." That day I was walking through the woods along the lake Silvaplana; at a powerful pyramidal rock not far from Surlei I stopped. It was then that this idea came to me." *Ecce Homo*, KSA, VI, 335. English translation: Kaufmann, 1989, p. 295.

[15] Cited in *Chronik zu Nietzsches Leben*, KSA, XV, p. 139.

[16] See fragments 27 [80], 27 [82], 29 [40], 29 [66], among many others, all of them included in volume 11 of the KSA.

[17] *Cf. supra*, p. 177 note 1.

[18] KSA, VI, p. 160.

[19] Cf. KSA, VI, p. 335. English translation: *The Basic Writings of Nietzsche*, p. 751.

[20] The only exceptions are fragments 5 [54], 5 [71] (which we speak about at the end of this work), and 7 [54] in volume 12 of the KSA, and fragment 10 [13] in volume 13.

[21] KSA, XIII, 22 [14].

[22] "If I reckon back a few months from this day, I find as an omen a sudden and profoundly decisive change in my taste, especially in music." *Ecce Homo*, KSA, VI, 335. English translation: Kaufmann, 1989, p. 295.

[23] Cf. KSA II, pp. 67, 70, 75.

[24] *Ueber die Grundlage der Moral*, Arthur Schopenhauer *Samtliche Werke*, Wissenschaftliche Buchgessellschaft, Darmstadt, 1980, Band 3:708. English translation: *On the Basis of Morality*, translated by E.F.J. Payne, Berghahm Books: Providence, 1995, p. 110.

[25] Kant, *Groundwork for the Metaphysics of Morals*, translated by Allen W. Wood, Yale University Press: New Haven, 2002, p. 66.

[26] *Human, All-too-Human*, KSA, II, p. 64. English Translation: *Human All-too-Human*, R.J. Hollingdale, Cambridge University Press: Cambridge, 1999, pp. 34–5.

[27] *Ibid.*

²⁸ Ibid.

²⁹ Ibid., p. 58.

³⁰ Heidegger makes various comments about this chapter in *Thus Spoke Zarathustra*: in *Nietzsche metaphysische Grundstellung im abendländischen Denken: Die ewige Wiederkehr des Gleichen (Sommersemester 1937), Gesamtausgabe XLIV*, in *Was Heisst Denken?*, Max Niemeyer Verlag: Tübingen, 1954, and expecially in the essay on Zarathustra in Vorträge und Aufsätze, Gesamtausgabe VII. English translation: *What is Called Thinking?*, translated by J. Glenn Gray, Harper & Row: New York, 1968. An important study of Heidegger's *meditation on Nietzsche about the* interpretation of time as irreversible and as a revelation of the fundamentally temporal condition of human existence can be found in "La présence de Nietzsche dans Sein und Zeit" by Jacques Taminiaux, in *Lectures de l'ontologie fondamentale. Essais sur Heidegger*, Jerôme Millon: Grenoble, 1989.

³¹ *Thus Spoke Zarathustra*, II, KSA, IV, p. 180. English translation: in *The Portable Nietzsche*, pp. 251–2.

³² Ibid., p. 252.

³³ Ibid.

³⁴ Ibid.

³⁵ Jankélévitch, *L'irréversible et le nostalgie*, Flammarion: Paris, 1974, p. 273. (My translation)

³⁶ *Thus Spoke Zarathustra*, II, KSA IV, pp. 179–80. English translation: *The Portable Nietzsche*, p. 251.

³⁷ Ibid., 252.

³⁸ It was Gilles Deleuze who made the idea of *typology* in Nietzsche central and under the rubric of which all of the theses of the theory of the will are brought together. He distinguishes active types, whose will to power is expressed through affirmation, and reactive types, which rest in the principle of negation, and creates a framework in which all of the typological figures of *Thus Spoke Zarathustra* and *The Geneology of Morals* are represented. The first group includes *the artist, the aristocrat, the sovereign individual* and *the legislator*. Among the reactive types are *the man who never finishes anything, the perpetual accuser, the man who multiplies his pain, the guilty man, the domesticated man, the aesthetic man* and *the non-artist*. Cf. *Nietzsche et la Philosophie*, p. 166. The weakness of Deleuze's reading is in the blurring of the difference between the various works of the 1881–5 period, that is *The Gay Science* and *Thus Spoke Zarathustra*, and those which are organized around the theory of the will to power, posterior to 1885, of which *The Genealogy of Morals* is the most important and paradigmatic. This blurring hinders our understanding of the basic ambivalence in Nietzsche's analysis of time in *Thus Spoke Zarathustra*. As we have tried to point out here, this work already contains a typological understanding of time, even if, simultaneously, time is conceived as a universal determination. Nietzsche will abandon the phenomenological perspective. And this abandonment will lead to the immense typology which is *The Genealogy of Morals*.

³⁹ Deleuze defines reactive forces precisely as those "that are separated from that of which they are capable." *Nietzsche et la Philosophie*, p. 140.

⁴⁰ See, for an excellent balance of the exegetical problems born of the attempts to conceive of the idea of the Eternal Return as the fundamental substance of

Nietzsche's final philosophy, M.C. Sterling, "Recent discussions of eternal recurrence: some critical comments" in *Nietzsche-Studien*, Band 6, Walter de Gruyter: Berlin/New York, 1977, pp. 261-91.

[41] KSA, IX, 11 [338]. Cf. tb. 11 [203] ou 11 [160]. English translation by Keith Ansell Pearson and Duncan Large in *The Nietzsche Reader*, p. 241.

[42] KSA, III, p. 570. English translation: *The Portable Nietzsche*, pp. 101-2.

[43] *Ibid.*

[44] KSA, IX, II [165]. English translation by Diane Morgan, Keith Ansell Pearson and Duncan Large in *The Nietzsche Reader*, p. 241.

[45] KSA, IX, 11 [163]. English translation by Keith Ansell Pearson and Duncan Large in *ibid.*, p. 241.

[46] Cf. tb. KSA, IX, 11 [161], 11 [160], 11 [203].

[47] *Thus Spoke Zarathustra*, III, KSA, IV, p. 249. English translation: *The Portable Nietzsche*, p. 310.

[48] KSA, IV, p. 181. English translation: *The Portable Nietzsche*, p. 253.

[49] KSA, IV, p. 278. English translation, *The Portable Nietzsche*, p. 333.

[50] KSA, IV, pp. 199-200. English translation: *Thus Spoke Zarathustra*, ed. and trans. by R.S. Hollingdale, Penguin: London, 1961, pp. 178-9.

[51] *Ibid.*, 179.

[52] Cf. works of Stambaugh and Lowith cited above.

[53] *Nietzsche Philosophie*, Kohlhammer Verlag: Stuttgart, 1960, p. 146.

[54] *Ibid.*, p. 103. [My translation.]

[55] *Nietzsche I*, Gunther Neske Verlag: Tübingen, 1961, p. 273. [My translation.]

[56] For a more complete understanding of the doctrine of the will to power, see Chapter 2, above.

[57] KSA, XIII, 11 [77], English translation: Kate Sturge, *Writings from the Late Notebooks*, Cambridge University Press: Cambridge 2003, p. 214.

[58] KSA, XI, 36 [20], English translation: Walter Kaufmann and R.J. Hollingdale, *The Will to Power*, Random House: New York, 1967, p. 340.

[59] KSA, XIII, 14 [95], English translation: *The Will to Power*, Random House: New York, 1967, p. 337.

[60] KSA, XI, 36 [18], English translation: Sturge, *Writings from the Late Notebooks*, p. 24.

[61] KSA, XIII, 14 [79], English translation: Sturge, *Writings from the Late Notebooks*, p. 216.

[62] See Volker Gerhardt, "Da Vontade de Poder: para a Génese e Interpretação da Filosofia do Poder em Nietzsche" in António Marques, ed., *Cem anos após o Projecto "Vontande de Poder – Transmutação de todos of Valores,"* Verga: Lisbon, 1989, pp. 11-32.

[63] *The Basic Writings of Nietzsche*, p. 220.

[64] *Ibid.* p. 221.

[65] In Ansell Pearson and Large, eds, *The Nietzsche Reader* For a more detailed commentary on this important fragment, see the following chapter.

[66] KSA, XII, p. 5. 71.

[67] This is Gianni Vattimo's interpretation in his commentary on the Lenzer Heide fragment in his *Introduzione a Nietzsche*, Laterza: Roma, 1985, pp. 94-100.

⁶⁸ Lenzer Heide
⁶⁹ Lenzer Heide, paragraph 9.
⁷⁰ *Ibid.*, para. 11.
⁷¹ *Ibid.*, para. 15.
⁷² *Ibid.*
⁷³ *Ibid.*, para. 9.
⁷⁴ *Ibid.*, para. 14.

6 Nihilism According to Nietzsche

¹ KSA, VI, p. 135. English translation: *Twilight of the Idols*, translated by R.J. Hollongdale, Penguin Books: London, 2003, p. 98.

² KSA, XIII, pp. 255–6. *The Will to Power* p. 25.

³ *The Anti-Christ, Ecce Homo, Twilight of Idols and other writings*, ed. Aaron Ridley and Judith Norman, translation by Judith Norman, Cambridge University Press: Cambridge, p. 64.

⁴ Nachgelassene Fragmente, 11 [411], Band XIII, p. 190. [My translation.]

⁵ *European Nihilism*, English transl. by Duncan Large in Keith Ansell-Pearson and Duncan Large (eds) *The Nietzsche Reader*, Blackwell: London, 2006, pp. 385–9. (Translator's note: all further paragraph references in this chapter refer to the Blackwell Ansell-Pearson/Large edition of *European Nihilism* – also referred to as the Lenzer Heide fragment.)

Bibliography

Friedrich Nietzsche

Werke, Kritische Studienausgabe (KSA), eds, Georgio Colli and Mazzino Montinari, 15 vols, de Gruyter, Berlin and New York, 1967–77.

For the texts written before *The Birth of Tragedy*: Hans Joachim Mette and Karl Schlechta edition, *Friedrich Nietzsche, Werke und Briefe, Historisch-Kritische Gesamtausgabe* (HKW), C.H. Beck'sche Verlagsbuch, Munich, 1937.

Sämtliche Briefe: Kritische Studienausgabe, eds, Giorgio Colli and Mazzino Montinari, 8 vols, de Gruyter, Berlin and New York, 1986.

Fatum und Geschichte, HKW, II. English translation: "Fate and History: Thoughts," by George, J. Stack, in Keith Ansell Pearson and Duncan Large, eds, *The Nietzsche Reader*, Blackwell, London, 2006.

Die Geburt der Tragödie, KSA, I. English translation: *The Birth of Tragedy*, by Walter Kaufmann, in *The Basic Writings of Nietzsche*, Modern Library, New York, 2000.

Vom Nutzen und Nachteil der Historie für das Leben, KSA I. English translation: "On the Uses and Disadvantages of History for Life." in *Untimely Meds*, R.J. Hollingdale, Cambridge University Press, Cambridge, 1997.

Schopenhauer als Erzieher, KSA, I. English translation "Schopenhauer as Educator," in R. J. Hollingdale, Cambridge University Press, Cambridge, 1997.

Menschliches, Allzumenschliches I & II, KSA, II. English translation: *Human, All-too-Human*, by R.J. Hollingdale, Cambridge University Press, Cambridge, 1995.

Morgenröte, KSA, III. English translation: *Daybreak*, by R.J. Hollingdale, Cambridge University Press, Cambridge, 1997.

Die fröhliche Wissenschaft, KSA, III. English translation: *The Gay Science*, by Josefine Nauckhoff, edited by Bernard Williams, Cambridge University Press, Cambridge, 2001.

Also sprach Zarathustra, KSA, IV. English translation: *Thus Spoke Zarathustra*, by Walter Kaufmann in *The Portable Nietzsche*, Viking Books, New York, 1976.

Jenseits von Gut und Böse, KSA, V. English translation: *Beyond Good and Evil*, by Marion Faber, Oxford University Press, Oxford, 1998.

Götzen-Dämmerung, Der Antichrist, Ecce Homo, KSA, VI. English translation: *The Anti-Christ, Ecce Homo, Twilight of Idols and other writings*, ed. Aaron Ridley and Judith Norman, translated by Judith Norman, Cambridge University Press, Cambridge, 1999.

Dionysos-Dithyramben, KSA, VI. English translation: *Dithyrambs of Dionysus*, by R.J. Hollingdale, Black Swan Books, Redding Ridge, 1984.

For the posthumous work:

The Will to Power, translated by Walter Kaufman and R.J.Hollingdale, Vintage Books, New York, 1967.

Writings from the Late Notebooks, translated by Kate Sturge, Cambridge University Press, Cambridge, 2003.

"Notes from 1881," translated by Duncan Large, Keith Ansell-Pearson, Diane Morgan, in Keith Ansell-Pearson and Duncan Larghe (eds) *The Nietzsche Reader*, Blackwell, London, 2006, pp. 238–41.

"European Nihilism," translated by Duncan Large, in Keith Ansell-Pearson and Duncan Large, eds, *The Nietzsche Reader*, Blackwell, London, 2006, pp. 385–389.

Secondary Works

AAVV. *Nietzsche aujourd'hui?*, 2 vols, Col 10/18, UGE, Paris, 1973.

Abel, Gunter, *Nietzsche, Die Dynamik der Willen zur Macht und die ewige Wiederkehr*, Walter de Gruyter, Berlin and New York, 1984.

Allen Gillespie, Michael and Strong, Tracy B., eds, *Nietzsche's New Seas: Explorations in Philosophy, Aesthetics, and Politics*, University of Chicago Press, Chicago and London, 1988.

Allison, David B., ed., *The New Nietzsche: Contemporary Styles of Interpretation*, MIT Press, Cambridge, Massachusetts and London, 1985.

Andler, Charles, *Nietzsche, sa vie et sa pensée*, Gallimard, Paris, 1958.

Ansell Pearson, Keith, *Viroid Life: Perspectives on Nietzsche and the Transhuman Condition*, Routledge, London, 1997.

Ansell Pearson, Keith and Caygill, Howard, eds, *The Fate of the New Nietzsche*, Aldershot, Avebury, 1993.

Barnes, Jonathan, "La doctrine du Retour Eternel," in *Les Stoïciens et leur Logique*, Vrin, Paris, 1978, pp. 3–20.

Behler, Ernst, "Nietzsche and Deconstruction," in Volker Dürr, Reinhold Grimm, and Kathy Harms, eds, *Nietzsche: Literature and Values*, University of Wisconsin Press, Madison, 1988.

Boyer, Alain, Comte-Sponville, A., Descombes, V., Ferry, L., Legros, R., Raynaud, Ph., Renaut, A., Taguieff, P.A. *Pourquoi nous ne sommes pas nietzschéens*, Grasset, Paris, 1991. English translation: *Why We Are Not Nietzscheans*, translated by Robert de Loaiza, University of Chicago Press, Chicago, 1997.
Bréhier, Emile, *Chrysippe*, Félix Alcan, Paris, 1910.
Burckhardt, Jacob, *The Civilization of the Renaissance in Italy* (1860), translated by Peter Murray, Penguin, London, 1990.
Colli, Giorgio, *Dopo Nietsche*, Adelphi, Milan, 1974.
——*Scritti su Nietzsche*, Adelphi Editore, Milan, 1980.
——*La ragione errabonda. Quaderni postumi*, a cura di Enrico Colli, Adelphi, Milan, 1990.
Courtine, Jean-François, *Extase de la Raison. Essais sur Schelling*, Galilée, Paris, 1990.
Cox, Christoph, *Nietzsche: Naturalism and Interpretation*, University of California Press, Berkeley, Los Angeles and London, 1999.
Crowther, Paul, "The Kantian Sublime, the Avant Garde and the Postmodern: A Critique of Lyotard," *New Formations*, Spring 1989, 7: 67–75.
Dahlhaus, Carl, *Musikästhetik*, Laaber Verlag, Laaber, 1979. English translation: *Aesthetics of Music*, translated by William W. Austin, Cambridge University Press, Cambridge, 1982.
Deleuze, Gilles, *Nietzsche et la Philosophie*, PUF, Paris, 1962. English translation: *Nietzsche and Philosophy*, translated by Hugh Tomlinson, Athlone Press, London, 1983.
——*Différence et Répétition*, PUF, Paris, 1969. English translation: *Difference and Repetition*, translated by Paul Patton, Columbia University Press, New York, 1994.
——*Logique du Sens*, Minuit, Paris, 1969. English translation: *The Logic of Sense*, translated by Mark Lester and Charles Stivale, Columbia University Press, New York, 1990.
——*Mille Plateaux*, Minuit, Paris, 1980 (with Felix Guattari). English translation: *A Thousand Plateaus – Capitalism and Schizophrenia*, translated by Brian Massumi, University of Minnesota Press, Minneapolis, 1987.
——*Foucault*, Minuit, Paris, 1986. English translation: by Sean Hand, University of Minnesota Press, Minneapolis, 1988.
——*Pourparlers*, Minuit, Paris, 1990, English translation: *Negotiations*, translated by Martin Joughin, Columbia University Press, New York, 1995.
——*Qu'est-ce que le Philosophie?*, Minuit, Paris, 1991(with Felix Guattari). English translation: *What is Philosophy?* translated by Hugh Tomlinson and Graham Burchell, Columbia University Press, New York, 1994.
——*Critique et Clinique*, Minuit, Paris, 1993. English translation: *Essays*

Critical and Clinical, translated by D. Smith and M. Greco, University of Minnesota Press, Minneapolis, 1997.

Derrida, Jacques, *Marges de la Philosophie*, Minuit, Paris, 1972. English translation: *Margins of Philosophy*, translated by Alan Bass, University of Chicago Press, Chicago, 1982.

—— *La Vérité en Peinture*, Flammarion, Paris, 1978. English translation: *The Truth in Painting*, translated by Geoff Bennington and Ian MacLeod, University of Chicago Press, Chicago, 1987.

Derrida, J., Lacoue-Labarthe, Ph., Nancy, J-L. Lyotard, J-F. *et al.*, *La Faculté de juger*, Minuit, Paris, 1985.

Droit, Roger-Pol, ed., *Présences de Schopenhauer*, Grasset, Paris, 1989.

Farrell Krell, David and Wood, David, eds, *Exceedingly Nietzsche: Aspects of Contemporary Nietzsche-Interpretation*, Routledge, London and New York, 1988.

Festa, Nicola, *I frammenti degli stoici antichi*, Georg Olms Verlag, Hildesheim, 1971.

Fink, Eugen, *Nietzsche's Philosophy*, translated by Goetz Richter, Continuum, London and New York, 2003.

Frank, Manfred, *Die Grenzen der Verständigung. Ein Geistergespräch zwischen Lyotard und Habermas*, Suhrkamp, Frankfurt am Main, 1988.

Goldschmidt, Victor, *Le système stoïcien et l'idée de temps*, Vrin, Paris, 1977.

Golomb, Jacob, *Nietzsche's Enticing Psychology of Power*, Magnes Press, Jerusalem, Iowa State University Press, Ames, 1989.

Gooding-Williams, Robert, *Zarathustra's Dionysian Modernism*, Stanford University Press, Stanford, California, 2001.

Granier, Jean, *Le probléme de la Verité dans la philosophie de Nietzsche*, Seuil, Paris, 1966.

Habermas, Jürgen, *Der philosophische Diskurs der Moderne. Zwölf Vorlesungen*, Suhrkamp, Frankfurt, 1985. English translation: *The Philosophical Discourse of Modernity*, translated by Frederick G. Lawrence, MIT Press, Cambridge, Massachusetts, 1987.

—— "Die Moderne – ein unvollendetes Projekt," in *Die Moderne – ein unvollendetes Projekt. Philosophisch-politische Aufsätze*, Reclam Verlag, Leipzig, 1990. English translation: "Modernity: An Unfinished Project", in *Habermas and the Unfinished Project of Modernity: Critical Essays on The Philosophical Discourse of Modernity*, ed., Maurizio Passerin d'Entreves and Seyla Benhabib, MIT Press, Cambridge, Massachusetts, 1997.

Hales, Steven D. and Rex Welshon, *Nietzsche's Perspectivism*, University of Illinois Press, Urbana and Chicago, 2000.

Hanslick, Eduard, *Vom Musicalisch-Schönen. Ein Beitrag zur Revision der Ästhetik der Tonkunst*, Breitkopf & Härtel, Wiesbaden, 1989, (1st edn, Leipzig, 1854). English translation: *Beautiful in Music. A contribution to the revisal of Musical Aesthetics*, translated by Gustav Cohen, Novello, Ewer and Co., London and New York, 1891.

Harr, Michel. *Nietzsche et la Métaphysique*, Gallimard, Paris, 1993. English Translation: *Nietzsche and Metaphysics*, translated by Michael Gendre, SUNY Press, New York, 1996.

Hatab, Lawrence J., *Nietzsche and Eternal Recurrence: The Redemption of Time and Becoming*, University Press of America, Washington, DC, 1978.

Havas, Randall, *Nietzsche's Genealogy: Nihilism and the Will to Knowledge*, Cornell University Press, Ithaca, New Yord and London, 1995.

Heidegger, Martin, *Was Heisst Denken?*, Max Niemeyer Verlag, Tübingen, 1954. English translation: *What is called Thinking?* translated by J. Glenn Gray, Harper & Row, New York, 1968.

——*Nietzsche*, 2 vols, Verlag Günther Neske, Pfullingen, 1961.

Hill, Kevin R., *Nietzsche's Critiques: the Kantian Foundations of his Thought*, Oxford University Press, Oxford and New York, 2003.

Hollinrake, Richard, *Nietzsche, Wagner and the Philosophy of Pessimism*, George Allen and Unwin, London, 1982.

Houlgate, Stephen, *Hegel, Nietzsche and the Criticism of Metaphysics*, Cambridge University Press, Cambridge and New York, 1986.

Janaway, Christopher, ed., *Willing and Nothingness: Schopenhauer as Nietzsche's Educator*, Oxford University Press, Oxford and New York, 1988.

Jankélévitch, Vladimir, *L'irréversible et le nostalgie*, Flammarion, Paris, 1974.

Juranville, Alain, *Physique de Nietzsche*, Denoel/Gonthier, Paris, 1973.

Kant, Immanuel, *Kritik der reinen Vernunft*, English translation: *Critique of Pure Reason*, translated by F. Max Müller, Anchor Books, New York, 1966.

——*Kritik der Urteilskraft*. English translation: *Critique of Judgment*, translated by Werner S. Pluhar, Hackett Publishing Company, Indianapolis, 1987.

——*Grundlegung zur Metaphysik der Sitten*, W. Weischedel, Band 6. English translation: *Groundwork for the Metaphysics of Morals*, translated by Allen W. Wood, Yale University Press, New Haven, 2002.

Kemal, Salim, Ivan Gaskell, and Daniel W. Conway, eds., *Nietzsche, Philosophy and the Arts*, Cambridge University Press, Cambridge and New York, 1998.

Klossowski, Pierre, *Nietzsche et le cercle vicieux*, Mercure de France, Paris, 1969. English translation: *Nietzsche and the Vicious Circle*, translated by Daniel W. Smith, Athlone Press, London, 1997.

Kofman, Sarah, *Nietzsche et la Métaphore*, Payot, Paris, 1972, English translation: *Nietzsche and Metaphore*, translated by Duncan Large, Athlone Press, London, 1993.

——*Explosions*, I & II, Galilée, Paris, 1991.

Lampert, Laurence, *Nietzsche's Teaching: An Interpretation of "Thus Spoke Zarathustra,"* Yale University Press, New Haven, Connecticut and London, 1986.

Love, Frederick R., *Young Nietzsche and the Wagnerian Experience*, University of North Carolina Press, Chapel Hill, 1963.

Löwith, Karl, *Nietzsches Philosophie der ewigen Wiederkehr des Gleichen*, Kohlhamer, Stuttgart, 1956. English translation: *Nietzsche's Philosophy of the Eternal Recurrence of the Same*, translated by J. Harvey Lomax, University of California Press, Berkeley, Los Angeles and London, 1997.

——*From Hegel to Nietzsche: The Revolution in Nineteenth-Century Thought*, translated by David E. Green, Rinehart & Winston, New York, 1964.

Lyotard, Jean-François, *L'Inhumain. Causeries sur le temps*, Galilée, Paris, 1988. English translation: *The Inhuman: Reflections on Time*, translated by Geoffrey Bennington and Rachel Bowlby, Polity Press, Cambridge, 1991.

——*Leçons sur l'Analytique du sublime*, Galilée, Paris, 1991. English translation: *Lessons on the Analytic of the Sublime: Kant's Critique of Judgment* [sections 23–29], translated by Elizabeth Rottenberg, Stanford University Press, California, 1994.

——"Réponse à la question: qu'est-ce que le postmoderne?" in *Critique*, 419, April 1982.

Magnus, Bernd, *Nietzsche's Existential Imperative*, Indiana University Press, Bloomington and London, 1978.

Martin, Nicholas, *Nietzsche and Schiller: Untimely Aesthetics*, Oxford University Press, Oxford and New York, 1996.

May, Keith M., *Nietzsche and the Spirit of Tragedy*, St Martin's Press, New York, 1990.

Moles, Alistair, *Nietzsche's Philosophy of Nature and Cosmology*, Lang, New York, 1990.

Montinari, Mazzino, "Nietzsche und Wagner vor hundert Jahren," in *Nietzsche – Studien*, 7 (1978), pp. 288–307.

——*Che cosa ha veramente ditto Nietzsche*, Casa Editrice Astrolábio-Ubaldini Editore, Rome, 1975.

——*Nietzsche*, Editori Riuniti, Rome, 1996.

Morel, Georges, *Nietzsche, Introduction à une première lecture*, Aubier-Montaigne, Paris, 1971.

Morrison, Robert G., *Nietzsche and Buddhism: A Study in Nihilism and Ironic Affinities*, Oxford University Press, Oxford and New York, 1997.

Nancy, Jean-Luc and Deguy, Michel, eds, *Du Sublime*, Belim, Paris, 1988. English translation: *Of the Sublime: Presence in Question*, translated by Jeffrey S. Librett, SUNY Press, New York, 1993.

Nattiez, Jean-Jacques, *Le Combat de Chronos et d'Orphée*, Christian Bourgois Editeur, Paris, 1993.

Nehamas, Alexander, *Nietzsche: Life as Literature*, Harvard University Press, Cambridge, Massachusetts and London, 1985.

Philonenko, Alexis, *Le transcendental et la pensée moderne*, PUF, Paris, 1990.

Poellner, Peter, *Nietzsche and Metaphysics*, Oxford University Press, Oxford, 1995.
Porter, James I., *The Invention of Dionysus: An Essay on The Birth of Tragedy*, Stanford University Press, Stanford, California, 2000.
Pries, Christine, ed., *Das Erhabene. Zwischen Grenzerfahrung und Grössenwahn*, Akademie Verlag, Berlin, 1995.
Rampley, Mathew, *Nietzsche, Aesthetics and Modernity*, Cambridge University Press, Cambridge and New York, 2000.
Reuber, Rudolf, *Aesthetische Lebensformen bei Nietzsche*, Wilhelm Fink Verlag, Munich, 1989.
Ribeiro dos Santos, Leonel, *A Razão Sensível. Estudos Kantianos*, Colibri, Lisboa, 1994.
Richir, Marc, *Du sublime en politique*, Payot, Paris, 1991.
Ridley, Aron, *Nietzsche's Conscience: Six Character Studies from the Genealogy*, Cornell University Press, Ithaca, New York and London, 1998.
Rochlitz, Rainer, "De l'expression au sens. Perspectives Esthétiques chez Habermas," in *Revue Internationale de Philosophie*, 4/1995, n. 194.
Rorty, Richard, "Habermas, Lyotard et la Postmodernité," in *Critique*, 442, March 1984.
Rosen, Stanley, *The Mask of Enlightenment: Nietzsche's Zarathustra*, Cambridge University Press, Cambridge and New York, 1995.
Sallis, John, *Crossings, Nietzsche and the Space of Tragedy*, University of Chicago Press, Chicago and London, 1991.
Sambursky, Samuel, *Physics of the Stoics*, Routledge and Kegan Paul, London, 1959.
Schacht, Richard, ed., *Nietzsche, Genealogy, Morality: Essays on Nietzsche's "Genealogy of Morals,"* University of California Press, Los Angeles and London, 1994.
Schiller, Friedrich, *Briefe über die ästhetische Erziehung des Menschen*. English translation: *On the Aesthetic Education of Man: In a Series of Letters*, translated by Elizabeth M. Wilkinson and L.A. Willoughby, Clarendon Press, Oxford, 1983.
Schmidt, Bertram, *Der ethische Aspekt der Musik. Nietzsches «Geburt der Tragoedie» und die Weiner Klassische Musik*, Königshausen & Neumann, Würzburg, 1991.
Schopenhauer, Arthur, *Die Welt als Wille und Vorstellung I*, Sämtliche Werk (S.W.) Wissenschaftliche Buchgesellschaft, Darmstadt, 1980, Band I and II. English translation: *The World as Will and Representation*, translated by E.F. Payne, Dover Publications, Inc., New York, 1969.
——*Ueber die Grundlage der Moral*, Sämtliche Werke, Band III. English translation: *On the Basis of Morality*, translated by E.F.J. Payne, Berghahm Books, Providence, 1995.

———*Parerga und Paralipomena*, Sämtliche Werk (S.W.) Wissenschaftliche Buchgesellschaft, Darmstadt, 1980, Band IV.

Schrift, Alan D., ed., *Why Nietzsche Still? Reflections on Drama, Culture, and Politics*, University of California Press, Berkeley, Los Angeles and London, 2000.

Shapiro, Gary, *Nietzschean Narratives*, Indiana University Press, Bloomington and Indianapolis, 1989.

———*Alcyone: Nietzsche on Gifts, Noise, and Women*, SUNY Press, Albany, 1991.

———*Archeologies of Vision: Foucault and Nietzsche on Seeing and Saying*, University of Chicago Press, 2003.

Silk, M.S. and Stern J.P., *Nietzsche on Tragedy*, Cambridge University Press, Cambridge and New York, 1981.

Simmel, Georg, *Schopenhauer and Nietzsche*, translated by Helmut Loiskandl, Deena Weinstein, and Michael Weinstein, University of Massachusetts Press, Amherst, 1986.

Spanneut, Michel, *Permanence du stoïcisme, de Zenon à Malraux*, ed. J. Duculot, S. A., Gembloux, 1973.

Stambaugh, Joan, *Nietzsche's Thought of Eternal Return*, The Johns Hopkins University Press, Baltimore and London, 1972.

Steiner, George, *Antigones*, Clarendon Press, New York, 1986.

Taminiaux, Jacques, *Lectures de l'ontologie fondamentale. Essais sur Heidegger*, Jerôme Millon, Grenoble, 1989.

Tejera, Victorino, *Nietzsche and Greek Thought*, Nijhoff, Dordrecht, 1987.

Tsekourakis, Damianos, *Studies in the terminology of early Stoic ethics*, Franz Steiner Verlag, Wiesbaden, 1974.

Vattimo, Gianni, *Al di la del soggetto. Nietzsche, Heidegger e l'hermeneutica*, Feltrinelli, Milan, 1981.

———*Introduzione a Nietzsche*, Laterza, Rome, 1985.

———*La fine della modernità*, Garzanti, Milan, 1985. English translation: *The End of Modernity: Nihilism and hermeneutics in post-modern culture*, translated by Jon R. Snyder, Polity Press, Cambridge, 1988.

———*Il soggeto et la maschera. Nietzsche e il problema della liberazione*, Bompiani, Milan, 2003.

———*Nichilismo et emancipazione. Etica, politica, diritto*, Garzanti, Milan, 2003.

von Arnim, Hans, *Stoicorum Veterum Fragmenta*, III, Teubner, Stuttgart, 1964.

Wagner, Richard, *Beethoven*, in Jubilaeumsausgabe, Band 9, Frankfurt am Main, Insel Verlag, 1983. English translation: *Beethoven*, translated by Edward Dannreuthe, ed. William Reeves, London, 1903.

Wellmer, Albrecht, *Zur Dialektik von Moderne und Postmoderne nach Adorno*, Frankfurt am Main, Suhrkamp, 1988. English translation: "The Dialectic of Modernism and Postmodernism: The Critique of Reason since

Adorno," in *The Persistence of Modernity: Essays on Aesthetics, Ethics and Postmodernism*, translated by David Midgley, Polity Press, Cambridge, 1991.

Whitlock, Greg, *Returning to Sils-Maria: A Commentary to Nietzsche's "Also sprach Zarathustra,"* Lang, New York, 1990.

Williams, Linda L., *Nietzsche's Mirror: The World as Will to Power*, Rowman & Littlefield, Lanham, Maryland and Oxford, 2000.

Winchester, James J. *Nietzsche's Aesthetic Turn: Reading Nietzsche after Heidegger, Deleuze, and Derrida*, SUNY Press, Albany, 1994.

Young, Julian, *Nietzsche's Philosophy of Art*, Cambridge University Press, Cambridge and New York, 1992.

Index

Abel, Gunter 190
actual, the
  distinction between empirical and
    intelligible character 39–42, 46,
    51, 54, 72–6, 106
  as phenomenal manifestation of
    eternity 26, 34, 83
Adorno, Theodor 5, 7
aesthetics
  aesthetic education and political
    utopia 3–6
  aesthetic of nostalgia 117
  aesthetic of pessimism 12, 22, 29
  of the beautiful 2, 10
  consciousness of finitude of the
    aesthetic subject 19
  Dionysian *see* Dionysus and the
    Dionysian
  of existence 87
  formalist aesthetic 31
  individuation between the aesthetic
    and the ethical 40–3
  justification of existence 42
  Kantian concept of aesthetic
    judgment 1–6
  Kantian concept of ethical judgment
    3, 5
  negative representation 2–3
  in postmodern debate 1–10
  Schopenhauerian transformation of
    Kantian 13–20, 26
  sensus communis as aesthetic
    foundation to ethical judgment
    in Kant 3, 5
  of the sublime *see* sublime, the
  theological interpretation of 33
  of the transcendental-pragmatic 2
  universality of the aesthetic 2, 4,
    14–15
  of the unrepresentable 9, 10
amor fati 66, 85–7, 91, 94
Andler, Charles 86
Antichrist, The 99, 100, 101, 103
Apollo and the Apollonian
  Apollo as an ethical divinity 77
  Dionysian/Apollonian polarity 10,
    34, 77
  individuation 41, 42
  justification of appearance 34
art
  Dionysian 10
  Kantian aesthetic and the
    interpretation of 2–3
  Schopenhauerian cartography of
    forms of 23, 27
  theophanic condition of 33
atomism 52, 53–4, 56
*Attempt at the Revaluation of All Values,
  The* 99

Bataille, G. 7
Baumgarten, Alexander 14
beauty
  the beautiful and the sublime 1–3,
    10–11, 12–15, 18, 26, 30–2
  Kantian aesthetic judgment and 1–6
  Kantian aesthetic of the beautiful 2, 30
  as manifestation of an Idea
    (Schopenhauer) 12–16
  musical 31
  Schopenhauerean aesthetic of the
    beautiful 14–15, 18, 21–2, 26

becoming, process of 43, 76
  "become who you are" 88, 89, 93, 97, 98
  chance as the innocence of becoming 68
  as circular 47 *see also* Eternal Return/Recurrence
Beethoven (essay by Wagner) 12, 29–30, 32–3
Beethoven, Ludwig van 29, 32
Beyond Good and Evil
  critique of stoic's maxim 85–6, 95–8
  Eternal Return 103, 138, 139
  intelligible character 51
  psychology 138
  will to power 127
Birth of Tragedy, The
  "artist's metaphysics" 5
  atemporal reality 77
  Dionysian ecstasy 41–2, 77, 82
  Habermas and the abandonment of 7, 8
  individuation in 40–2
  oblique treatment of sublime condition of music 29–30
  postmodern reading of 5–11
  premises of postmodern aesthetic theory 7
  Schopenhauerian roots to aesthetic of 11–12, 16
  the sublime and the beautiful in 9, 10–11
  tragedy as musical drama 29, 30, 34
Bréhier, Émile 93
Buddhism 147, 153–4

calculability in nature 126, 127
causality, principle of 17, 45–6
  individual as origin and end of chain of causation 49
chance 68
Christian morality 89–93, 100, 128, 132, 148
  self-dissolution of Christian morals 135
Chrysippus 88, 95

Cicero 96
  and Montinari, Mazzino 99, 137
Comte-Sponville, A. 8
contemplation
  disinterested contemplation of forms 2, 18
  intuitive contemplation of Ideas 18, 32
  pure contemplation 21–2, 28
contingency 68

Dawn, The 44, 105
Daybreak 91
decadence 86, 132, 133–5, 137
Deleuze, G.
  in Nietzsche's legacy 7
  on Nietzsche's relationship to Stoicism 86–7
Derrida, Jacques
  "artist's metaphysics" 5
  as French Nietzschean 7
Descombes, V. 8
determinism 73, 91–2
  see also necessity
Diocles of Magnesia 88
Diogenes Laertius, essay on 88, 93, 95, 98
Dionysus 99
Dionysus and the Dionysian
  Dionysian/Apollonian polarity 10, 34, 77
  Dionysian ecstasy 41–2, 77, 82
  Dionysian experience 29, 64
  Eternal Return and 103
  as the experience of the sublime 8–11, 34
  as symbol of unity of the will (Schopenhauer) 41, 77
  Yes to all existence 64, 86
Dithyrambs of Dionysus 66
drama
  musical 9, 29–34
  tragic 24, 33, 42
dreams 16, 25

Ecce Homo
  amor fati 97

Eternal Return 93, 103, 104, 138, 157
  revaluation of all values 99, 100, 139
  tragedy xii, xiii
ecstasy, Dionysian 10, 34, 41–2, 77, 82
energy-quantum, will to power 53–4, 60–1, 126, 129
Epictetus 90–1, 92
  maxims 86, 87
Epicurus 88
Eternal Return/Recurrence
  ambiguity and decision 116–18
  anthropological perspective 118, 124
  demon's message 115
  eternity and 66
  as an experience of nostalgia 110–11, 117, 120
  as an experience of remorse 108–15
  genesis of the idea 80, 91, 92–3, 102–3
  individuality and 46–50
  the instant as the true perspective to idea of 120–5
  necessity and 65–7, 72
  nihilism and xiv, 101, 128–32, 147–57
  and the over-human 115, 118–23
  phenomenal consciousness and 124
  place in project of revaluation of all values 99–104, 125–32, 138
  reformulation of Stoic idea of 65, 86, 92–4
  selectivity and 131
  spirit of revenge and 71
  strange disappearance of idea xiv, 102–4, 124, 138
  and the tragic xii–xiv, 122
  typological perspective 124
  will to power and 63, 126–9
eternity
  as ever present 68, 75, 82
  as fatum 66
  as ideality (Schopenhauer) 26
  as immutability of character 39–40, 73–5
  individuality and 62–4
  as infinite repetition 48–50
  as intemporality 77–83
  as a mode of necessity 66, 75–7
ethics
  of Antiquity 87, 90–3
  ethic of immanence (based on physics) 85–6, 93–8
  ethic of pessimism 11, 74, 107
  individuation and 40–3, 45
  of the Portico 85
  Socratic 133
  Stoic ethic vs. Christian morality 89–93
  the sublime as an ethical experience 19–21
  see also morality
European Nihilism, The see Lenzer Heide fragment

fate
  fatum 67–82, 97
  love of (*amor fati*) 66, 85–7, 91, 94
Fate and History 67, 77
Ferry, Luc 8
Fink, Eugen 123, 124
force 57–62
  hierarchy of forces 59–62, 136, 144–6
Foucault, Michel 5, 7, 87
free will
  error of 105–6
  fatum and 67–73, 75–6
freedom 66, 69, 72, 73
  defined by actuality and immutability 75, 83
  guilt and the intuitive condition of 106
  morality and 105–7
Freedom of the Will and Fate 67
French Nietzscheanism 7

Gast, Peter 137, 146
Gay Science, The
  Eternal Return xii, 94, 102, 114–18, 148
  naturalism and 44, 105
Genealogy of Morals, The
  disappearance of idea of Eternal Return 125–32

new concept of tragedy xii
revaluation of all values 100
typology of the will 124–5, 138–9,
141–3
God
arbitrary manifestation of 68
"death of God" 37
divine presence experienced through art 33
man between automaton and God 70, 72
Goethe, Johann Wolfgang von 78
Granier, Jean 86
Greek tragedy 9, 34, 42
guilt, phenomenology of xii, 105–8, 110–12, 114–17, 119, 143

Habermas, Jürgen
"Modernity: an Unfinished Project?" (lecture) 5–6
The Philosophical Discourse of Modernity 5, 6, 7–8
postmodern debate 1–12
return to Kant 6–7, 9
the "transcendental-pragmatic" 1–2
Hanslick, Eduard 31–2
Hegel, Georg Wilhelm Friedrich 37, 85, 87
inverted Hegelianism 134
Heidegger, Martin
hermeneutical ontology of time 108–9, 123–4
the over-human and end of humanism 101
postmodern debate 5, 7
hierarchy of forces 59–62, 136, 144–6
history
antiquarian 80–1
critical 81
fate and 67–8, 77–8
life and 77–82
monumental 79–80
supra-historical awareness 82
Human, All Too Human
break with Schopenhauer 44–7, 112
individuation 44

monism of the world of representation 45
remorse as origin of morality 105–8, 114
Stoic morality 86
Husserl, Edmund 123

idealism 46, 66, 76
Ideas *see* Platonic Ideas
Illuminism 5
illusion 15–16, 25
in experience of self as temporality 109–10
of freedom 107
of remorse 113
Immoralist, The 99
individuality
essence of world within the individual 51–3, 54
essential relations of the individual 57–9
eternity and 62–4
hierarchy of 61–2
as identity in repetition 46–50 *see also* Eternal Return/Recurrence
imaginary and real individuals 53–4
immanent quest for 37–8
the individual without qualities 44–6
individuals as only real beings 38
in Kant 106–8
nomadic individualities 54–5
perception and 57–9
perspective and 59–61
in Schopenhauer 39–40
spontaneity and 55–7, 62, 63
in the theory of the will to power 50–64
individuation 38, 39–46, 51–5
innocence 108
chance as the innocence of becoming 68
Nietzsche's naturalism and the access to innocence of nature 65–7, 91–2, 94
intelligible character 39–40, 73–6, 77
distinction between empirical and

intelligible character 39–42, 46, 51, 54, 72–6, 106
intuition
  of the beautiful 26
  of freedom 106
  of the sublime 26
  understanding and 16–18, 51

Jankélévitch, Vladimir 111

Kant, Immanuel
  concept of freedom 106–7
  Critique of Judgment 1–10, 13, 25, 30
  Critique of Pure Reason 74, 106
  distinction between beautiful and sublime 1–3, 10, 13–15
  empirical and intelligible character 39–40, 73–6
  formalism of Kantian morality 87
  individuality 106–8
  as target in Nietzsche's "practice of war" 85
  theory of the sublime 2–3, 7, 8, 9, 13, 19–20
  vicious circle in foundation of morality through freedom 106–7
Klossowski, Pierre 7
knowledge
  converted into pure contemplation 28
  decried by life 82
  innocence and 108
  Nietzsche's naturalism and the access to innocence of nature 65–7, 91–2, 94
  nullified will as pure subject of 40
  Schopenhauerean aesthetic and theory of 16–18
  self-destruction of nihilism and 144–5
  serving life 78–9
  the sublime and 10–11
Kofman, Sarah 7

Lacoue-Labarthe, Philippe 7, 8
Leibniz, Gottfried Wilhelm 38
Lenzer Heide fragment (*The European Nihilism*) 128–30, 132, 136–57

life
  beauty and the intensification of 13
  cursed 105
  evocation of nostalgia through events of 117
  history and 77–82
  individuals as systems of 52, 53, 55
  nature and 96
  remorse as revolt of life against itself 105
  saying *Yes* to existence 64, 86, 129, 152
  tragedy of 24–5
  as will to power 96
Luther, Martin 135
Lyotard, Jean-François
  "artist's metaphysics" 5
  controversy with Habermas 5, 6–7, 8–9
  as French Nietzschean 7, 9
  "negative representation" 1, 2–3
  and the sublime 1–3, 7–9

Mahler, Gustav xii
man
  as analogy of world in itself 51–2
  between automaton and God 70, 72
  death of 101
  the Stoic wise man vs. the Christian religious man 89–93
  supra-historical 82
metaphysics
  of the artist 5, 8
  in *Birth of Tragedy* 34, 40–2
  Dionysian ecstasy as metaphysical experience 34, 40–2
  duality of atemporal essence and existence in time 77–80
  Kantian concept of metaphysics and the limits of human knowledge 26–7, 105–7
  naturalist *see* naturalism
  Nietzsche's critique and return to Kant's theory of knowledge 44–5
  Nietzsche's philosophy as last modern metaphysics of necessity 65 *see also* necessity

of pessimism 105 *see also* ethics: ethic of pessimism
theory of will to power as return to 50–1
of the will (Schopenhauer) 39–40
Mill, John Stuart 87
Mixed Opinions and Maxims 44, 105
modernity
  abandonment of rational legitimization of 6–7
  corrosion of the metaphysical 5
  objectivity of aesthetic experience 2
  and postmodernity 1–12, 101 *see also* postmodernism
Montinari, Mazzino
  Collie, Giorgio and 99, 137
morality
  as an anthropological given 111
  Christian 89–93, 100, 128, 132, 135, 148
  of compassion 87
  as the condemnation of existence 105
  as consequence of a certain type of will 142–4
  in the face of powerlessness against men 130–2, 153
  formalism of Kantian morality 87
  freedom and 105–7
  genealogy of 139–46
  Nietzsche's critique 105–8
  remorse as evidence for morality 105–7
  Stoic 89–93
  time and 108–10
  as universal condition of human being in time 108–15
  will to power and 152–3
  see also ethics
Morel, Georges 86
Mosaic law 33
motivation 17–18
music 27–34

Nancy, Jean-Luc 7, 8
naturalism
  as response to Kantian/Schopenhauerean duality 44–5
  as revelation of the innocence of the world 65–7, 91–2, 94, 108
nature, living by 95–8
necessity
  as determinism 73, 91–2
  as eternal repetition 65–7, 72
  eternity as mode of 66, 75–7
  as *fatum see* fate
  as immutability of character 73–5
  as irrevocability of the past 108–15
  life and 77–8
  as local and instantaneous copossibility 125–7
  of nature 94
  will to power 126, 149–51
negative representation 1, 2–3, 25
  converted into representation without an object 28
  see also unrepresentable, the
Nietzsche's works
  The Antichrist 99, 100, 101, 103
  The Attempt at the Revaluation of All Values 99
  Beyond Good and Evil see Beyond Good and Evil
  The Birth of Tragedy see Birth of Tragedy, The
  The Dawn 44, 105
  Daybreak 91
  Dionysus 99
  Ecce Homo see Ecce Homo
  The European Nihilism (Lenzer Heide fragment) 128–30, 132, 136–57
  Fate and History 67, 77
  Freedom of the Will and Fate 67
  The Gay Science see Gay Science, The
  The Genealogy of Morals see Genealogy of Morals, The
  Human, All Too Human 44–7, 86, 105–8, 112, 114
  The Immoralist 99
  Lenzer Heide fragment (*The European Nihilism*) 128–30, 132, 136–57

Mixed Opinions and Maxims 44, 105
poems 66
Thus Spoke Zarathustra see Thus Spoke Zarathustra
Twilight of the Idols 100, 103, 134, 138, 139
Untimely Meditations 41–3, 76, 77–83, 134
The Wanderer and His Shadow 44, 105
We That Say Yes 99
The Will to Power 63–4, 99–101, 137–9
nihilism
  decadence and 132, 133–5, 137
  Eternal Return and xiv, 101, 128–32, 147–57
  forms of 37, 139–42, 144–8
  Lenzer Heide fragment 136–57
  Lyotard's nihilistic sublime 1
  as a negative dialectic 145–6
  overcoming of 101, 132, 143–6
  in *The Will to Power* 99–101, 137–9
  will to power and 103, 104, 124, 127–9
nostalgia 110–11, 115–20

On the Genealogy of Morality see Genealogy of Morals, The
over-human, the (Übermensch)
  anthropological description of time as ground of concept 108–15
  disappearance of idea 101, 115, 118–23
  and the end of humanism 101

Pautrat, Bernard 7
perception
  as appearance 14, 27, 29
  as property of every force 57–60
perspectivism
  as ground for individuality of every force 57, 59–62
  as typology 142–7
pessimism
  aesthetic of 12, 22, 29
  ethic of 11, 74
  and metaphysical condemnation of individuated life 39–40

and tragedy in Schopenhauer xi, 11, 29, 32
Wagner's vocabulary of 32, 33–4
philology of Stoicism 87–9
Pindar 88, 97, 98
Plato 85
  Nietzsche's turning from Platonism 87
Platonic Ideas 17, 18, 20, 22
  music as an Idea 33
  the One as an Idea 37, 53
Platonism of general forms 68
political utopia 3–6
Portico school 85, 90–3, 94, 98
postmodernism
  equivoques of postmodern reading of Nietzsche 6–12
  and the return to Kant and the sublime 1–12
power 57–62

realism 14, 16
redemption
  of eternity 64
  of nature 142
  of the past 118–20
  of the raging will by idea of Eternal Return 71
  of the sublime by the beautiful 34
reflexive judgment, theory of 4, 13, 14
relation, concept of
  dynamic relations 56–62
  external relations as all that exist 45
  self-subsistent spatio-temporal relations 49
religion
  as art's escape valve 33
  Buddhism 147, 153–4
  Christian morality *see* Christian morality
remorse 105–15
  redemptive message directed against 118–19
Renaut, Alain 8
representation
  as all there is 19

appearance of 15–16, 46
experience of absolute absence of 10
metaphysical world and world of
representation 44
music as the representation of the
unrepresentable 27–8
negative representation *see* negative
representation
the sublime as a representation of the
unrepresentable 25–6, 33
utopian 3
will and 16–18
see also unrepresentable, the
revaluation of all values
amor fati 87
in *Birth of Tragedy* xiii
eternal return xiv, 103–4, 115, 127–32, 148–57
genesis of the project 99–101, 103
nihilism 133–6, 141–8
will to power 125–32
Rey, Jean-Michel 7
Romanticism 5, 9, 10, 74

Schiller, Friedrich
On the Aesthetic Education of Man 3–5, 6
Schillerean romanticism 10 *see also* romanticism
Schopenhauer, Arthur
"Aesthetics of Poetry" 24
On the Basis of Morality 75, 105
cartography of the forms of art 23, 27
"Critique of Kantian Philosophy" 14
eternity as ever present 75, 82
experience of remorse as evidence for morality 105–7
freedom as immutability of character 73–5
individuation 39–40
model of necessity 73–5
morality of compassion 87
music 27–9
Nietzsche's break with 44–5, 105–8
One Will 37
paradox of individuality 39–40

reification of Kantian concept of
intelligible character 39–40, 74, 77
as target in Nietzsche's "practice of war" 85
theory of the sublime 11, 12–22, 25–6
tragedy and the sublime 23–5
transformation of Kantian aesthetic 13–20, 26
transformation of the sublime/beautiful polarity 10
The World as Will and Representation 12–13, 16, 20–9, 72
Shakespeare, William 23
Socrates 85
Spencer, Herbert 87
Spinoza, Benedict de 37, 65, 151
maxim of *amor fati* 66, 85
Steiner, George ix
Stoicism 85–98
idea of Eternal Recurrence 93–4
as a philological problem 87–9
reformulation of Stoic idea of Eternal Recurrence 65
Stoic ethic vs. Christian morality 89–93
Strauss, Richard xii
sublime, the
the aesthetic as an experience of 35
beauty that redeems the sublime 34
Dionysian experience of 8–11, 34
distinction between beauty and 1–3, 10–11, 12–15, 18, 26, 30–2
as an ethical experience 19–21, 35
Kantian aesthetic of 2–3, 7, 8, 9
music and 27–34
postmodernity and 1–12
Schopenhauerian theory of 11, 12–27
tragedy as symbol of 23–5
truth of 10, 21–3
the unrepresentable and 25–7 *see also* music
in Wagner's music 29–34
suprahistorical awareness 82

taste, judgment of 1, 2, 3–5, 6, 14, 17

theodicy 68
theology
　rejection of theological perspective 68
　theological interpretation of aesthetics 33
　see also Christian morality
thing-in-itself
　fatum as 72-3, 75
　Kantian 10, 72-3, 74
　in ontology of music 27-9
　reification of 39-40
　Universal as 37
　as will (Schopenhauer) 31, 34, 39-40, 73-5
　as will to power 50-1
　see also individuality
Thus Spoke Zarathustra
　anthropological understanding of time 118, 124
　chance as the innocence of becoming 68
　Eternal Return 66, 101, 102-3, 108-15, 118-25
　irrevocability and irreversibility 111-20
　the over-human 114-15, 123, 130
　spirit of revenge 71, 109-15
time
　the ahistorical instant 77-83
　anthropology of 118, 124
　duality of atemporal essence and existence in time 77-80
　fatum as a figure of the past 71
　the instant as the true perspective to idea of Eternal Return 120-5
　irreversibility of 71, 111-12
　morality and 108-10
　nostalgia and 111, 115-20
　phenomenology of 123-5
　as real property of things in becoming 44-50
　revolt against the irrevocability of the past 71, 108-15
　and space as appearances 19-21, 32

　and space as pure forms of sensibility 2, 15-18, 39-40
　and the spirit of revenge 71, 109-15
　typologies of temporality 115-20
tragedy
　Greek 9, 34, 42
　as musical drama 29-34
　in Schopenhauer 23-5
　silence vii, xi-xiii
　the sublime and 6-12, 23-7
　Wagner's crossing of tragedy and the metaphysics of music 33
truth
　appearance and 41
　of the sublime 10, 21-3
Twilight of the Idols
　decadence 134
　Eternal Return 103, 138
　genesis of the project of revaluation of all values 100, 139

understanding, intuitive 16-18
unrepresentable, the
　aesthetic of 9, 10
　God and 33
　moral law and 3, 33
　music and 27-8, 33-4
　the sublime and 25-7, 33
Untimely Meditations
　Eternal Return 80
　historicism 134
　individuality 41-3
　metaphysical hierarchy 76
　time 77-83
utilitarianism 87
utopia, political 3-6

values
　inversion of 37
　revaluation of *see* revaluation of all values
　universal validity of value judgments 5

Wagner Case, The 85, 139
Wagner, Richard 29-34

Wanderer and His Shadow, The 44, 105
We That Say Yes 99
will
  the creative will 119
  fatalism 65–73
  freedom 73–5 *see also* free will; freedom
  given up in the sublime 21
  individuation 39–43, 51–4
  nature as 95–8
  opposition to time 109–15
  representation and 16–19
  revolt of the will against itself 105, 108–9
  Schopenhauer 39–40
  spontaneity (Kant) 73–5
  suspended in response to the beautiful 18
  thing-in-itself as 31, 34, 39–40, 73–5
  the unified will 26
  will to live 24, 79
Will to Power, The
  nihilism 99–101, 137–9
  the tragic *Yes* 63–4
will to power 38
  action at a distance 57–8
  atomism 53–4 *see also* atomism
  calculability 62, 126
  and the death of man 101
  Eternal Return and 63, 126–9
  general and singular perspectives 127
  hierarchy of forces 61–2, 144–6
  individuality 54–64
  individuation and 51–4
  inner and outer finality 86
  instantaneity of the will 126
  morality and 152–3, 156
  necessity 126, 149–51
  and Nietzsche's return to metaphysics 50–1
  nihilism and 103, 104, 124, 127–9
  perspectivism 59–61
  quantum of energy 53–4, 60–1, 60–1, 126, 129
  and the revaluation of all values 125–32
  spontaneity and 56–7
  as thing-in-itself 50–1
  the world as 96–8, 143
world perspectives
  internal 51–2
  mechanistic 45, 50, 52, 56
  naturalism and the innocence of the world 65–7, 91–2, 94, 108
  of the necessary 65, 92
  as philosophical problem 98
  rejection of theological 68
  world as will to power 96–8, 143

Zeno, maxims of 85, 87